SEVENTH EDITION

Concise
Guide to
APA Style

THE OFFICIAL APA STYLE GUIDE FOR STUDENTS

7 SEVENTH EDITION

Concise Guide to APA Style

THE OFFICIAL APA STYLE GUIDE FOR STUDENTS

AMERICAN PSYCHOLOGICAL ASSOCIATION
Washington, DC

Published by
American Psychological Association
750 First Street, NE
Washington, DC 20002
https://www.apa.org

Order Department
https://www.apa.org/pubs/books
order@apa.org

For additional ordering information, including international distributors, see
https://www.apa.org/pubs/ordering

Typeset in Aria and Avenir

APA Style Director: Emily L. Ayubi
APA Style Content Development Managers: Chelsea L. Bromstad Lee, Hayley S. Kamin, and Timothy L. McAdoo
APA Style Editors: Anne T. Woodworth and Ayanna A. Adams
Reviewer: Donell Campbell
Director, Print & Electronic Book Production: Jennifer M. Meidinger
Production Manager: Daniel Brachtesende
Printer: Hess Print Solutions, Brimfield, OH
Cover and Interior Designer: Debra Naylor, Naylor Design, Inc., Washington, DC
Compositor: Robert Kern, TIPS Technical Publishing, Inc., Carrboro, NC
Indexer: Gray Van Dyke, TIPS Technical Publishing, Inc., Carrboro, NC

The correct reference for this book is as follows:
American Psychological Association. (2020). *Concise guide to APA Style* (7th ed.). https://doi.org/10.1037/0000173-000

Library of Congress Cataloging-in-Publication Data

Names: American Psychological Association, issuing body.
Title: Concise guide to APA style / American Psychological Association.
Other titles: Concise rules of APA style.
Description: Washington, DC : American Psychological Association, [2020] | Earlier editions published as: Concise rules of APA style. | Includes bibliographical references and index.
Identifiers: LCCN 2019043805 (print) | LCCN 2019043806 (ebook) | ISBN 9781433832734 (spiral bound) | ISBN 9781433832765 (ebook)
Subjects: LCSH: Psychology--Authorship--Style manuals. | Social sciences--Authorship--Handbooks, manuals, etc.
Classification: LCC BF76.7 .C66 2020 (print) | LCC BF76.7 (ebook) | DDC 808.06/615--dc23
LC record available at https://lccn.loc.gov/2019043805
LC ebook record available at https://lccn.loc.gov/2019043806

https://doi.org/10.1037/0000173-000

Printed in the United States of America
10 9 8 7 6 5 4 3 2 1

BRIEF CONTENTS

CONTENTS

6   Numbers and Statistics   119

7   Tables and Figures   131

9 Reference List   211

10 Reference Examples 243

INTRODUCTION

Effective writing is critical for success in many academic and professional pursuits. APA Style is a set of guidelines for clear and precise scholarly communication that helps writers, both new and experienced, achieve excellence in writing. It is used by millions of people around the world in psychology and in fields ranging from nursing to social work, communications to education, business to engineering, and other disciplines for writing student papers, dissertations, theses, and journal articles. The *Concise Guide to APA Style, Seventh Edition* is adapted from the *Publication Manual of the American Psychological Association, Seventh Edition* (APA, 2020), which is the authoritative resource for APA Style. We developed the *Concise Guide* for novice writers—especially students—to learn APA Style and apply it when writing and formatting their papers and other course assignments.

Why Use APA Style?

APA Style provides a foundation for effective scholarly communication because it helps writers present their ideas in a clear, concise, and organized manner. Uniformity and consistency enable readers to (a) focus on the ideas being presented rather than formatting and (b) scan works quickly for key points, findings, and sources. Style guidelines encourage writers to fully disclose essential information and allow readers to dispense with minor distractions, such as inconsistencies or omissions in punctuation, capitalization, reference citations, and presentation of statistics.

When style works best, ideas flow logically, sources are credited appropriately, and papers are organized predictably and consistently. People are described using language that affirms their worth and dignity. Tables and figures present data in an engaging, consistent manner.

Whether you use APA Style for a single class or throughout your career, we encourage you to recognize the benefits of a conscientious approach to writing. Although the guidelines span many areas and take time and practice to learn, we hope that they provide a balance of directiveness and flexibility and will eventually become second nature.

APA Style for Students

All students, no matter what career they pursue, can benefit from mastering scholarly writing as a way to develop their critical thinking skills and hone the precision and clarity of their communication. The *Publication Manual* has long been the authoritative source for APA Style as used in scholarly writing. The *Concise Guide* focuses on the APA Style guidelines specific to students and other novice writers, including how to format a student title page, cite classroom or intranet sources, and write common types of student papers (e.g., annotated bibliographies, response papers, and dissertations and theses). Those interested in learning about more advanced topics, including ethical standards, research reporting standards, and the publication process, should refer to the *Publication Manual*.

Utility and Accessibility

We have created the seventh edition of the *Concise Guide* with the practical needs of our users in mind. Within chapters, content is organized using numbered sections to help users quickly locate answers to their questions. This ease of navigability and depth of content mean that the guide can be used as both a reference work and a textbook on scholarly writing.

This edition promotes accessibility for everyone, including users with disabilities. In consultation with accessibility experts, we ensured that the guidelines support users who read and write works in APA Style through a variety of modalities, including screen readers and other assistive technologies. For example, we present a streamlined format for in-text citations intended to reduce the burden of both writing and reading them. We provide guidance on how to use adequate contrast in figures to meet Web Content Accessibility Guidelines (Web Accessibility Initiative, 2018). We also support the use of a variety of fonts and default settings in common word-processing programs, meaning that users need to make fewer adjustments to their systems to be ready to write in APA Style. Above all, our aim is to support the many ways in which people communicate. We encourage writers to be conscientious and respectful toward both the people about whom they are writing and the readers who will benefit from their work.

What's New in the Seventh Edition?

Brief descriptions of new and updated content are provided next on a chapter-by-chapter basis. For a more comprehensive overview of content changes, see the APA Style website (https://apastyle.apa.org).

Chapter 1: Student Paper Types, Elements, and Format

Chapter 1 is designed to help students select, format, and organize paper elements.

- General guidelines on how to apply APA Style to student papers are provided, including descriptions of common types of student papers.
- New formatting guidance is provided for annotated bibliographies.
- Guidance on a new student title page containing the course name and number, professor name, and assignment due date provides a format relevant to course assignments.
- A running head is not required for student papers.
- Font specifications are more flexible to address accessibility needs.
- An updated heading format for Levels 3, 4, and 5 improves readability and assists writers who use the heading-styles feature of their word-processing program.
- A new sample student paper is provided, with labels to show how specific elements appear when implemented.

Chapter 2: Writing Style and Grammar

Chapter 2 provides guidance on writing style and grammar.

- The singular "they" is endorsed, consistent with inclusive usage.
- More detailed guidance helps writers avoid anthropomorphism.
- Strategies to improve writing help strengthen the quality of papers.

Chapter 3: Bias-Free Language Guidelines

Chapter 3 presents guidance on bias-free language to encourage authors to write about people with inclusivity and respect.

- Existing guidance on age, disability, gender, racial and ethnic identity, and sexual orientation has been updated to reflect best practices.
- New guidance is provided on participation in research, socioeconomic status, and intersectionality.

Chapter 4: Punctuation, Lists, and Italics

Chapter 4 provides guidelines on punctuation, lists, and italics.

- Updated guidance answers a common question: Use one space after punctuation at the end of a sentence, unless an instructor or publisher requests otherwise.
- Updated guidelines provide greater flexibility for lettered, numbered, and bulleted lists.
- Formatting of linguistic examples has changed; quotation marks, rather than italics, are now used around examples to promote accessibility.

Chapter 5: Spelling, Capitalization, and Abbreviations

Chapter 5 covers spelling, capitalization, and abbreviations.

- Common technology-related spelling examples are presented for ease of reference.
- Expanded guidance is provided on the capitalization of proper nouns, job titles, diseases and disorders, and more.
- Guidelines for the presentation of abbreviations address common questions, such as how to include a citation with an abbreviation.

Chapter 6: Numbers and Statistics

Chapter 6 provides guidelines for presenting numbers and statistics in a paper.

- Guidelines for the presentation of numbers have been updated to be consistent throughout a work (e.g., there is no longer an exception for presenting numbers in an abstract).
- More examples are provided of numbers expressed in numerals versus words.

- Expanded guidance includes more examples of how to present currency, with and without symbols.

Chapter 7: Tables and Figures

Chapter 7 provides guidance on creating tables and figures.

- More than 20 new sample tables and figures are presented, in dedicated sections, covering a variety of research types and topics.
- The presentation of tables and figures in text is more flexible (either placed after the reference list on separate pages or embedded in the text).
- Formatting of tables and figures is parallel, including consistent styles for numbers, titles, and notes.
- The accessible use of color in figures is addressed.

Chapter 8: Works Credited in the Text

Chapter 8 discusses appropriate levels of citation as well as plagiarism, self-plagiarism, and other unethical writing practices. General guidelines on copyright and permission are also addressed.

- In-text citations have been simplified; all in-text citations for works with three or more authors are shortened to the name of the first author plus "et al." (except where this would create ambiguity).
- Examples of paraphrasing demonstrate how to achieve clear attribution without overcitation.
- More examples of formatting are shown, including examples of short quotations and block quotations.

Chapter 9: Reference List

Chapter 9 covers the four elements of a reference list entry (author, date, title, and source) and formatting of the reference list.

- The number of authors included in a reference entry has changed; up to 20 authors are now included before names are omitted with an ellipsis.
- The presentation of digital object identifiers (DOIs) and URLs has been standardized. Both are presented as hyperlinks; the label "DOI:" is no longer used, and the words "Retrieved from" are used only when a retrieval date is also needed.

- Updated guidance explains when to include DOIs and URLs for works retrieved from most academic research databases as well as from proprietary databases such as ERIC or UpToDate.

Chapter 10: Reference Examples

Chapter 10 provides more than 100 examples of APA Style references, each with accompanying parenthetical and narrative in-text citations.

- Templates are provided for every reference category.

- References are streamlined; for example, journal article references always include the issue number, and book references omit the publisher location.

- Audiovisual materials receive expanded coverage, including new examples for YouTube videos, PowerPoint slides and lecture notes, TED Talks, and more.

- Social media, webpages, and websites are addressed in new categories. For consistency and ease of formatting, blogs and other online platforms that publish articles are part of the periodicals category.

- Common legal reference examples are provided (e.g., the Every Student Succeeds Act).

APA Style Online

The APA Style website (https://apastyle.apa.org) is the premier and authoritative online destination for APA Style. In addition to numerous free resources and instructional aids, it contains supplemental content that is referred to throughout the manual, including additional reference examples, sample papers, and guidance on using color effectively and accessibly in figures.

The APA Style blog (https://apastyle.apa.org/blog) and related social media accounts will continue to answer questions about and share insights into APA Style with the publication of the seventh edition, providing authoritative content from members of the APA Style team.

Academic Writer (https://digitallearning.apa.org/academic-writer) is APA's cloud-based tool for teaching and learning effective writing. Developed by the creators of APA Style, this product helps all writers compose research papers and master the application of seventh-edition APA Style.

Notes to Users

The *Concise Guide* refers to numerous products and services that are not affiliated with the American Psychological Association but that our readers may encounter or use during the process of research, writing, and publication. The trademarks referenced in the *Concise Guide* are the property of their respective owners. The inclusion of non-APA products is for reference only and should not be construed as an endorsement of or affiliation between APA and the owners of these products and their respective brands.

Finally, some eagle-eyed users have asked why every aspect of APA Style is not applied throughout the *Concise Guide*. The *Concise Guide* is a published work, whereas the guidelines for APA Style are meant to be applied to student papers or to manuscripts being submitted for publication. Considerations for published works such as this book (e.g., typesetting, line spacing, length, fonts, use of color, margins) differ from those of student papers or draft manuscripts and thus necessitate deviations from APA Style formatting. Also, in this guide—in which we are writing about writing—it is often necessary to distinguish between explanatory text and examples through the use of font, color, and other design elements. Wherever possible, however, we have endeavored to demonstrate APA Style while writing about it and to present the information in a way that is accessible for our many users around the world.

1

STUDENT PAPER TYPES, ELEMENTS, AND FORMAT

Students are important members of the scholarly community. Although most student work is not formally published, by writing papers students engage in critical thinking, self-reflection, and scientific inquiry and thereby prepare to make unique contributions to the repository of knowledge. Students should pay careful attention to the format and organization of their papers. Consistency in the order, structure, and format of the elements of a paper allows readers to focus on its content rather than its presentation. Using APA Style guidelines to achieve consistency in the presentation of paper elements is essential to crafting an effective scholarly work.

This chapter provides an overview of the elements of an APA Style student paper. We first present ways to apply APA Style to student papers and describe common types of student papers. Next, we outline the required elements of a student paper, followed by descriptions of how to write and format each paper element. We then discuss formatting and organizational principles for writing papers. A sample APA Style student paper is included at the end of this chapter; additional sample papers are available on the APA Style website (https://apastyle.apa.org).

General Guidelines for Student Papers

1.1 Application of APA Style to Student Papers

Although the *Publication Manual* originated as a guide for authors seeking publication in scholarly journals, it has been widely adopted by academic instructors, departments, and institutions that require students to use APA Style when writing scholarly papers. Likewise, the manual has historically addressed researchers working in the field of psychology; however, students and researchers use APA Style in other fields and disciplines, including social work, nursing and other health-related fields, communications, education, business, engineering, and technology. Students write many of the same kinds of papers that are published in journals (e.g., literature review articles; for more information on articles published in scholarly journals, see Sections 1.1–1.9 of the *Publication Manual*). Students may also write papers that are not typically published (e.g., essays, response or reaction papers, dissertations and theses, annotated bibliographies; described in Sections 1.2–1.4).

Most APA Style guidelines can be applied to student papers. However, because the scope of what constitutes a student paper is broad and flexible, and because students submit papers to their academic institutions rather than to an APA journal, we do not designate formal requirements for the nature or contents of an APA Style student paper. Thus, questions about paper length, required sections, and so forth are best answered by the instructor or institution setting the assignment. Students should follow the guidelines and requirements developed by their instructors, departments, and/or academic institutions when writing papers, including dissertations and theses; these guidelines and requirements may entail adaptations of or additions to the APA Style guidelines described in this guide. We encourage writers, students, instructors, departments, and academic institutions outside of the journal publication context to adapt APA Style to fit their needs.

1.2 Student Essays

Undergraduate students commonly write many types of essays as well as response and reaction papers. The descriptions that follow are generally representative of these types of papers; check with your assigning instructor or institution for specific guidelines.

Cause-and-Effect Essays. In cause-and-effect essays, writers discuss how specific events lead to particular outcomes while often advocating for a position. A clear and strong thesis provides a solid foundation for this type of essay. The paper is generally structured by describing each cause and its collateral effect, with logical transitions between them.

Comparative Essays. In comparative essays, writers compare and contrast two (or more) topics with the goal of linking disparate items under a central thesis. The paper can be structured to focus separately on Topic 1 and then Topic 2, or the topics may be interwoven as the writer discusses specific aspects of each.

Expository Essays. In expository essays, writers explain or provide information on a specific topic with evidence used to reinforce the claims made. The paper is structured in multiple paragraphs and includes an introduction, body, and conclusion.

Narrative Essays. In narrative essays, writers convey a story from a clear point of view. The paper is structured to include a beginning, middle, and end; has a clearly defined purpose; and is written in concise, evocative language.

Persuasive Essays. In persuasive essays, writers present arguments intended to convince readers to adopt a certain viewpoint or take a particular action. Persuasive essays have a similar paper structure to expository essays and include clear arguments connected by logical transitions.

Précis. In précis, writers concisely summarize essential points, statements, or facts from a single work. The paper should include a brief thesis and sections that match those of the original work (e.g., Method, Results, Discussion), but it should be much shorter than the original work and be written in the writer's own words.

Response or Reaction Papers. In response or reaction papers, writers summarize one or more works and describe their personal reactions or responses to them, such as how the work or works affected them, are relevant to their life, and so forth. This type of paper is typically short (i.e., three pages or so) and written in the first person (see Section 2.16).

1.3 Annotated Bibliographies

An annotated bibliography is a type of student paper in which reference list entries are followed by short descriptions of the work called *annotations.* The annotations inform readers about the relevance and quality of the sources the writer has used. Annotated bibliographies can also constitute one element of a research paper in fields that require bibliographies rather than reference lists.

Most APA Style guidelines are applicable to annotated bibliographies.

- For guidance on font, line spacing, and paper margins, see Sections 1.18, 1.20, and 1.21, respectively.

- For guidance on writing the text of your annotations, consult the writing style and grammar guidelines in Chapter 2.

- For guidance on discussing people's personal characteristics such as age, gender, or disability status, see the bias-free language guidelines in Chapter 3.

- For guidance on punctuation, capitalization, and so forth, see the mechanics of style guidelines in Chapters 4 to 6.

- For guidelines on creating and properly ordering references in an annotated bibliography, see Chapter 9.

- For templates and examples of reference entries, see Chapter 10. In general, it is not necessary to cite the work being annotated in the annotation because the origin of the information is clear through context. However, do include in-text citations (see Chapter 8) to clarify the source if you refer to multiple works within an annotation.

Instructors generally set all other requirements for annotated bibliographies (e.g., number of references to include, length and focus of each annotation). In the absence of other guidance, format an annotated bibliography as follows:

- Format and order references in an annotated bibliography in alphabetical order, the same as you would order entries in a reference list (see Sections 9.42–9.43).

- Write each annotation as a new paragraph below its reference entry. Indent the entire annotation 0.5 in. from the left margin, the same as you would a block quotation (see Section 8.27). Do not indent the first line of the annotation further.

- If the annotation spans multiple paragraphs, indent the first line of the second and any subsequent paragraphs an additional 0.5 in., the same as you would a block quotation with multiple paragraphs.

See Figure 1.1 for an example of an annotated bibliography.

Figure 1.1 Sample Annotated Bibliography

Workplace Stress: Annotated Bibliography

Barber, L. K., Grawitch, M. J., & Maloney, P. W. (2016). Work–life balance: Contemporary perspectives. In M. J. Grawitch & D. W. Ballard (Eds.), *The psychologically healthy workplace: Building a win– win environment for organizations and employees* (pp. 111–133). American Psychological Association. https://doi.org/10.1037/14731-006

This book chapter provides an overview of the psychosociological concept of work–life balance. The authors discuss findings from studies showing harmful effects of work–life conflict on psychological and behavioral health as well as beneficial effects of work–life facilitation, wherein one role makes a positive contribution to the other. The chapter concludes with a description of work-life balance initiatives that organizations have adopted to help employees manage their dual work and nonwork obligations and some of the key factors influencing their effectiveness.

Carlson, D. S., Thompson, M. J., & Kacmar, K. M. (2019). Double crossed: The spillover and crossover effects of work demands on work outcomes through the family. *Journal of Applied Psychology*, *104*(2), 214–228. https://doi.org/10.1037/apl0000348

Carlson et al. (2019) conducted an empirical study to examine the multiple paths through which work and family variables can affect work outcomes. Whereas Barber et al. (2016) explored how work obligations can increase stress or enhance fulfillment at home, Carlson et al. viewed work demands as raising family stress, with potential negative consequences on work performance. Results supported a model in which direct effects of work demands and spillover effects of work demands to work-to-family conflict led to lower job satisfaction and affective commitment, as well as crossover effects of work-to-family conflict, spousal stress transmission, and later family-to-work conflict on organizational citizenship and absenteeism. Overall, the study demonstrated a link from work demands to work outcomes when considering the family, but those paths differed depending on whether attitudinal or behavioral work outcomes were examined.

1.4 Dissertations and Theses

Dissertations or theses are typically required of graduate students, but undergraduate students completing advanced research projects may also write them or similar types of papers. Academic institutions or departments have detailed guidelines for how to format and write dissertations and theses, and the requirements and acceptable format vary by discipline. Some dissertations and theses are hundreds of pages long and contain thorough literature reviews and exhaustive reference lists, whereas others follow a multiple-article format consisting of several shorter, related papers that are intended for individual publication. Students should follow the guidelines of their institution or department first and follow APA Style guidelines in the absence of other specific guidance. More information on adapting dissertations and theses for publication in a scholarly journal can be found in Section 12.1 of the *Publication Manual*.

1.5 Student Paper Required Elements

Student papers usually include, at minimum, a title page (see Section 1.6), which contains the paper title (see Section 1.7), author names and affiliations (see Sections 1.8–1.9), and course and assignment information (i.e., course name and number, professor's name, assignment due date; see Section 1.6); page headers with the page number (see Section 1.17); text (see Section 1.11); and a reference list (see Section 1.12). They may also include tables (see Chapter 7), figures (see Chapter 7), footnotes (see Section 1.13), and/or appendices (see Section 1.14). Student papers do not typically include a running head, an author note, or an abstract unless specifically requested by the instructor or institution. Information on paper elements usually required only in a professional paper (i.e., author note, running head, keywords, supplemental materials) can be found in Sections 2.7, 2.8, 2.10, and 2.15 of the *Publication Manual*.

Paper Elements

1.6 Title Page

A title page is required for all APA Style papers. There are both professional and student versions of the title page. The *Concise Guide* includes information on only a student title page; for guidance on a professional title page, see Sections 2.3 to 2.8 of the *Publication*

Manual. Students should follow the guidelines of their instructor or institution when determining what elements to include on the title page and how to format them. If not instructed otherwise, students should include the following elements on the title page (see Figure 1.2):

- title of the paper (see Section 1.7);

- name of each author of the paper (the byline; see Section 1.8 for formatting the byline);

- affiliation for each author, typically the university attended (including the name of any department or division; see Section 1.9);

- course number and name for which the paper is being submitted (use the format shown on institutional materials; e.g., PSY204, PSYC 4301, NURS 303);

- instructor name (check with the instructor for the preferred form; e.g., Dr. Hülya F. Akış; Professor Levin; Kwame Osei, PhD; Mariam Sherzai, RN);

- assignment due date, written in the month, date, and year format used in your country (usually November 4, 2020, or 4 November 2020; we recommend spelling out the month, although 2020-11-04 is the format in countries that use the international standard date); and

- page number in the header (also included on all pages; see Section 1.17).

Format. See the sections for the title, byline, affiliation, and page numbers for formatting instructions for these elements. Place the course number and name, instructor name, and assignment due date on separate lines on the title page, centered and in that order, starting one line below the affiliation (see Section 1.20 for more on line spacing). Do not add extra lines between these elements.

1.7 Title

The *title* should summarize the main idea of your paper simply and, if possible, in a way that is engaging for readers. For research papers, it should be a concise statement of the main topic of the research and identify the variables or theoretical issues under investigation and the relationship between them.

Although there is no prescribed limit for title length in APA Style, keep your titles focused and succinct. Include essential terms in the title that clarify the topic of your paper for readers.

Figure 1.2 Sample Student Title Page

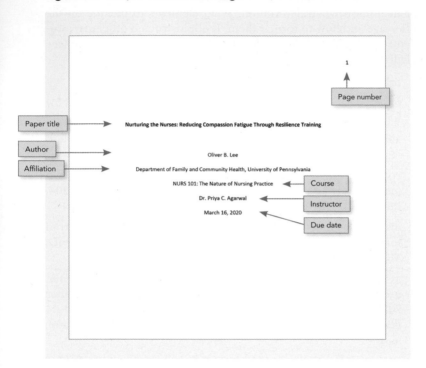

Avoid words that serve no purpose; they increase the title length and can mislead readers. For example, the words "introduction," "method," and "results" do not normally appear in a title, nor should such phrases as "a study of" or "an experimental investigation of." Occasionally, terms such as "literature review," "research synthesis," or "meta-analysis" convey important information for potential readers and are included in the title. Avoid using abbreviations in a title; spelling out all terms helps readers more readily comprehend a title's meaning. When an animal name—for example, "Rat"—is in the title, also include the scientific name in italics and parentheses: Rat (*Rattus norvegicus*). See Table 1.1 for examples of effective versus ineffective paper titles.

Format. Write the paper title in title case (see Section 5.7), bold, centered, and positioned in the upper half of the title page (e.g., three or four lines down from the top margin of the page). If the title is longer than one line, the main title and the subtitle can be separated on

Table 1.1 Effective and Ineffective Paper Titles

Effective title	Ineffective title	Rationale
Effect of Depression on the Decision to Join a Clinical Trial	A Study of the Effect of Depression on the Decision to Join a Clinical Trial	More direct: Unnecessary words have been cut.
Transition to Higher Education for Students With Autism: A Systematic Literature Review	Higher Education for Students With Autism	More precise: The focus of the research has been clarified; the type of research (literature review) has been specified.
Closing Your Eyes to Follow Your Heart: Avoiding Information to Protect a Strong Intuitive Preference	Closing Your Eyes to Follow Your Heart	More informative: A creative title has been balanced with a substantive subtitle.
Predator Stress Negatively Impacts Cognitive Performance in Rats (*Rattus norvegicus*)	Does Predator Stress Impact Cognitive Performance in Rats?	More explanatory: The title tells readers the direction of the relationship between the variables. It also includes the scientific name of the animal used in the study.

double-spaced lines if desired. Note that the paper title also appears at the top of the first page of text (see Sections 1.11 and 1.27).

Running Head. Although a running head is not required of student papers in APA Style, some instructors or institutions may request it. The *running head* is an abbreviated version of the paper title that appears at the top of every page to identify it for readers. When including a running head, place it in the page header, flush left and across from the right-aligned page number. Write the running head in all-capital letters. The same running heads appears in all page headers.

The running head should contain a maximum of 50 characters, counting letters, punctuation, and spaces between words. If the title is already 50 characters or fewer, the full title can be used as the running head. Avoid using abbreviations in the running head; however, the ampersand symbol (&) may be used rather than "and" if desired.

The running head does not have to consist of the same words in the same order as the title; rather, the idea of the title should be conveyed in a shortened form. For example, the article title "Restless Nights: Sleep Latency Increases and Sleep Quality Decreases With Caffeine Intake" could be shortened to a running head of "CAFFEINE-INDUCED REDUCTIONS IN SLEEP EFFICIENCY." For examples of a running head on a paper, see the professional title page and sample paper in Chapter 2 of the *Publication Manual* and on the APA Style website (https://apastyle.apa.org).

1.8 Author Name (Byline)

Every paper includes the name of the author or authors—the *byline*. The preferred form of an author's name is first name, middle initial(s), and last name; this form reduces the likelihood of mistaken identity (e.g., that authors with the same first and last names are the same person). Use the same form of your name for all papers. If you change your name, present your new name in a consistent form as well. Omit all academic degrees or licenses (e.g., PhD, RN, LCSW, BA, BS) from the byline.

Authors are responsible for determining the order of authorship (i.e., the order in which two or more authors' names appear in the byline) on papers that will be submitted to an instructor. Students who contribute equally to a group project may put their names in any order in the byline (e.g., alphabetical order, reverse alphabetical order). Students who contribute different amounts to a group project should list their names in the order of contribution.

Format. Write the byline on the title page after the paper title. Include one blank double-spaced line between the paper title and the byline. Follow these guidelines for byline formatting:

- If the paper has one author, write the author name centered and in standard (i.e., nonbold, nonitalic) font.
- If the paper has multiple authors, write all names on the same line (flowing onto additional lines if needed), centered, and in standard font. For two authors, separate the names with the word "and"; for three or more authors, separate the names with commas and include "and" before the final author's name.
- For names with suffixes, separate the suffix from the rest of the name with a space, not a comma (e.g., Roland J. Thorpe Jr.).

See Table 1.2 for examples of how to set up author bylines and affiliations.

Table 1.2 Examples of Author Bylines and Affiliations

Variation	Example
One author, one affiliation	Maggie C. Leonard Department of Psychology, George Mason University
One author, no institutional affiliation	Isabel de Vries Rochester, New York, United States
Two authors, shared affiliation	Mackenzie J. Clement and Talia R. Cummings College of Nursing, Michigan State University
Two authors, different affiliations	Wilhelm T. Weber[1] and Latasha P. Jackson[2] [1] Max Planck Institute for Human Development, Berlin, Germany [2] College of Education, University of Georgia
Three or more authors, shared affiliation	Madina Wahab, DeAndre L. Washington Jr., and Julian H. Lee School of Public Health, University of California, Berkeley
Three or more authors, different affiliations	Savannah C. St. John[1], Fen-Lei Chang[2,3], and Carlos O. Vásquez III[1] [1] Educational Testing Service, Princeton, New Jersey, United States [2] MRC Cognition and Brain Sciences Unit, Cambridge, England [3] Department of Psychology, University of Cambridge

1.9 Author Affiliation

The *affiliation* identifies where the author(s) studied (or worked, in the case of professional authors) when the paper was written or the work was conducted, which is usually a university or other institution. Follow these guidelines when presenting affiliations:

- Academic affiliations (e.g., universities, teaching hospitals affiliated with a university) should include the name of any department or division and the name of the institution, separated by a comma. It is not necessary to include the location of the institution unless the location is part of the institution's name.

- Nonacademic institutional affiliations (e.g., hospitals or agencies not affiliated with a university, independent laboratories, other organizations) should include the name of any department or division, the name of the institution, and the location of the institution, separated by commas.

- When providing a location (as for nonacademic institutions), give the city; state, province, or territory as applicable; and country.

Spell out state, province, and territory names rather than abbreviating them.

Format. The format of the affiliation depends on the number of authors and whether different authors have different affiliations, as follows. Begin the affiliation(s) on a new line after the byline. Place different affiliations on their own lines. Do not add blank lines between affiliations or between the byline and the first affiliation. See Table 1.2 for examples of how to set up author bylines and affiliations.

All Authors Share One Affiliation. If the paper has one author with one affiliation, or if all authors of a multiauthored paper share one affiliation, include the affiliation centered and in standard font on its own line, beginning one line below the byline. Do not include a superscript numeral.

Multiple Authors With Different Affiliations. If the paper has two or more authors with different affiliations (even if only the department is different within the same university), use superscript Arabic numerals to connect author names to the appropriate affiliation(s). List authors' affiliations in the order the authors appear in the byline; for example, for a paper with two authors who have different affiliations, list the affiliation of the first author first, followed by the affiliation of the second author, with each affiliation centered and in standard font on its own line, beginning one line below the byline. Place a superscript numeral 1 after the first author's surname, without a space between the name and the numeral (when a paper has three or more authors and thus commas appear after author names, put the numeral after the surname and before the comma). Then put a superscript numeral 1 before the corresponding affiliation (with a space between the numeral and the start of the affiliation). Repeat this process for the second author using the numeral 2 (and so on when a paper has more authors).

If some, but not all, authors share an affiliation, list the affiliation once and reuse the superscript numeral in the byline. Identify authors with two affiliations in the byline by separating the appropriate superscript numerals with a superscript comma and space. If the paper has only one author, or if there are multiple authors but all authors share the same affiliation, then superscript numerals are not used.

1.10 Abstract

An *abstract* is a brief, comprehensive summary of the contents of your paper. An abstract is not usually required for student papers unless requested by the instructor or institution.

The abstract needs to be dense with information. A good abstract is

- **accurate:** Ensure that the abstract correctly reflects the purpose and content of the paper. Do not include information that does not appear in the text.

- **nonevaluative:** Report rather than evaluate; do not add to or comment on what is in the text.

- **coherent and readable:** Write in clear and deliberate language. Use verbs rather than their noun equivalents and the active rather than the passive voice (e.g., "investigated" instead of "an investigation of"; "we present results" instead of "results are presented"; see Section 2.13). Use the present tense to describe conclusions drawn or results with continuing applicability; use the past tense to describe specific variables manipulated or outcomes measured.

- **concise:** Be brief, and make each sentence maximally informative, especially the lead sentence. Begin the abstract with the most important points. Do not waste space by repeating the title. Include only the four or five most important concepts, findings, or implications.

Format. Abstracts typically are limited to 250 words. Place the abstract on its own page after the title page (i.e., page 2). Write the section label "Abstract" in bold title case (see Section 5.7), centered at the top of the page, and place the abstract below the label.

Abstracts are usually written as a single paragraph without indentation of the first line. Some instructors may require a structured abstract, which is also written as a single paragraph without indentation and includes labels to identify various sections (e.g., Objective, Method, Results, Conclusions); unless instructed otherwise, write the labels in bold italic font.

1.11 Text (Body)

The *text*, or body of the paper, contains the writer's main contribution. The text can be organized in many ways, and the organization generally depends on the paper type (see Sections 1.2–1.4). Most papers include an introduction, consisting of one or a few focused paragraphs that address the paper's importance, contextualization within the existing literature, and aims. Often the introduction for a research paper contains a literature review of relevant background studies on the topic of the paper; this review provides enough information for readers to understand the paper's content but does not go into detail about every study.

Beyond the introduction, the paper should include paragraphs or sections explaining its main premises. There are many possible formats for the rest of the text; for example, a quantitative research paper typically includes sections called "Method," "Results," and "Discussion," whereas a qualitative research paper may include a section called "Findings" instead of "Results," or it may have different section headings altogether. A brief student paper (e.g., a response paper) may not have section headings or may have sections with headings different from those described in this guide. For example, a comparative essay may contain headings for each topic as well as subheadings for specific aspects of each topic. See Section 1.25 for more on organization.

Format. The text should start on a new page after the title page (if your paper does not include an abstract) or after the abstract (if your paper includes one). On the first line of the first page of the text, write the title of the paper again in title case (see Section 5.7), bold, and centered. The text then starts on the next line, left-aligned and written as double-spaced paragraphs, with the first line of each paragraph indented by one tab key (0.5 in.; see Sections 1.22–1.23). Use headings as needed and appropriate within the text to separate sections and to reflect the organizational structure of the content (see Sections 1.26–1.27). Do not start a new page or add extra line breaks when a new heading occurs; each section of the text should follow the next without a break.

1.12 Reference List

The *reference list* provides a reliable way for readers to identify and locate the works cited in a paper. References are used to document and substantiate statements made about the literature, just as data in the paper are used to support interpretations and conclusions. The references cited in the paper do not need to be exhaustive but should be sufficient to support the need for your paper and to enable readers to place it in the context of previous research and theorizing. Each entry in the reference list should have a corresponding citation in the text. For detailed guidance on citing sources in the text and preparing the reference list, consult Chapters 8 and 9, respectively.

Format. Start the reference list on a new page after the text and before any tables, figures, and/or appendices. Write the section label "References," capitalized, in bold, and centered at the top of the page. Double-space all reference list entries (including between and within references). Use a hanging indent for all references, meaning that the first line of each reference is flush left and subsequent lines are indented by 0.5 in. Automatically apply the hanging indent using the paragraph-formatting function of your word-processing program. For the order of works in the reference list, see Sections 9.43 to 9.48.

1.13 Footnotes

A *footnote* is a brief note that provides additional content or copyright attribution. Any type of paper may include footnotes as needed.

Content Footnotes. Content footnotes supplement or enhance substantive information in the text; they should not include complicated, irrelevant, or nonessential information. Because they can be distracting, content footnotes should be included only if they strengthen the discussion. A content footnote should convey just one idea; if you find yourself creating paragraphs as you are writing a footnote, then the main text or an appendix would likely be a more suitable place to present the information.

Copyright Attribution. When authors reproduce lengthy quotations and/or test or scale items in the text, a copyright attribution is usually required and should be presented in a footnote. A reproduced table or figure also requires a copyright attribution, but this attribution appears in the table or figure note. Further directions on seeking permission to reproduce material and appropriate wording for the copyright attribution appear in Sections 8.35 to 8.39.

Footnote Callout Numbering and Format. Number all footnotes consecutively in the order in which their callouts appear in the text with superscript Arabic numerals. Footnote callouts should be superscripted, like this,[1] following any punctuation mark except a dash. A footnote callout that appears with a dash—like this[2]—always precedes the dash. (The callout falls inside a closing parenthesis if it applies only to matter within the parentheses, like this.[3]) Do not put a space before the footnote callout in text. Do not place footnote callouts in headings. To refer to a footnote again after it has been called out, identify it in the text by the footnote number (e.g., write "see Footnote 3"); do not repeat the footnote callout or the whole footnote.

Place each footnote at the bottom of the page on which it is discussed using the footnote function of your word-processing program. Footnotes may alternatively be placed in consecutive order on a separate page after the references. In this case, write the section label "Footnotes," capitalized, in bold, and centered at the top of the page, then write the footnotes themselves as double-spaced indented paragraphs that begin with a superscript footnote number; put a space between the footnote number and the text that follows. Be sure that the number of the footnote callout corresponds with the number that appears with the footnoted text.

1.14 Appendices

Material that supplements the paper's content but that would be distracting or inappropriate in the text of the paper can be included in an *appendix*. In general, an appendix is appropriate for materials that are relatively brief and easily presented in print. Include an appendix only if it helps readers understand, evaluate, or replicate the study or theoretical argument being made. Some examples of material suitable for an appendix are (a) lists of stimulus materials (e.g., those used in psycholinguistic research); (b) instructions to participants; (c) tests, scales, or inventories developed for the study being reported; (d) data sets, maps, or long tables; (e) detailed descriptions of complex equipment; (f) detailed demographic descriptions of subpopulations in the study; and (g) other items that are too detailed or complex to report within the body of the paper. Be sure that you have followed all relevant ethical standards for materials placed in the appendices, including copyright attribution, accurate representation of data, and protection of human participants (e.g., as the standards apply to images or videos of identifiable people; for more information on ethical standards in research, see Sections 1.1–1.25 of the *Publication Manual*).

Format. Begin each appendix on a separate page after any references, footnotes, tables, and figures. Give each appendix a label and a title. If a paper has one appendix, label it "Appendix"; if a paper has more than one appendix, label each appendix with a capital letter (e.g., "Appendix A," "Appendix B") in the order in which it is mentioned in the text. Each appendix should be mentioned (called out by its label) at least once in the text (e.g., "see Appendix A"). The appendix title should describe the appendix content. Place the appendix label and title in bold, title case (see Section 5.7), and centered on separate lines at the top of the page on which the appendix begins.

The appendix may consist of text, tables, figures, or a combination of these. A text appendix may contain headings. If an appendix contains text, write the paragraphs as regular indented paragraphs, the same as in the body of the paper. If a text appendix contains tables, figures, footnotes, and/or displayed equations, give each one a number preceded by the letter of the appendix in which it appears (e.g., Table A1 is the first table within Appendix A or of a sole appendix that is not labeled with a letter; Equation B1 is the first equation within Appendix B; Figure C2 is the second figure of Appendix C). In a sole text appendix, which is not labeled with a letter, precede all table, figure, footnote, and equation numbers with the letter "A" to distinguish them from those of the main text. All tables and figures within a text appendix must be mentioned in the appendix and numbered in order of mention. The tables and figures in a text appendix should be embedded within the text, as described in Section 7.6.

If an appendix consists of a table only or a figure only, then the appendix label takes the place of the table or figure number, and the appendix title takes the place of the table or figure title. Thus, if Appendix B is a table-only appendix, the table is referred to as Appendix B rather than as Table B1. Likewise, if Appendix C is a figure-only appendix, the figure is referred to as Appendix C rather than as Figure C1. If multiple tables and/or figures (but no text) are combined into one appendix, label and title the appendix and also number and title the tables and/or figures within the appendix (e.g., Tables D1 and D2 are two tables in Appendix D).

Format

1.15 Importance of Format

Use the guidelines in this section to format all APA Style papers. A well-prepared paper encourages instructors and readers to view your work as professional. In contrast, mechanical flaws can lead instructors and readers to misinterpret content and question your understanding of the material or attention to detail. Depending on the requirements of the instructor, students may receive a lower grade because of formatting errors in their papers.

1.16 Order of Pages

Arrange the pages of the paper in the following order:

- title page (page 1)
- abstract (if needed, start on a new page after the title page)

- text (start on a new page after the abstract or, if the paper does not have an abstract, on a new page after the title page)
- references (start on a new page after the end of the text)
- footnotes (if needed, start on a new page after the references)
- tables (if needed, start each on a new page after the footnotes)
- figures (if needed, start each on a new page after the tables)
- appendices (if needed, start each on a new page after the references or after any tables and/or figures)

APA Style provides options for the display of footnotes, tables, and figures. Footnotes may appear either in the footer of the page where they are first mentioned (see Section 1.13) or on a separate page after the references. Tables and figures may be embedded within the text after they are first mentioned, or each table and figure can be displayed on a separate page after the footnotes (or after the references if there is no footnotes page; see Section 7.6).

1.17 Page Header

All papers should contain the page number, flush right, in the header of every page. Use the automatic page-numbering function of your word-processing program to insert page numbers in the top right corner; do not type page numbers manually. The title page is page number 1.

If requested, the running head also appears in the page header (see Section 1.7) along with the page number. When both elements appear, the running head should be flush left and the page number should be flush right. Student papers need only the page number in the page header unless the instructor or institution also requires a running head.

1.18 Font

APA Style papers should be written in a font that is accessible to all users. Historically, sans serif fonts have been preferred for online works and serif for print works; however, modern screen resolutions can typically accommodate either type of font, and people who use assistive technologies can adjust font settings to their preferences. Thus, a variety of font choices are permitted in APA Style; check with your instructor or institution for any requirements regarding font.

Use the same font throughout the text of the paper. Options include

- a sans serif font such as 11-point Calibri, 11-point Arial, or 10-point Lucida Sans Unicode or

- a serif font such as 12-point Times New Roman, 11-point Georgia, or normal (10-point) Computer Modern (the latter is the default font for LaTeX).

We recommend these fonts because they are legible and widely available and because they include special characters such as math symbols and Greek letters.

An APA Style paper may contain other fonts or font sizes under the following circumstances:

- Within figure images, use a sans serif font with a type size between 8 and 14 points.

- When presenting computer code, use a monospace font, such as 10-point Lucida Console or 10-point Courier New.

- When presenting a footnote in a page footer, the default footnote settings of your word-processing program are acceptable (e.g., 10-point font with single line spacing).

Because different fonts take up different amounts of space on the page, we recommend using word count rather than page count to gauge paper length (see Section 1.24). See the APA Style website (https://apastyle.apa.org) for further discussion of font and accessible typography.

1.19 Special Characters

Special characters are accented letters and other diacritical marks, Greek letters, math signs, and symbols. Type special characters using the special character functions of your word-processing program or a plug-in such as MathType. Characters that are not available should be presented as images. For more information on Greek letters and mathematical symbols, see Sections 6.10 and 6.11.

1.20 Line Spacing

Double-space the entire paper, including the title page, abstract, text, headings, block quotations, reference list, table and figure notes, and appendices, with the following exceptions:

- **title page:** Elements of the title page are double-spaced, and an additional double-spaced blank line appears between the title and byline (see Figure 1.2).

- **table body and figure image:** The table body (cells) and words within the image part of a figure may be single-spaced, one-and-a-half-spaced, or double-spaced, depending on what format creates the most effective presentation of the data. If text appears on the same page as a table or figure, insert a double-spaced blank line between the text and the table or figure (for more information on placement of tables and figures, see Section 7.6).

- **footnotes:** Footnotes that appear at the bottom of the page on which they are called out should be single-spaced and formatted with the default settings of your word-processing program. Footnotes that appear on their own page after the references should be formatted like regular paragraphs of text—that is, indented and double-spaced.

- **displayed equations:** It is permissible to use triple- or quadruple-spacing in special circumstances, such as before and after a displayed equation.

It is not necessary to add blank lines before or after headings, even if a heading falls at the end of a page. Do not add extra spacing between paragraphs.

1.21 Margins

Use 1-in. (2.54-cm) margins on all sides (top, bottom, left, and right) of the page. This is the default page margin in most word-processing programs. The page header is placed within these margins; insert page numbers using the automatic page-numbering function of your word-processing program (see Section 1.17 for more). Dissertations and theses may have different requirements if they are to be bound (e.g., 1.5-in. left margins).

1.22 Paragraph Alignment

Align the text to the left and leave the right margin uneven ("ragged"). Do not use full justification, which adjusts the spacing between words to make all lines the same length (flush with the margins). Do not manually divide words at the end of a line, and do not use the hyphenation function to break words at the ends of lines. Do not manually insert line breaks into long DOIs or URLs; however, breaks in DOIs or URLs applied automatically by a word-processing program are permissible.

1.23 Paragraph Indentation

Indent the first line of every paragraph 0.5 in. For consistency, use the tab key or the automatic paragraph-formatting function of your word-processing program. The default settings in most word-processing programs are acceptable. The remaining lines of the paragraph should be left-aligned.

Exceptions to these paragraph indentation requirements are as follows:

- On the title page, the title (in bold), byline, affiliations, course number and name, instructor, and assignment date should be centered (see Figure 1.2).
- At the top of the first page of text, the title (in bold) should be centered (see Figure 1.3).
- Section labels, such as "Abstract" and "References," should be centered (and in bold; see Section 1.27).
- The first line of the abstract should be flush left (not indented; see Section 1.10).
- The entirety of a block quotation should be indented from the left margin 0.5 in. If the block quotation spans more than one paragraph, the first line of the second and any subsequent paragraphs of the block quotation should be indented another 0.5 in. so that those first lines are indented a total of 1 in. (see Section 8.27).
- Level 1 headings should be centered (and in bold), and Level 2 and 3 headings should be left-aligned (and in bold or bold italic, respectively; see Section 1.26).
- Table and figure numbers (in bold; see Section 7.10), titles (in italic; see Sections 7.11 and 7.25), and notes (see Sections 7.14 and 7.28) should be flush left.
- Reference list entries should have a hanging indent of 0.5 in. (see Section 1.12).
- Appendix labels and titles should be centered (and in bold; see Section 1.14).

1.24 Paper Length

The length for student papers is specified by the assignment guidelines. If a paper exceeds the target length, try shortening it by stating points clearly and directly, confining discussion to the specific problem under investigation, deleting or combining data displays, eliminating repetition across sections, and writing in the active voice. For guidance on improving sentence and paragraph length, see Section 2.6. If your paper is still too long, you may need to focus on a narrower topic or, if the instructor allows, divide the paper into two or more papers, each with a specific focus.

Paper length targets may be specified by either page count or word count; we recommend word count because different fonts are slightly different sizes and may produce variations in the number of pages. However, follow the directions of your assigning instructor or institution for determining paper length. In general, to determine the page count, count every page, including the title page and reference list. Likewise, to determine word count, count every word from beginning to end, including all in-text citations, reference entries, tables, figures (other than words in a figure image, which may not be captured by word count), and appendices. Use the word-count function of your word-processing program to determine the word count. Do not count text in the page header (i.e., running head and page numbers) or manually add any words within figure images to the word count (these words are generally not included in the automatic word count in programs such as Microsoft Word, Academic Writer, or Google Docs).

Organization

1.25 Principles of Organization

In scholarly writing, sound organizational structure is the key to clear, precise, and logical communication. Before beginning to write, consider the best paper length and structure for your findings. Ordering your thoughts logically at both sentence and paragraph levels will also strengthen the impact of your writing.

Headings in a document identify the topic or purpose of the content within each section. Headings help readers become familiar with how a paper's content is organized, allowing them to easily find the information they seek. Headings should be succinct yet long enough to describe the content; see the sample student paper at the end of this chapter for examples of effective headings. Concise headings help readers anticipate key points and track the development of your argument. Headings that are well formatted and clearly worded aid both visual and nonvisual readers of all abilities. It is important for headings to be clearly distinguishable from the text. For a deeper discussion of how to effectively create and use headings (and related text) for all users (including those using assistive technologies), visit the APA Style website (https://apastyle.apa.org).

There are five levels of heading in APA Style (see Section 1.26), and all topics of equal importance should have the same level of heading. For example, in a comparative essay, the heading for each topic being compared should be at the same level, with parallel wording. Avoid having only one subsection heading within a section, just like in an outline; use at least two subsection headings within a section, or use none (e.g., in an outline, a section numbered with a Roman numeral would be divided into either a minimum of A and B subsections or no subsections; an A subsection could not stand alone).

1.26 Heading Levels

APA Style headings have five possible levels: Level 1 headings are used for top-level or main sections, Level 2 headings are subsections of Level 1, and so on (see Table 1.3). Regardless of the number of levels of subheading within a section, the heading structure for all sections follows the same top-down progression. Each section starts with the highest level of heading, even if one section has fewer levels of subheading than another section. For example, in a psychology paper with Level 1 Method, Results, and Discussion headings, the Method and Results sections may each have two levels of subheading (Levels 2 and 3), and the Discussion section may have only one level of subheading (Level 2). Thus, there would be three levels of heading for the paper overall.

Headings in the Introduction. Do not begin a paper with an "Introduction" heading; because the first paragraphs of a paper are understood to be introductory, the paper title at the top of the first page of text acts as a de facto Level 1 heading (see Figure 1.3). For subsections within the introduction, use Level 2 headings for the first level of

Figure 1.3 Use of Headings in a Sample Introduction

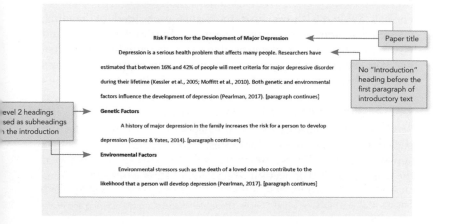

Table 1.3 Format for the Five Levels of Heading in APA Style

Level	Format
1	<div align="center">**Centered, Bold, Title Case Heading**</div>Text begins as a new paragraph.
2	**Flush Left, Bold, Title Case Heading** Text begins as a new paragraph.
3	***Flush Left, Bold Italic, Title Case Heading*** Text begins as a new paragraph.
4	**Indented, Bold, Title Case Heading, Ending With a Period.** Text begins on the same line and continues as a regular paragraph.
5	***Indented, Bold Italic, Title Case Heading, Ending With a Period.*** Text begins on the same line and continues as a regular paragraph.

Note. In title case, most words are capitalized (see Section 5.7).

subsection, Level 3 for subsections of any Level 2 headings, and so on. After the introduction (regardless of whether it includes headings), use a Level 1 heading for the next main section of the paper (e.g., Method).

Number of Headings in a Paper. The number of levels of heading needed for a paper depends on its length and complexity; three is average. If only one level of heading is needed, use Level 1; if two levels are needed, use Levels 1 and 2; if three levels are needed, use Levels 1, 2, and 3; and so forth. Use only the number of headings necessary to differentiate distinct sections in your paper; short student papers may not require any headings. Do not label headings with numbers or letters.[1]

Format. Table 1.3 shows how to format each level of heading, Figure 1.3 demonstrates the use of headings in the introduction, and Figure 1.4 lists all the headings used in a sample paper in correct format. The sample student paper at the end of this chapter also shows the use of headings in context.

1.27 Section Labels

Section labels include "Abstract," the paper title at the top of the first page of text, "References," "Footnotes," and "Appendix A" (and other appendix labels). Place section labels on a separate line at the top of the page on which the section begins, in bold and centered.

---

[1] The sections and headings in the *Concise Guide* are numbered to aid indexing and cross-referencing.

Figure 1.4 Format of Headings in a Sample Paper

Sample Student Paper

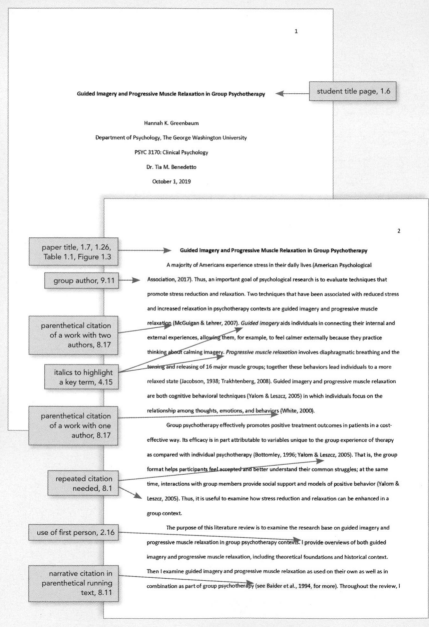

1

Guided Imagery and Progressive Muscle Relaxation in Group Psychotherapy ◀—— student title page, 1.6

Hannah K. Greenbaum

Department of Psychology, The George Washington University

PSYC 3170: Clinical Psychology

Dr. Tia M. Benedetto

October 1, 2019

2

paper title, 1.7, 1.26, Table 1.1, Figure 1.3 ——▶ **Guided Imagery and Progressive Muscle Relaxation in Group Psychotherapy**

A majority of Americans experience stress in their daily lives (American Psychological

group author, 9.11 ——▶ Association, 2017). Thus, an important goal of psychological research is to evaluate techniques that

promote stress reduction and relaxation. Two techniques that have been associated with reduced stress

and increased relaxation in psychotherapy contexts are guided imagery and progressive muscle

parenthetical citation of a work with two authors, 8.17 —— relaxation (McGuigan & Lehrer, 2007). *Guided imagery* aids individuals in connecting their internal and

external experiences, allowing them, for example, to feel calmer externally because they practice

thinking about calming imagery. *Progressive muscle relaxation* involves diaphragmatic breathing and the

italics to highlight a key term, 4.15 —— tensing and releasing of 16 major muscle groups; together these behaviors lead individuals to a more

relaxed state (Jacobson, 1938; Trakhtenberg, 2008). Guided imagery and progressive muscle relaxation

are both cognitive behavioral techniques (Yalom & Leszcz, 2005) in which individuals focus on the

parenthetical citation of a work with one author, 8.17 —— relationship among thoughts, emotions, and behaviors (White, 2000).

Group psychotherapy effectively promotes positive treatment outcomes in patients in a cost-

effective way. Its efficacy is in part attributable to variables unique to the group experience of therapy

as compared with individual psychotherapy (Bottomley, 1996; Yalom & Leszcz, 2005). That is, the group

format helps participants feel accepted and better understand their common struggles; at the same

repeated citation needed, 8.1 —— time, interactions with group members provide social support and models of positive behavior (Yalom &

Leszcz, 2005). Thus, it is useful to examine how stress reduction and relaxation can be enhanced in a

group context.

use of first person, 2.16 —— The purpose of this literature review is to examine the research base on guided imagery and

progressive muscle relaxation in group psychotherapy contexts. I provide overviews of both guided

imagery and progressive muscle relaxation, including theoretical foundations and historical context.

narrative citation in parenthetical running text, 8.11 —— Then I examine guided imagery and progressive muscle relaxation as used on their own as well as in

combination as part of group psychotherapy (see Baider et al., 1994, for more). Throughout the review, I

Sample Student Paper *(continued)*

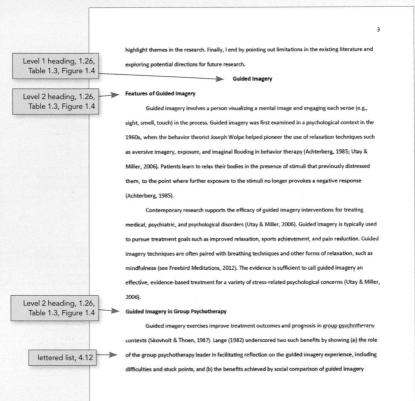

3

highlight themes in the research. Finally, I end by pointing out limitations in the existing literature and exploring potential directions for future research.

Guided Imagery

Features of Guided Imagery

Guided imagery involves a person visualizing a mental image and engaging each sense (e.g., sight, smell, touch) in the process. Guided imagery was first examined in a psychological context in the 1960s, when the behavior theorist Joseph Wolpe helped pioneer the use of relaxation techniques such as aversive imagery, exposure, and imaginal flooding in behavior therapy (Achterberg, 1985; Utay & Miller, 2006). Patients learn to relax their bodies in the presence of stimuli that previously distressed them, to the point where further exposure to the stimuli no longer provokes a negative response (Achterberg, 1985).

Contemporary research supports the efficacy of guided imagery interventions for treating medical, psychiatric, and psychological disorders (Utay & Miller, 2006). Guided imagery is typically used to pursue treatment goals such as improved relaxation, sports achievement, and pain reduction. Guided imagery techniques are often paired with breathing techniques and other forms of relaxation, such as mindfulness (see Freebird Meditations, 2012). The evidence is sufficient to call guided imagery an effective, evidence-based treatment for a variety of stress-related psychological concerns (Utay & Miller, 2006).

Guided Imagery in Group Psychotherapy

Guided imagery exercises improve treatment outcomes and prognosis in group psychotherapy contexts (Skovholt & Thoen, 1987). Lange (1982) underscored two such benefits by showing (a) the role of the group psychotherapy leader in facilitating reflection on the guided imagery experience, including difficulties and stuck points, and (b) the benefits achieved by social comparison of guided imagery

Level 1 heading, 1.26, Table 1.3, Figure 1.4

Level 2 heading, 1.26, Table 1.3, Figure 1.4

Level 2 heading, 1.26, Table 1.3, Figure 1.4

lettered list, 4.12

Sample Student Paper *(continued)*

4

experiences between group members. Teaching techniques and reflecting on the group process are unique components of guided imagery received in a group context (Yalom & Leszcz, 2005).

Empirical research focused on guided imagery interventions supports the efficacy of the technique with a variety of populations within hospital settings, with positive outcomes for individuals diagnosed with depression, anxiety, and eating disorders (Utay & Miller, 2006). Guided imagery and relaxation techniques have even been found to "reduce distress and allow the immune system to function more effectively" (Trakhtenberg, 2008, p. 850). For example, Holden-Lund (1988) examined effects of a guided imagery intervention on surgical stress and wound healing in a group of 24 patients. Patients listened to guided imagery recordings and reported reduced state anxiety, lower cortisol levels following surgery, and less irritation in wound healing compared with a control group. Holden-Lund concluded that the guided imagery recordings contributed to improved surgical recovery. It would be interesting to see how the results might differ if guided imagery was practiced continually in a group context.

Guided imagery has also been shown to reduce stress, length of hospital stay, and symptoms related to medical and psychological conditions (Scherwitz et al., 2005). For example, Ball et al. (2003) conducted guided imagery in a group psychotherapy format with 11 children (ages 5–18) experiencing recurrent abdominal pain. [...]

psychotherapy sessions [...]

diaries and parent and c[...]

pain. Despite a small san[...]

that guided imagery in a [...]

*Labels (call-outs):*
- short quotation, 8.25, 8.26
- repeated narrative citation with the year omitted, 8.16
- "et al." citations for works with three or more authors, 8.17
- Level 1 heading, 1.26, Table 1.3, Figure 1.4
- Level 2 heading, 1.26, Table 1.3, Figure 1.4
- secondary source citation, 8.6
- narrative citation with the year in the narrative, 8.11
- "for more" citation, 8.11

5

met once in a group to learn guided imagery and then practiced guided imagery individually on their own (see Menzies et al., 2014, for more). Thus, it is unknown whether guided imagery would have different effects if implemented on an ongoing basis in group psychotherapy.

Progressive Muscle Relaxation

Features of Progressive Muscle Relaxation

Progressive muscle relaxation involves diaphragmatic or deep breathing and the tensing and releasing of muscles in the body (Jacobson, 1938). Edmund Jacobson developed progressive muscle relaxation in 1929 (as cited in Peterson et al., 2011) and directed participants to practice progressive muscle relaxation several times a week for a year. After examining progressive muscle relaxation as an intervention for stress or anxiety, Joseph Wolpe (1960; as cited in Peterson et al., 2011) theorized that relaxation was a promising treatment. In 1973, Bernstein and Borkovec created a manual for helping professionals to teach their clients progressive muscle relaxation, thereby bringing progressive muscle relaxation into the fold of interventions used in cognitive behavior therapy. In its current state, progressive muscle relaxation is often paired with relaxation training and described within a relaxation framework (see Freebird Meditations, 2012, for more).

Research on the use of progressive muscle relaxation for stress reduction has demonstrated the efficacy of the method (McGuigan & Lehrer, 2007). As clients learn how to tense and release different muscle groups, the physical relaxation achieved then influences psychological processes (McCallie et al., 2006). For example, progressive muscle relaxation can help alleviate tension headaches, insomnia, pain, and irritable bowel syndrome. This research demonstrates that relaxing the body can also help relax the mind and lead to physical benefits.

Progressive Muscle Relaxation in Group Psychotherapy

Limited, but compelling, research has examined progressive muscle relaxation within group psychotherapy. Progressive muscle relaxation has been used in outpatient and inpatient hospital

Sample Student Paper *(continued)*

6

settings to reduce stress and physical symptoms (Peterson et al., 2011). For example, the U.S. Department of Veterans Affairs integrates progressive muscle relaxation into therapy skills groups (Hardy, 2017). The goal is for group members to practice progressive muscle relaxation throughout their inpatient stay and then continue the practice at home to promote ongoing relief of symptoms (Yalom & Leszcz, 2005).

[long paraphrase, 8.24]

Yu (2004) examined the effects of multimodal progressive muscle relaxation on psychological distress in 121 elderly patients with heart failure. Participants were randomized into experimental and control groups. The experimental group received biweekly group sessions on progressive muscle relaxation, as well as tape-directed self-practice and a revision workshop. The control group received follow-up phone calls as a placebo. Results indicated that the experimental group exhibited significant improvement in reports of psychological distress compared with the control group. Although this study incorporated a multimodal form of progressive muscle relaxation, the experimental group met biweekly in a group format; thus, the results may be applicable to group psychotherapy.

Progressive muscle relaxation has also been examined as a stress-reduction intervention with large groups, albeit not therapy groups. Rausch et al. (2006) exposed a group of 387 college students to

[time abbreviation, 5.16]

20 min of either meditation, progressive muscle relaxation, or waiting as a control condition. Students exposed to meditation and progressive muscle relaxation recovered more quickly from subsequent

[block quotation, 8.25, 8.27]

stressors than did students in the control condition. Rausch et al. (2006) concluded the following:

> A mere 20 min of these group interventions was effective in reducing anxiety to normal levels
> . . . merely 10 min of the interventions allowed [the high-anxiety group] to recover from the
> stressor. Thus, brief interventions of meditation and progressive muscle relaxation may be
> effective for those with clinical levels of anxiety and for stress recovery when exposed to brief,
> transitory stressors. (p. 287)

Thus, even small amo

anxiety.

Guided

Combinations

muscle relaxation, have been shown to improve psychiatric and medical symptoms when delivered in a group psychotherapy context (Bottomley, 1996; Cunningham & Tocco, 1989). The research supports the existence of immediate and long-term positive effects of guided imagery and progressive muscle relaxation delivered in group psychotherapy (Baider et al., 1994). For example, Cohen and Fried (2007)

[narrative citation, 8.11; paraphrasing, 8.23]

examined the effect of group psychotherapy on 114 women diagnosed with breast cancer. The researchers randomly assigned participants to three groups: (a) a control group, (b) a relaxation psychotherapy group that received guided imagery and progressive muscle relaxation interventions, or (c) a cognitive behavioral therapy group. Participants reported less psychological distress in both intervention groups compared with the control group, and participants in the relaxation psychotherapy group reported reduced symptoms related to sleep and fatigue. The researchers concluded that relaxation training using guided imagery and progressive muscle relaxation in group psychotherapy is effective for relieving distress in women diagnosed with breast cancer. These results further support the utility of guided imagery and progressive muscle relaxation within the group psychotherapy modality.

[Level 1 heading, 1.26, Table 1.3, Figure 1.4]

Conclusion

Limitations of Existing Research

Research on the use of guided imagery and progressive muscle relaxation to achieve stress reduction and relaxation is compelling but has significant limitations. Psychotherapy groups that implement guided imagery and progressive muscle relaxation are typically homogeneous, time limited, and brief (Yalom & Leszcz, 2005). Relaxation training in group psychotherapy typically includes only one

Sample Student Paper *(continued)*

8

usually expected to practice the techniques by themselves (see Menzies et al., 2014). Future research

should address how these relaxation techniques can assist people in diverse groups and how the impact

of relaxation techniques may be amplified if treatments are delivered in the group setting over time.

Future research should also examine differences in inpatient versus outpatient psychotherapy

groups as well as structured versus unstructured groups. The majority of research on the use of guided

imagery and progressive muscle relaxation with psychotherapy groups has used unstructured inpatient

groups (e.g., groups in a hospital setting). However, inpatient and outpatient groups are distinct, as are

structured versus unstructured groups, and each format offers potential advantages and limitations

(Yalom & Leszcz, 2005). For example, an advantage of an unstructured group is that the group leader

can reflect the group process and focus on the "here and now," which may improve the efficacy of the

relaxation techniques (Yalom & Leszcz, 2005). However, research also has supported the efficacy of

structured psychotherapy groups for patients with a variety of medical, psychiatric, and psychological

disorders (Hashim & Zainol, 2015; see also Baider et al., 1994; Cohen & Fried, 2007). Empirical research ◀—— "see also" citation, 8.12

assessing these interventions is limited, and further research is recommended.

Directions for Future Research ◀—— Level 2 heading, 1.26, Table 1.3, Figure 1.4

There are additional considerations when interpreting the results of previous studies and

planning for future studies of these techniques. For example, a lack of control groups and small sample

sizes have contributed to low statistical power and limited the generalizability of findings. Although the

current data support the efficacy of psychotherapy groups that integrate guided imagery and

progressive muscle relaxation, further research with control groups and larger samples would bolster

confidence in the effica[...]

participants over time, re[...]

attrition. These factors a[...]

rates and changes in me[...]

personal communication, 8.9

9

participation (L. Plum, personal communication, March 17, 2019). Despite these challenges, continued

research examining guided imagery and progressive muscle relaxation interventions within group

psychotherapy is warranted (Scherwitz et al., 2005). The results thus far are promising, and further

investigation has the potential to make relaxation techniques that can improve people's lives more

effective and widely available.

Sample Student Paper *(continued)*

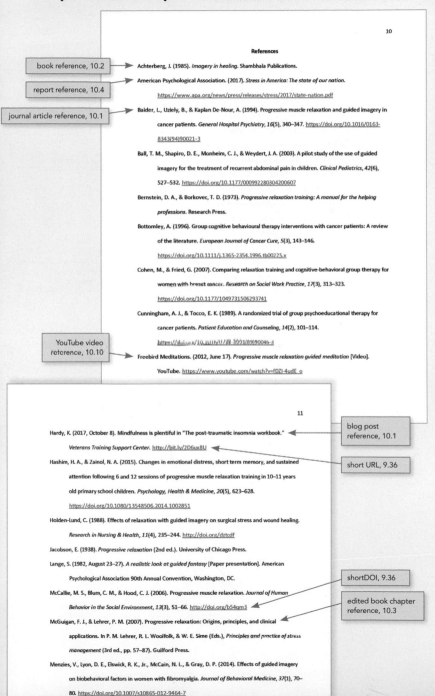

10

References

book reference, 10.2 → Achterberg, J. (1985). *Imagery in healing*. Shambhala Publications.

report reference, 10.4 → American Psychological Association. (2017). *Stress in America: The state of our nation*.
https://www.apa.org/news/press/releases/stress/2017/state-nation.pdf

journal article reference, 10.1 → Baider, L., Uziely, B., & Kaplan De-Nour, A. (1994). Progressive muscle relaxation and guided imagery in
cancer patients. *General Hospital Psychiatry*, *16*(5), 340–347. https://doi.org/10.1016/0163-
8343(94)90021-3

Ball, T. M., Shapiro, D. E., Monheim, C. J., & Weydert, J. A. (2003). A pilot study of the use of guided
imagery for the treatment of recurrent abdominal pain in children. *Clinical Pediatrics*, *42*(6),
527–532. https://doi.org/10.1177/000992280304200607

Bernstein, D. A., & Borkovec, T. D. (1973). *Progressive relaxation training: A manual for the helping
professions*. Research Press.

Bottomley, A. (1996). Group cognitive behavioural therapy interventions with cancer patients: A review
of the literature. *European Journal of Cancer Cure*, *5*(3), 143–146.
https://doi.org/10.1111/j.1365-2354.1996.tb00225.x

Cohen, M., & Fried, G. (2007). Comparing relaxation training and cognitive-behavioral group therapy for
women with breast cancer. *Research on Social Work Practice*, *17*(3), 313–323.
https://doi.org/10.1177/1049731506293741

Cunningham, A. J., & Tocco, E. K. (1989). A randomized trial of group psychoeducational therapy for
cancer patients. *Patient Education and Counseling*, *14*(2), 101–114.
https://doi.org/10.1016/0738-3991(89)90046-3

YouTube video reference, 10.10 → Freebird Meditations. (2012, June 17). *Progressive muscle relaxation guided meditation* [Video].
YouTube. https://www.youtube.com/watch?v=fDZ1-4udE_o

11

Hardy, K. (2017, October 8). Mindfulness is plentiful in "The post-traumatic insomnia workbook." ← blog post reference, 10.1
Veterans Training Support Center. http://bit.ly/2D6ux8U ← short URL, 9.36

Hashim, H. A., & Zainol, N. A. (2015). Changes in emotional distress, short term memory, and sustained
attention following 6 and 12 sessions of progressive muscle relaxation training in 10–11 years
old primary school children. *Psychology, Health & Medicine*, *20*(5), 623–628.
https://doi.org/10.1080/13548506.2014.1002851

Holden-Lund, C. (1988). Effects of relaxation with guided imagery on surgical stress and wound healing.
Research in Nursing & Health, *11*(4), 235–244. http://doi.org/dztcdf

Jacobson, E. (1938). *Progressive relaxation* (2nd ed.). University of Chicago Press.

Lange, S. (1982, August 23–27). *A realistic look at guided fantasy* [Paper presentation]. American
Psychological Association 90th Annual Convention, Washington, DC.

McCallie, M. S., Blum, C. M., & Hood, C. J. (2006). Progressive muscle relaxation. *Journal of Human
Behavior in the Social Environment*, *13*(3), 51–66. http://doi.org/b54qm3 ← shortDOI, 9.36

McGuigan, F. J., & Lehrer, P. M. (2007). Progressive relaxation: Origins, principles, and clinical ← edited book chapter reference, 10.3
applications. In P. M. Lehrer, R. L. Woolfolk, & W. E. Sime (Eds.), *Principles and practice of stress
management* (3rd ed., pp. 57–87). Guilford Press.

Menzies, V., Lyon, D. E., Elswick, R. K., Jr., McCain, N. L., & Gray, D. P. (2014). Effects of guided imagery
on biobehavioral factors in women with fibromyalgia. *Journal of Behavioral Medicine*, *37*(1), 70–
80. https://doi.org/10.1007/s10865-012-9464-7

Sample Student Paper *(continued)*

12

recovery. *International Journal of Stress Management, 13*(3), 273–290.

https://doi.org/10.1037/1072-5245.13.3.273

Scherwitz, L. W., McHenry, P., & Herrero, R. (2005). Interactive guided imagery therapy with medical

patients: Predictors of health outcomes. *The Journal of Alternative and Complementary

Medicine, 11*(1), 69–83. https://doi.org/10.1089/acm.2005.11.69

Skovholt, T. M., & Thoen, G. A. (1987). Mental imagery and parenthood decision making. *Journal of

Counseling & Development, 65*(6), 315–316. http://doi.org/fzmtjd

Trakhtenberg, E. C. (2008). The effects of guided imagery on the immune system: A critical review.

International Journal of Neuroscience, 118(6), 839–855. http://doi.org/fxfsbq

Utay, J., & Miller, M. (2006). Guided imagery as an effective therapeutic technique: A brief review of its

history and efficacy research. *Journal of Instructional Psychology, 33*(1), 40–43.

White, J. R. (2000). Introduction. In J. R. White & A. S. Freeman (Eds.), *Cognitive-behavioral group

therapy: For specific problems and populations* (pp. 3–25). American Psychological Association.

https://doi.org/10.1037/10352-001

Yalom, I. D., & Leszcz, M. (2005). *The theory and practice of group psychotherapy* (5th ed.). Basic Books.

Yu, S. F. (2004). *Effects of progressive muscle relaxation training on psychological and health-related

quality of life outcomes in elderly patients with heart failure* (Publication No. 3182156) [Doctoral

dissertation, The Chinese University of Hong Kong]. ProQuest Dissertations and Theses Global.

shortDOI, 9.36

doctoral dissertation reference, 10.5

2 ⌃⌄

WRITING STYLE AND GRAMMAR

Being able to communicate ideas clearly and succinctly is essential for all successful writers. This chapter provides general writing principles that help improve writing style. First, we focus on the importance of continuity and flow as a means of achieving smooth expression, including the use of transitional words to connect related sentences and ideas. We next discuss techniques for writing clearly and concisely, with recommendations for ways to reduce wordiness and redundancy and to establish appropriate tone. We end by providing general rules for grammar and usage and suggested strategies for improving your writing.

Effective Scholarly Writing

Effective scholarly writing balances continuity and flow with conciseness and clarity. By implementing the techniques and principles described in Sections 2.1 to 2.11, writers can become more effective communicators.

2.1 Continuity and Flow

Effective writing is characterized by *continuity*, the logical consistency of expression throughout a written work, and by *flow*, the smooth cadence of words and sentences. Inconsistencies, contradictions, omissions, and irrelevancies in your writing style and presentation of ideas can make your arguments seem less credible. A work that lacks continuity and flow may seem disorganized or confusing, and details may seem incomplete or inconsistent. Readers will better understand your ideas if you aim for continuity in words, concepts, and thematic development from the opening statement to the conclusion. Explain relationships between ideas clearly, and present ideas in a logical order to improve your paper's readability.

2.2 Transitions

To improve continuity and flow in your writing, check transitions between sentences, paragraphs, and ideas to ensure that the text is smooth and clear rather than abrupt or disjointed. When editing your writing, use additional transitional devices to make it less choppy. Text that sounds choppy or disjointed may indicate that you have abandoned an argument or theme prematurely—instead consider amplifying its discussion.

Punctuation marks contribute to continuity and flow by signaling transitions and demonstrating relationships between ideas. They also reflect the pauses, inflections, subordination, and pacing normally heard in speech. Use the full range of punctuation. Neither overuse nor underuse one type of punctuation, such as commas or dashes: Overuse may annoy readers, whereas underuse may cause confusion. Instead, use punctuation to support meaning.

Likewise, transitional words and phrases help maintain the flow of ideas, especially when the material is complex or abstract. For example, using a pronoun that refers to a noun in the preceding sentence not only serves as a transition but also avoids repetition. Be sure the referent is obvious. Other transitional words and phrases include the following:

- time links (e.g., "then," "next," "after," "while," "since")
- cause–effect links (e.g., "therefore," "consequently," "as a result")
- addition links (e.g., "in addition," "moreover," "furthermore," "similarly")
- contrast links (e.g., "but," "conversely," "nevertheless," "however," "although")

Use adverbs carefully as introductory or transitional words (e.g., "certainly," "consequently," "conversely," "fortunately," "importantly," "interestingly," "more importantly," "regrettably," and "similarly"). Writers often overuse adverbs, so ask yourself whether the introduction or transition is needed. For example, both "importantly" and "interestingly" can often be changed to enhance the message of a sentence or simply omitted without a loss of meaning.

2.3 Noun Strings

Noun strings, meaning several nouns placed one after another to modify a final noun, can confuse readers and force them to question how the words relate to one another. Although skillful hyphenation can clarify the relationships between words, often the best option is to untangle the string. One approach to untangling is to move the final noun earlier in the string and show relationships between the other nouns by using verbs and prepositions. For example, "culturally sensitive qualitative interview techniques" can be rearranged to "culturally sensitive techniques for qualitative interviews." Consider how each of the following nearly uninterpretable noun strings could be better structured:

Noun string	Better sentence structure
skinfold test body fat percentage examination	• a caliper examination to determine body fat percentage • a skinfold test to determine body fat percentage • determination of body fat percentage using calipers to measure skinfold thickness
preliminary online collegiate instructional methods survey results	• preliminary results of an online survey of collegiate instructional methods • preliminary results of an online survey to assess college students' preferred instructional methods

2.4 Conciseness and Clarity

Say only what needs to be said in your writing: The writer who is more concise—that is, more frugal with words—writes a more readable paper. Students increase their chances of academic success when they write concisely. Likewise, writing that is precise and clear is more accurate and transparent. Together, conciseness and clarity in your writing ensure that readers understand your meaning.

Some writers may fear that writing concisely will make their papers too short. However, adding extraneous material or "fluff" to make your paper longer will dilute its focus and meaning and will not improve your chances of getting a favorable grade. If your paper is too short when written concisely, your ideas and themes may need to be further developed to add substance.

Where possible, tighten language to eliminate wordiness, redundancy (see Section 2.5), evasiveness, overuse of the passive voice, circumlocution, and clumsy prose. Shorten or eliminate overly detailed descriptions of equipment or apparatuses, participants, or procedures; elaborations of the obvious; and irrelevant observations or asides.

Short words and short sentences are easier to comprehend than long ones (see Section 2.6). A long technical term, however, may be more precise than several short words, and technical terms are inseparable from scientific reporting. However, a paper with too much jargon or terminology familiar to only a few specialists does not sufficiently contribute to the literature because its meaning is unclear (see Section 2.9). Rather, the technical terms in a paper should be either readily understood by readers across disciplines or defined for readers who may be unfamiliar with them.

Concise writing must also be clear. Be deliberate in your word choices, making certain that every word means exactly what you intend. For example, in informal style, "feel" broadly substitutes for "think" or "believe," but in academic style, such latitude in word choice is not acceptable. Likewise, using a word with multiple meanings can cause confusion. For example, some writers use the word "significant" to mean "important," whereas others use "significant" only in the context of statistical significance testing; ensure that your intended meaning is clear. Choose words and phrases carefully, and specify the intended meaning if there is potential for ambiguity.

If you use a word or phrase multiple times, do so consistently (e.g., do not switch between "participants in the music condition" and "participants who heard the music while completing the task"—choose one presentation and use it consistently). Some writers deliberately use synonyms or near-synonyms to avoid repeating a word or phrase. The intention is commendable, but in practice the use of synonyms can lead to imprecision: By using synonyms, you may unintentionally suggest a subtle difference. Therefore, use synonyms with care.

Word choice is especially important when talking about people who are members of specific groups, such as in a Method section. Carefully consider the descriptors you use, making sure they are accurate, consistent with current preferred terminology, and in line with how the individuals you are writing about describe themselves. In no case should you use biased, pejorative, or demeaning language (see Chapter 3).

Strive for a professional tone and professional language (see Sections 2.7–2.9). Avoid heavy alliteration, rhyming, poetic expressions, and clichés. Use metaphors sparingly; although they can help simplify complicated ideas, metaphors can also be distracting or unclear. Avoid mixed metaphors (e.g., "a theory representing one branch of a growing body of evidence") and words with surplus or unintended meanings (e.g., "outstanding" for "remaining"), which may distract or mislead readers. Use figurative expressions with restraint and colorful expressions with care; because these expressions can be open to interpretation and even cultural differences, they generally do not add to understanding for all possible readers. Instead, make direct, logical comparisons (see Section 2.10) and clearly attribute actions (see Section 2.11).

2.5 Wordiness and Redundancy

Wordiness can impede readers' understanding by forcing them to sort through unnecessary words to decipher your ideas. Unconstrained wordiness lapses into embellishment and flowery writing, which are inappropriate in academic style. Consider the following examples of wordy and concise language:

Wordy	Concise
at the present time	now
for the purpose of	for, to
there were several students who completed	several students completed

Whereas *wordiness* refers to using more words than are necessary, *redundancy* means using multiple words with the same meaning. Writers often use redundant language to be emphatic. Instead, use sentence structure to convey emphasis, for example, by placing the words to be emphasized at the beginning or end of a sentence. When possible and appropriate for the context, use the active voice (see Section 2.13) to reduce wordiness and redundancy. In the following examples, the highlighted words are redundant and should be omitted:

they were both alike   one and the same
a sum total   in close proximity to
four different groups saw   completely unanimous
were exactly the same as   positioned very close
absolutely essential   period of time
has been previously found   summarize briefly
small in size   the reason is because

2.6 Sentence and Paragraph Length

There is no minimum or maximum sentence length in APA Style. Overuse of short, simple sentences produces choppy prose, however, and overuse of long, involved sentences results in difficult, sometimes incomprehensible, language. Varied sentence length helps readers maintain interest and comprehension. When involved concepts require long sentences, the components should proceed logically. Avoid including multiple ideas in a single sentence; instead, break the sentence into shorter ones. Direct, declarative sentences with simple, common words are usually best.

Similar cautions apply to paragraph length. Single-sentence paragraphs are abrupt and should be used infrequently. Paragraphs that are too long (i.e., longer than one double-spaced manuscript page) risk losing readers' attention. A new paragraph signals a shift to a new idea and provides a pause for readers—a chance to assimilate one step in the conceptual development before beginning another. Look for a logical place (or places) to break up a long paragraph or reorganize the material.

2.7 Tone

Although scholarly writing differs in form and content from creative or literary writing, it does not need to lack style or be dull. When writing a scholarly paper, keep in mind that scholarly prose and creative or literary writing serve different purposes. Devices that are often used in creative writing—for example, setting up ambiguity; inserting the unexpected; omitting the expected; and suddenly shifting the topic, tense, or person—do not support the objective of clear communication in scholarly writing. Similarly, devices or embellishments that attract attention to words and sounds instead of to ideas are inappropriate in scholarly writing.

When describing your research, present the ideas and findings in a direct and straightforward manner, while also aiming for an interesting and compelling style—for example, by fully elaborating on an idea or concept (see Section 2.2), making word choices that reflect your involvement with the problem (see Section 2.4), and varying sentence and paragraph lengths (see Section 2.6). Use language that conveys professionalism and formality (see Section 2.8). For example, scholarly writing often contrasts the positions of different researchers, and these differences should be presented in a professional, noncombative manner: Stating "Gerard (2019) did not address" is acceptable, whereas "Gerard (2019) completely overlooked" is not.

One way to achieve the right tone is to imagine a specific reader you intend to reach and write in a way that will inform and persuade that individual. For example, your reader might be a researcher in a related field who is trying to keep abreast of the literature but is not familiar with the jargon or insider perspectives of your field. What would help this reader understand your work and appreciate its importance?

2.8 Contractions and Colloquialisms

Avoid using contractions and colloquialisms, which detract from a professional tone in scholarly writing. *Contractions*—shortened forms of one or two words in which an apostrophe is used in place of missing letters—generally do not appear in scholarly writing because they convey an informal tone. To avoid contractions and improve your writing, evaluate words with apostrophes carefully. Excluding the exceptions noted next, rewrite a word like "can't" into "cannot." Use apostrophes to indicate possession (e.g., "the student's work"), but remember that possessive pronouns do not include apostrophes (e.g., write "its purpose was" not "it's purpose was"). However, contractions can be appropriately used in some circumstances, such as in reproducing a direct quotation that contains a contraction (e.g., when quoting a research participant, do not change a participant's use of "let's go" to "let us go"), referring to a contraction as a linguistic example (e.g., when discussing confusion of "who's" with "whose"), or referring to an idiom or common saying that contains a contraction (e.g., "you can't take it with you").

Likewise, avoid *colloquialisms*, which are informal expressions used in everyday speech and writing (e.g., "to write up" instead of "to report," "gonna" instead of "going to"). These expressions often diffuse meaning, as in the case of approximations of quantity; "quite a large part," "practically all," and "very few" are interpreted differently by different readers or in different contexts. Approximations weaken statements, especially those describing empirical observations. Instead, use precise, scholarly language.

2.9 Jargon

Jargon is specialized terminology that is unfamiliar to those outside a specific group. Overuse of jargon, even in papers in which that vocabulary is relevant, hinders comprehension. Jargon also may be euphemistic if substituted for a familiar term (e.g., "period of economic adjustment" instead of "recession"), and you should avoid using jargon in this way. Bureaucratic jargon has had the greatest publicity, but academic or scientific jargon may also grate on readers, encumber communication, and waste space. Use language that allows readers to understand your writing even if they are not experts in your field, and define on first use any specialized terms that are key to your topic.

2.10 Logical Comparisons

Ensure that the comparisons you make are expressed clearly and logically. Ambiguous or illogical comparisons result from the omission of key words or from nonparallel structure (see Section 2.24). Consider, for example, "Twelve-year-olds were more likely to play with age peers than 6-year-olds." Does this sentence mean that 12-year-olds were more likely than 6-year-olds to play with age peers? Or does it mean that 12-year-olds were more likely to play with age peers and less likely to play with 6-year-olds? Ambiguity occurs when parallelism is overlooked for the sake of brevity, as in "The responses of transgender participants were more positive than cisgender participants." One correct way to write this sentence would be "The responses of transgender participants were more positive than those of cisgender participants." Thoughtful attention to good sentence structure and word choice reduces the chance of this kind of ambiguity.

2.11 Anthropomorphism

Do not attribute human characteristics to animals or to inanimate sources—doing so is called *anthropomorphism*.

Correct	Incorrect	Rationale
Pairs of rats (cage mates) were allowed to forage together.	Rat couples (cage mates) were allowed to forage together.	"Rat couples" implies a misleading parallel between human romantic couples and pairs of rats.
The theory addresses	The theory concludes	A theory might address, indicate, or present, but it is the researchers (not the theory itself) who conclude.

Pair active verbs with human actors (e.g., write "we extrapolated the rate of change" rather than "the study extrapolated the rate of change"). However, many acceptable constructions in widespread use do not constitute anthropomorphism because they do not impede understanding or mislead readers. When describing the content of different sections of a paper, you may write, for example, "this section addresses" or "the chapter focuses on" as well as "in this section we address" or "in this chapter, we focus on" (see Section 4.3 for comma use with introductory phrases). Similarly, when describing the results of a study, you may write, for example, "the results suggest," "the data provide," "the research contributes," or "the study found."

Determining what constitutes anthropomorphism can be challenging, and even distinguished scholars may disagree. In ambiguous cases, we recommend that you keep the principle of clear communication at the forefront of your word choice and sentence structure.

Grammar and Usage

Incorrect grammar and careless construction of sentences distract readers, introduce ambiguity, and impede clear communication. The examples in this section represent common grammar and usage errors that often appear in papers submitted to academic instructors.

2.12 Verb Tense

Verbs are vigorous, direct communicators. The past tense is appropriate when expressing an action or a condition that occurred at a specific, definite time in the past, such as when discussing another researcher's work. The present perfect tense is appropriate to express a past action or condition that did not occur at a specific, definite time or to describe an action beginning in the past and continuing to the present.

Use verb tenses consistently, and stay within the chosen tense to ensure smooth expression. Sudden, unnecessary shifts in verb tense in the same paragraph or in adjacent paragraphs may confuse readers. Use the verb tenses shown in Table 2.1 to report information in various parts of your paper.

2.13 Active and Passive Voice

Voice describes the relationship between a verb and the subject and object associated with it. In the *active voice*, the subject of a sentence is presented first, followed by the verb and then the object of the verb (e.g., "students completed surveys"). In the *passive voice*, the object of the verb is presented first, followed by the verb (usually a form of "to be" + past participle + the word "by") and then the subject last (e.g., "surveys were completed by students"); sometimes, the subject is omitted altogether, resulting in confusion about who is performing the action.

Table 2.1 Recommended Verb Tenses in APA Style Papers

Paper section	Recommended tense	Example
Literature review (or whenever discussing other researchers' work)	Past	Quinn (2020) presented
	Present perfect	Many researchers have studied
Method Description of procedure	Past	Participants completed a survey
	Present perfect	Others have used similar approaches
Reporting of your own or other researchers' results	Past	Results showed Scores increased Hypotheses were supported
Personal reactions	Past	I felt surprised
	Present perfect	I have experienced
	Present	I believe
Discussion of implications of results or of previous statements	Present	The results indicate The findings mean
Presentation of conclusions, limitations, future directions, and other concluding statements	Present	We conclude Limitations of the study are Future research should explore

Choose voice carefully. Both active and passive voices are permitted in APA Style, but many writers overuse the passive voice. Use the active voice as much as possible to create direct, clear, and concise sentences. For example, use the active voice to describe the actions of participants and others involved in your study (see Section 3.6), as in "the patients took the medication orally," not "the medication was taken orally by the patients."

The passive voice is acceptable in expository writing when focusing on the object or recipient of the action rather than on the actor. For example, a description of the experimental setup in the Method section might read, "the speakers were attached to either side of the chair," which appropriately emphasizes the placement of the speakers, not who placed them. Similarly, "the tests were gathered promptly" emphasizes the importance of the tests and their timely collection. When it is important to know who performed the action, use the active voice.

2.14 Mood

Mood refers to the form of a verb writers use to express their attitude toward what they are saying (e.g., whether they believe what they are saying or just wish it were true). Use the indicative mood to make factual statements (e.g., "we addressed," "the findings demonstrate"). Use the subjunctive mood only to describe conditions that are contrary to fact or improbable; do not use the subjunctive to describe simple conditions or contingencies.

Correct	Incorrect	Rationale
If the campus were larger, we would have had access to more participants.	If the campus was larger, we would have had access to more participants.	The campus is not in fact larger; the writer is only wishing that this were so.

Use the word "would" with care. "Would" can be used in the indicative mood to mean "habitually," as in "The child would walk about the classroom," or in the conditional mood to express a condition of action, as in "We would sign the letter if we could." Do not use "would" to hedge; for example, change "it would appear that" to "it appears that."

2.15 Subject and Verb Agreement

A verb must agree in number (i.e., singular or plural) with its subject, regardless of intervening phrases such as "together with," "including," "plus," and "as well as."

Correct: The percentage of correct responses, as well as the speed of the responses, increases with practice.

Incorrect: The percentage of correct responses, as well as the speed of the responses, increase with practice.

Collective Nouns. Collective nouns (e.g., "series," "set," "faculty," "pair," "social media") can refer to several individuals or to a single unit. If the action of the verb applies to the group as a whole, treat the noun as singular and use a singular verb. If the action of the verb applies to members of the group as individuals, treat the noun as plural and use a plural verb. The context (i.e., your emphasis) determines whether the action applies to the group or to individuals.

Singular in context: The number of people in the state is growing.

A pair of animals was in each cage.

Plural in context: A number of people are watching.

A pair of animals were then yoked.

Use of "None." The subject pronoun "none" can be singular or plural. When the noun that follows it is singular, use a singular verb; when the noun is plural, use a plural verb.

Singular in context: None of the information was correct.

Plural in context: None of the children were finished in the time allotted.

Compound Subjects Joined by "Or" or "Nor." When a compound subject is composed of a singular and a plural noun joined by "or" or "nor," the verb agrees with the noun that is closer to the verb.

Correct: Neither the participants nor the confederate was in the room.

Neither the confederate nor the participants were in the room.

Incorrect: Neither the participants nor the confederate were in the room.

2.16 First- Versus Third-Person Pronouns

Pronouns replace nouns, and each pronoun should refer clearly to its antecedent. To avoid ambiguity in attribution, use the first person rather than the third person when describing the work you did as part of your research and when expressing your own views. If you are writing a paper by yourself, use the pronoun "I"; do not use the pronoun "we" to refer to yourself if you do not have coauthors (see also Section 2.17). If you are writing a paper with coauthors, use the pronoun "we." Do not refer to yourself or your coauthors in the third person as "the author(s)" or "the researcher(s)."

However, use the third person to refer to the specific contribution of a particular coauthor within a multiauthored paper. In the following example, Sonia J. Cousteau is one of the authors of the paper:

We assessed children's language abilities. Sonia J. Cousteau, who is a speech-language pathologist, trained all testers.

2.17 Editorial "We"

Do not use "we" to refer to people in general, as in "We live on the same planet, but we rarely truly understand each other"; this use is called the *editorial "we."* It is especially important to avoid the editorial "we" in multiauthored papers because readers may wonder whether you are referring to all people, members of your professional group(s), or yourself and your coauthors. Substitute a more specific noun or clarify your usage.

Correct: Psychological researchers typically study decision making in a laboratory setting.

Incorrect: We typically study decision making in a laboratory setting.

Some alternatives to "we" are "people," "humans," "researchers," "psychologists," "nurses," and so on. However, "we" is an appropriate and useful referent once a specific subject has been established.

> **Correct:** As nurses, we tend to rely on . . .
>
> **Incorrect:** We tend to rely on . . .

2.18 Singular "They"

Writers should always use the singular "they" to refer to a person who uses "they" as their pronoun (see Section 3.5 for more on gender and pronoun usage). Also use "they" as a generic third-person singular pronoun to refer to a person whose gender is unknown or irrelevant to the context of the usage. Although usage of the singular "they" was once discouraged in academic writing, many advocacy groups and publishers have accepted and endorsed it, including *Merriam-Webster's Dictionary* (Merriam-Webster, n.d.-b). The use of the singular "they" is inclusive of all people, helps writers avoid making assumptions about gender, and is part of APA Style.

When using the singular "they," use the forms "they," "them," "their," "theirs," and "themselves." The variant "themself" is also acceptable because the referent is clearly singular, although "themselves" is currently the more common usage. The following are examples of correct usage of the singular "they."

> Each participant turned in their questionnaire.
>
> Jaime shared their experiences as a genderqueer person.
>
> A child should learn to play by themselves [or themself] as well as with friends.
>
> Rowan, a transgender person, helped themselves [or themself] to the free coffee.

Do not use "he" or "she" alone as a generic third-person pronoun. Use "he or she" and "she or he" sparingly, and ensure that these pronouns match the pronouns of the people being described; if you do not know the pronouns used by the people being described, use "they" instead or rewrite the sentence. Do not use the combination forms "(s)he" and "s/he" or alternate "he" and "she" (unless you know that a person uses these forms); these choices may have unintentional implications.

Keep in mind that there are typically many possible ways to write a sentence. If the singular "they" as a generic third-person pronoun seems awkward or distracting, try one of the following strategies to rewrite the sentence.

Strategy	Gender neutral	Gender biased
Rephrasing	When an individual attends psychotherapy, that person can improve emotional regulation. Therapy can help an individual improve emotional regulation.	When an individual attends psychotherapy, she can improve emotional regulation.
Using plural nouns or plural pronouns	Therapists who are too much like their clients can lose their objectivity.	A therapist who is too much like his client can lose his objectivity.
Replacing the pronoun with an article	A researcher must apply for the grant by September 1.	A researcher must apply for his grant by September 1.
Dropping the pronoun	The researcher must avoid letting biases and expectations influence the interpretation of the results.	The researcher must avoid letting her own biases and expectations influence the interpretation of the results.

2.19 Pronouns for People and Animals ("Who" vs. "That")

Relative pronouns introduce subordinate clauses linked to nouns. Use the relative pronoun "who" for human beings; use the relative pronoun "that" or "which" for nonhuman animals (e.g., rats, chimpanzees) and for inanimate objects.

> *Correct:* The students who completed the task . . .
>
> *Correct:* The instructions that were included . . .
>
> *Incorrect:* The students that completed the task . . .

Use neuter pronouns to refer to animals (e.g., "the dog . . . it"). However, it is acceptable to use gendered pronouns if the animal has been named and its sex is known, as in the following example.

> The chimps were tested daily. Sheba was tested unrestrained in an open testing area, which was her usual context for training and testing.

2.20 Pronouns as Subjects and Objects ("Who" vs. "Whom")

Relative pronouns can be subjects or objects of verbs or prepositions. Use "who" as the subject of a verb and "whom" as the object of a verb or a preposition. You can determine whether a pronoun is the subject or object of a verb by turning the subordinate clause around and substituting a personal pronoun. If you can substitute "he," "she," or "they," then "who" is correct. In the following examples, "who" and its replacement personal pronoun are highlighted to show the substitutions. The sentence with the substitution is a way to verify whether the original sentence is correct.

Use of "who"	Original sentence	Substitution sentence
Correct	The participants who passed the exam were given course credit.	They passed the exam and were given course credit.
Incorrect	Eligible participants were mothers, each of who had a child under the age of 21 with cancer.	Eligible participants were mothers; each of they had a child under the age of 21 with cancer.

Likewise, if you can substitute "him," "her," or "them," then "whom" is correct.

Use of "whom"	Original sentence	Substitution sentence
Correct	Eligible participants were mothers, each of whom had a child under the age of 21 with cancer.	Eligible participants were mothers; each of them had a child under the age of 21 with cancer.
Incorrect	The participants whom passed the exam were given course credit.	Them passed the exam and were given course credit.

2.21 Pronouns in Restrictive and Nonrestrictive Clauses ("That" vs. "Which")

Relative pronouns (e.g., "who," "whom," "that," "which") introduce an element that is subordinate to the main clause of the sentence, and that subordinate clause may be either restrictive or nonrestrictive.

Restrictive clauses—also called "that" clauses—are essential to the meaning of the sentence. Restrictive clauses are not set off with commas.

Therapist self-disclosure that conflicts with the patient's story might hinder the therapeutic process.

In the example, only self-disclosure that conflicts with the patient's story, not all self-disclosure, might hinder the therapeutic process.

Nonrestrictive clauses—also called "which" clauses—add further information to the sentence but are not essential to its meaning. Nonrestrictive clauses are set off with commas.

> All interviews were conducted at participants' offices, which provided suitable privacy to secure participants' anonymity.

In the example, all interviews were conducted at the offices, and all offices provided suitable privacy.

Although some writers use "which" for both restrictive and nonrestrictive clauses, APA Style reserves "which" for nonrestrictive clauses and "that" for restrictive clauses. Consistent use of "that" for restrictive clauses and "which" for nonrestrictive clauses will help make your writing clear and precise.

2.22 Subordinate Conjunctions

Subordinate conjunctions (e.g., "since," "while," "although," "because," "whereas"), like relative pronouns (see Sections 2.19–2.21), introduce subordinate clauses. Select these conjunctions with care; interchanging conjunctions with more than one meaning may reduce the precision of your writing. Although some writers use "while" and "since" when they do not refer strictly to time, restricting your use of "while" and "since" to their temporal meanings can help readers.

"While" Versus "Although," "Despite," "And," or "But." Use "while" to link events occurring simultaneously.

> Individual goal striving in late adulthood may enrich life while reducing stagnation and boredom.

Otherwise, use "although," "despite," "and," or "but" in place of "while."

> *Precise:* Although goal progress predicted well-being for all genders, the associations tended to be stronger for women.
>
> Goal progress predicted well-being for all genders, but the associations tended to be stronger for women.
>
> *Imprecise:* While goal progress predicted well-being for all genders, the associations tended to be stronger for women.

"Since" Versus "Because." In cases where the meaning of "since" is ambiguous (it could be either "from a time in the past" or "because"), replace "since" with "because." If the meaning is not ambiguous, it is acceptable to use either "since" or "because" to mean "because."

Precise: Participants were leaving because the light turned green.

Imprecise: Participants were leaving since the light turned green.

2.23 Misplaced and Dangling Modifiers

An adjective or an adverb, whether a single word or a phrase, must clearly refer to the word that it modifies. Having modifiers without clear referents can make it hard for readers to follow the logic of your sentence.

Misplaced Modifiers. Because of their placement in a sentence, misplaced modifiers ambiguously or illogically modify a word. Eliminate misplaced modifiers by placing an adjective or an adverb as close as possible to the word it modifies.

Correct	Incorrect	Rationale
Using this procedure, the investigator tested the participants. The investigator tested the participants who were using the procedure.	The investigator tested the participants using this procedure.	The incorrect sentence is unclear about whether the investigator or the participants used this procedure.
On the basis of this assumption, we developed a model. Based on this assumption, the model . . .	Based on this assumption, we developed a model.	The incorrect construction says, "we are based on this assumption."

Many writers misplace the word "only." Place "only" next to the word or phrase it modifies.

Correct	Incorrect	Rationale
These data provide only a partial answer.	These data only provide a partial answer.	The answer is partial, not the providing of it.

Squinting modifiers are a type of misplaced modifier. Because of their ambiguous placement, they make it difficult to tell whether the modifier refers to the phrase before or after the modifier.

Correct	Incorrect	Rationale
My comprehension is improved when I read slowly.	Reading books slowly improves my comprehension.	It is unclear whether the reading or the improvement is slow.

GRAMMAR

Dangling Modifiers. Dangling modifiers have no referent in the sentence. Many of these result from the use of the passive voice (see Section 2.13). You can avoid many dangling modifiers by writing in the active voice.

Correct	Incorrect	Rationale
Using this procedure, I tested the participants.	Using this procedure, the participants were tested.	I, not the participants, used the procedure.
Armitage and Martinez (2017) found that the treatment group performed better, a result congruent with those of other studies.	Congruent with other studies, Armitage and Martinez (2017) found that the treatment group performed better.	The result, not Armitage and Martinez, is congruent.

2.24 Parallel Construction

To enhance readers' understanding, present parallel ideas in parallel or coordinate form. Use parallel structure in compound sentences, series and lists (see Sections 4.11–4.14), and table stubs (see Section 7.12).

Repetition of Parallel Elements. Ensure that all elements of the parallelism are present before and after the coordinating conjunction (e.g., "and," "but," "or," "nor"). For example, if the first part of the clause is introduced by "that," the second part of the clause should be as well. When a clause has two parts (and not three or more), do not use a comma or semicolon before the conjunction.

> *Correct:* Ford (2020) found that homework is positively related to achievement and that the association is stronger in middle and high school than in elementary school.

> *Incorrect:* Ford (2020) found that homework is positively related to achievement, and that the association is stronger in middle and high school than in elementary school.

Coordinating Conjunctions Used in Pairs. With coordinating conjunctions used in pairs ("between . . . and," "both . . . and," "neither . . . nor," "either . . . or," "not only . . . but also"), place the first conjunction immediately before the first part of the parallelism.

"Between" and "And."

> *Correct:* We recorded the difference between the performance of participants who completed the first task and the performance of those who completed the second task.

Incorrect: We recorded the difference between the performance of participants who completed the first task and the second task.

Correct: between 2.5 and 4.0 years old

Incorrect: between 2.5–4.0 years old

"Both" and "And."

Correct: The names were difficult both to pronounce and to spell.

Incorrect: The names were difficult both to pronounce as well as to spell.

Never use "both" with "as well as": The resulting construction is redundant.

"Neither" and "Nor"; "Either" and "Or."

Correct: Neither the responses to the auditory stimuli nor the responses to the tactile stimuli were repeated.

Incorrect: Neither the responses to the auditory stimuli nor to the tactile stimuli were repeated.

Correct: The respondents either gave the worst answer or gave the best answer.

Correct: The respondents gave either the worst answer or the best answer.

Incorrect: The respondents either gave the worst answer or the best answer.

"Not Only" and "But Also"

Correct: It is surprising not only that pencil-and-paper scores predicted this result but also that all other predictors were less accurate.

Incorrect: It is not only surprising that pencil-and-paper scores predicted this result but also that all other predictors were less accurate.

Elements in a Series. Elements in a series should also be parallel in form.

Correct: The participants were told to make themselves comfortable, to read the instructions, and to ask about anything they did not understand.

Incorrect: The participants were told to make themselves comfortable, to read the instructions, and that they should ask about anything they did not understand.

Strategies to Improve Your Writing

2.25 Reading to Learn Through Example

Good writing is a skill learned through practice. Reading is one of the most effective ways for students to improve their writing because it enables them to learn through example. For instance, a student tasked with writing a literature review would benefit from reading other literature reviews (including the literature review sections of longer works) to see the various ways in which information can be organized and discussed. Likewise, a writer who needs to present complex statistical information in a table would benefit from seeing how published authors have organized similar information in their tables. Careful reading in your chosen area of study will help you learn about not only new developments in the field but also ways to effectively convey information on the page.

2.26 Writing From an Outline

Writing from an outline ensures that the flow of your paper reflects the logic of your research or ideas. Creating and using an outline helps you identify main ideas, define subordinate ideas, focus your writing, avoid tangential excursions, and find omissions. In the outline, you can also designate the headings and subheadings you will use in your paper (see Sections 1.25–1.26 for more on principles of organization and levels of heading). Outlines can take many forms, including the traditional format with Roman numeral headings or a concept map.

2.27 Rereading the Draft

Rereading your own work after setting it aside for a few hours or days allows you to look at it from a fresh perspective. Taking the further step of reading your paper aloud may reveal faults that you previously overlooked and may help strengthen the tone and style of your writing. You can also try reading the sections of your paper in reverse order—from the conclusion back to the introduction—to ensure that you have set up arguments appropriately. Budget ample time when writing to allow yourself to take advantage of these strategies.

2.28 Seeking Help From Fellow Students

Students are encouraged to solicit feedback from their instructor and peers. After you have reread and revised your draft, you might give your paper to a fellow student for a critical review. Consider asking multiple students to read your paper and provide critiques to improve the feedback you receive. Seek help not only from students who are studying within your own field but also from those in related fields to ensure that your meaning is clear even to those who are less familiar with your topic.

2.29 Working With Writing Centers

Some writers, particularly new writers and those writing in a non-native language, may benefit from extra help with their writing. They might visit a tutor at their institution's writing center. A writing center tutor can assist with idiomatic language use, organization, and other areas. We highly recommend use of this service for students who would like to attain more success in the classroom.

2.30 Revising a Paper

Revising a draft into a polished paper takes time and effort. Writers should develop a revision plan. It is best to start with the big picture and work down to the details. Consider the following broad questions when reviewing your paper:

- Is the central point or thesis of your paper clear? Do the arguments follow logically from the thesis?

- Is the information well organized?

- Does the draft meet the parameters of the assignment? If there is a rubric for the assignment, does the paper address each element of the rubric?

3

BIAS-FREE LANGUAGE GUIDELINES

Writers must strive to use language that is free of *bias*, meaning the implied or irrelevant evaluation of the group or groups they are writing about. As an organization, APA is committed to both the advancement of science and the fair treatment of individuals and groups. These principles require that students and authors who use APA Style avoid perpetuating demeaning attitudes in their writing. It is unacceptable to use constructions that might imply prejudicial beliefs or perpetuate biased assumptions against persons on the basis of age, disability, gender, participation in research, racial or ethnic identity, sexual orientation, socioeconomic status, or some combination of these or other personal factors (e.g., marital status, immigration status, religion). Instead, writers should use affirming and inclusive language.

This chapter contains guidelines for writing about people respectfully and accurately. We start by providing general guidelines for writing without bias, followed by sections addressing the specific topics of age, disability, gender, participation in research, race and ethnicity, sexual orientation, socioeconomic status, and intersectionality. More examples of bias-free language can be found on the APA Style website (https://apastyle.apa.org).

Just as you have learned to check what you write for spelling, grammar, and wordiness, practice rereading your work for preconceptions about groups of people. When possible, ask people from the groups about which you are writing to read and comment on your material or consult self-advocacy groups to determine appropriate terminology. If you work directly with participants, ask them what terms they use to describe themselves. Language changes over time, and it is important to use the terms that individuals and/or communities use to describe themselves, their experiences, and their practices.

Some attempts to follow the guidelines in this chapter may result in wordiness or clumsy prose. As always, good judgment is required—these are not rigid rules. If your writing reflects respect for your participants and your readers, and if you write with appropriate specificity and precision, you will contribute to the goal of accurate, unbiased communication.

General Guidelines for Reducing Bias

3.1 Describe at the Appropriate Level of Specificity

Precision is essential in scholarly writing; when you refer to a person or persons, choose words that are accurate, clear, and free from bias or prejudicial connotations. Bias, like inaccurate or unclear language, can be a form of imprecision. For example, using "man" to refer to all human beings is not as accurate or inclusive as using the terms "individuals," "people," or "persons."

Focus on Relevant Characteristics. Be mindful to describe only relevant characteristics. Although it is possible to describe a person's age, disability, gender identity, participation in research, racial and ethnic identity, sexual orientation, socioeconomic status, or other characteristic without bias, it is not always necessary to include all of this information in your report. (For a more detailed discussion of participant characteristics to report in quantitative and qualitative studies, refer to Sections 3.6 and 3.14 of the *Publication Manual*, respectively.) For example, you would be unlikely to mention participants' sexual orientation in a study of cognition because sexual orientation is not relevant to cognition; however, you would likely mention participants' gender in a study of stereotype threat because gender is relevant to the examination of stereotype threat. Furthermore, there may be multiple relevant characteristics to discuss; when this is the case, address the ways in which the characteristics intersect, as appropriate (see Section 3.10).

Acknowledge Relevant Differences That Do Exist. Part of writing without bias is not only recognizing that differences should be mentioned only when relevant but also acknowledging relevant differences when they do exist. Evaluate the meaning of the word "difference" carefully in relation to the target population, not the dominant group. For example, a researcher who wants to generalize their study results to all people or all students should assess and report whether the sample studied is different from the target population and, if so, describe how it is different.

Be Appropriately Specific. Once you have determined which characteristics to describe, choose terms that are appropriately specific, which will depend on the research question and the present state of knowledge in the field. Do not mention characteristics gratuitously; however, when in doubt, be more specific rather than less because it is easier to aggregate data than to disaggregate them. Consider the appropriate level of specificity early in the research process—such as when designing the study—because it may not be possible to gather more data once the study is underway or finished. Using specific terms improves readers' ability to understand the generalizability of your findings and other researchers' ability to use your data in a meta-analysis or replication.

Examples of Specificity by Topic. Next, we present examples of specific language for the topics covered in these bias-free language guidelines; again, the proper choice will depend on the situation, and these examples represent just some of the possible options.

- When writing about age, exact ages or age ranges (e.g., 15–18 years old, 65–80 years old) are more specific than broad categories (e.g., under 18 years old, over 65 years old; see Section 3.3). Also include the age mean and median in addition to the range of ages to increase the specificity of the reporting.

- When writing about disability, names of conditions (e.g., Alzheimer's disease) are more specific than categories of conditions (e.g., types of dementia) or general references such as "people with disabilities" (see Section 3.4).

- When writing about gender identity, descriptors with modifiers (e.g., cisgender women, transgender women) are more specific than descriptors without modifiers (e.g., women) or general nongendered terms (e.g., people, individuals; see Section 3.5 for how to differentiate between gender and sex).

- When writing about people who took part in research, terms that indicate the context of the research (e.g., patients, participants, clients) are more specific than general terms (e.g., people, children, women; see Section 3.6).

- When writing about racial or ethnic groups, the nation or region of origin (e.g., Chinese Americans, Mexican Americans) is more specific than a generalized origin (e.g., Asian Americans, Latin Americans; see Section 3.7).

- When writing about sexual orientation, the names of people's orientations (e.g., lesbians, gay men, bisexual people, straight people) are more specific than broad group labels (e.g., gay; see Section 3.8).

- When writing about socioeconomic status, income ranges or specific designations (e.g., below the federal poverty threshold for a family of four) are more specific than general labels (e.g., low income; see Section 3.9).

3.2 Be Sensitive to Labels

Respect the language people use to describe themselves; that is, call people what they call themselves. Accept that language changes with time and that individuals within groups sometimes disagree about the designations they use. Make an effort to determine what is appropriate for your study or paper, particularly when these designations are debated within groups. You may need to ask your participants which designations they use and/or consult self-advocacy groups that represent these communities to research the issue if you are not working directly with participants. However, note that some individuals may use slurs or stigmatizing language to refer to themselves; researchers should use extreme caution before repeating this language because doing so can propagate that stigma (see Sections 3.3–3.4 for more on the use of stigmatizing language with regard to age and disability, respectively).

Acknowledge People's Humanity. Choose labels with sensitivity, ensuring that the individuality and humanity of people are respected. Avoid using adjectives as nouns to label people (e.g., "the gays," "the poor") or using labels that equate people with their condition (e.g., "amnesiacs," "schizophrenics," "the learning disabled," "drug users"). Instead, use adjectival forms (e.g., gay men, older adults) or nouns with descriptive phrases (e.g., people living in poverty, people with learning disabilities, people who use drugs). Some groups (e.g., the Deaf) have chosen to use a capitalized label to identify and promote a sense of unity and community (Solomon, 2012); use the label that the community uses, even when that label is adjectival (note, however, that not everyone who has hearing loss identifies as Deaf). In particular, the use of labels where disability is concerned is evolving, and people may disagree about the preferred approach. When writing about disability, person-first language (e.g., "a person with paraplegia" rather than "a paraplegic"), identity-first language (e.g., "an autistic person" rather than "a person with autism"), or both may be acceptable depending on the group you are writing about (see Section 3.4).

Provide Operational Definitions and Labels. If you provide operational definitions of groups early in your paper (e.g., "participants scoring a minimum of X on the Y scale constituted the high verbal group, and those scoring below X constituted the low verbal group"), the best practice is to describe participants thereafter in terms of the measures used to classify them (e.g., "the contrast for the high verbal group was statistically significant"), provided the terms are not inappropriate. A pejorative label should not be used in any form. Abbreviations or series labels for groups usually sacrifice clarity and may be problematic: "LDs" or "LD group" to describe people with specific learning difficulties is problematic; "HVAs" for "high verbal ability group" is difficult to decipher. "Group A" is not problematic, but it is also not descriptive. Instead, ensure that operational group labels are clear and appropriate (e.g., "group with dysgraphia").

Avoid False Hierarchies. Compare groups with care. Bias occurs when writers use one group (often their own group) as the standard against which others are judged (e.g., using citizens of the United States as the standard without specifying why that group was chosen). For example, usage of "normal" may prompt readers to make the comparison with "abnormal," thus stigmatizing individuals with differences. Likewise, contrasting lesbians with "the general public" or "normal women" portrays lesbians as marginal to society. More appropriate comparison groups for lesbians might be straight individuals, straight women, or gay men. Use parallel designations for groups, especially when presenting racial and ethnic information (see Section 3.7).

Be aware that the order of social group presentation may imply that the first-mentioned group is the norm or standard and that later-mentioned groups are abnormal or deviant. Thus, the phrases "men and women" and "White Americans and racial minorities" subtly reflect the perceived dominance of men and White people over other groups (furthermore, listing specific racial minority groups is preferable to writing about racial minorities in general; see Section 3.7). Similarly, when presenting group data, placing socially dominant groups such as men and White people on the left side of a graph or at the top of a table may also imply that these groups are the universal standard (Hegarty & Buechel, 2006). When referring to multiple groups, thoughtfully consider the order in which to present them. Do not put groups in order of social dominance by default; instead, consider options such as alphabetical order or sample size order. For ease of comprehension, list groups in the same order consistently throughout a paper.

Reducing Bias by Topic

3.3 Age

Age should be reported as part of the description of participants in the Method section. Be specific in providing age ranges, means, and medians (see also Section 3.1). Avoid open-ended definitions such as "under 18 years" or "over 65 years," unless referring, for instance, to broad research study eligibility criteria.

Terms for Different Age Groups. Different terms are used for individuals of different ages, and these terms are often gendered (see Section 3.5). Use the terms individuals use to self-describe, whether these are binary gender categories of boy–girl or man–woman or descriptive and possibly nonbinary categories of transgender, genderqueer, agender, or gender-fluid.

- For an individual of any age, appropriate terms are "person," "individual," and similar terms. In general, avoid using "males" and "females" as nouns; instead use "men" and "women" or other age-appropriate words (see Section 3.5). "Males" and "females" are appropriate terms when groups include individuals with a broad age range (e.g., "males" to describe a group that includes both boys and men).

- For an individual aged 12 years and younger, appropriate terms are "infant" (for a very young child), "child," "girl," "boy," "transgender girl," "transgender boy," "gender-fluid child," and so on.

- For an individual aged 13 to 17 years, appropriate terms are "adolescent," "young person," "youth," "young woman," "young man," "female adolescent," "male adolescent," "agender adolescent," and so on.

- For an individual aged 18 years and older, appropriate terms are "adult," "woman," "man," "transgender man," "trans man," "transgender woman," "trans woman," "genderqueer adult," "cisgender adult," and so on.

Terms for Older Adults. Older adults are a subgroup of adults, and the age groups of older adults may be described with adjectives. On first reference to a group of older people, be as specific as possible by including the age range, average age, and median age, when available. Terms such as "older persons," "older people," "older adults," "older patients," "older individuals," "persons 65 years and older," and "the older population" are preferred. Avoid using terms such as "seniors," "elderly," "the aged," "aging dependents," and similar "othering" terms because they connote a stereotype and suggest that members of the group are not part of society but rather a group apart (see Lundebjerg et al., 2017; Sweetland et al., 2017). Do not use these stigmatizing terms in your research even if your participants use them to refer to themselves (see Section 3.4 for similar guidance regarding disability). Likewise, avoid negativistic and fatalistic attitudes toward aging, such as age as being an obstacle to overcome (Lindland et al., 2015). Do not use "senile"; it is an outdated term with no agreed-upon meaning. Use "dementia" instead of "senility," and specify the type of dementia when known (e.g., dementia due to Alzheimer's disease). Be sure your language conveys that aging is a normal part of the human experience and is separate from disease and disorder.

Gerontologists may use combination terms for older age groups (e.g., "young-old," "old-old," "oldest old"); provide the specific ages of these groups when introducing them in your paper, and use the group names only as adjectives, not as nouns (i.e., refer to "young-old individuals," not to "the young-old"). When contrasting older adults with adults of other ages, describe that other age group specifically (e.g., young adults vs. older adults, middle-aged adults vs. older adults). You can use decade-specific descriptors if desired (e.g., octogenarian, centenarian). Generational descriptors such as "baby boomers," "Gen X," "millennials," "centennials," and "Gen Z" should be used only when discussing studies related to the topic of generations. For more information on writing about age, see "Guidelines for the Evaluation of Dementia and Age-Related Cognitive Change" (APA, 2012b) and "Guidelines for Psychological Practice With Older Adults" (APA, 2014).

3.4 Disability

Disability is a broad term that is defined in both legal and scientific ways and encompasses physical, psychological, intellectual, and socioemotional impairments (World Health Organization, 2001, 2011). The members of some groups of people with disabilities—effectively subcultures within the larger culture of disability—have particular ways of referring to themselves that they would prefer others to adopt. When you use the disability language choices made by groups of disabled individuals, you honor their preferences. For example, some Deaf individuals culturally prefer to be called "Deaf" (capitalized) rather than "people with hearing loss" or "people who are deaf" (Dunn & Andrews, 2015). Likewise, use the term "hard of hearing" rather than "hearing-impaired." Honoring the preference of the group is not only a sign of professional awareness and respect for any disability group but also a way to offer solidarity.

The language to use where disability is concerned is evolving. The overall principle for using disability language is to maintain the integrity (worth and dignity) of all individuals as human beings. Authors who write about disability are encouraged to use terms and descriptions that both honor and explain person-first and identity-first perspectives. Language should be selected with the understanding that the expressed preference of people with disabilities regarding identification supersedes matters of style.

Person-First Language. In person-first language, the person is emphasized, not the individual's disabling or chronic condition (e.g., use "a person with paraplegia" and "a youth with epilepsy" rather than "a paraplegic" or "an epileptic"). This principle applies to groups of people as well (e.g., use "people with substance use disorders" or "people with intellectual disabilities" rather than "substance abusers" or "the mentally retarded"; University of Kansas, Research and Training Center on Independent Living, 2013).

Identity-First Language. In identity-first language, the disability becomes the focus, which allows the individual to claim the disability and choose their identity rather than permitting others (e.g., authors, educators, researchers) to name it or to select terms with negative implications (Brown, 2011/n.d.; Brueggemann, 2013; Dunn & Andrews, 2015). Identity-first language is often used as an expression of cultural pride and a reclamation of a disability that once conferred a negative identity. This type of language allows for constructions such as "blind person," "autistic person," and "amputee," whereas in person-first language, the constructions would be "person who is blind," "person with autism," and "person with an amputation," respectively.

Choosing Between Person-First and Identity-First Language. Both person-first and identity-first approaches to language are designed to respect disabled persons; both are fine choices overall. It is permissible to use either approach or to mix person-first and identity-first language unless or until you know that a group clearly prefers one approach, in which case, you should use the preferred approach (Dunn & Andrews, n.d.). Mixing this language may help you avoid cumbersome repetition of "person with . . ." and is also a means to change how authors and readers regard disability and people within particular disability communities. Indeed, the level of disability identity integration can be an effective way to decipher the language that is preferred by the persons about whom you are writing. Those who embrace their disability as part of their cultural and/or personal identity are more likely to prefer identity-first language (Dunn & Andrews, 2015). If you are unsure of which approach to use, seek guidance from self-advocacy groups or other stakeholders specific to a group of people (see, e.g., Brown, 2011/n.d.). If you are working with participants directly, use the language they use to describe themselves.

Relevance of Mentioning a Disability. The nature of a disability should be indicated when it is relevant. For example, if a sample included people with spinal cord injuries and people with autism—two different groups with disabilities—then it makes sense to mention the presence of the particular disabilities. Within each group, there may be additional heterogeneity that should, under some circumstances, be articulated (e.g., different levels of spinal cord injury, different symptom severities of autism spectrum disorder).

Negative and Condescending Terminology. Avoid language that uses pictorial metaphors or negativistic terms that imply restriction (e.g., "wheelchair bound" or "confined to a wheelchair"; use the term "wheelchair user" instead) and language that uses excessive and negative labels (e.g., "AIDS victim," "brain damaged"; use the terms "person with AIDS" or "person with a traumatic brain injury" instead). Avoid terms that can be regarded as slurs (e.g., "cripple," "invalid," "nuts," "alcoholic," "meth addict"); use terms like "person with a physical disability," "person with a mental illness," "person with alcohol use disorder," or "person with substance use disorder" instead, or be more specific (e.g., "person with schizophrenia"). Labels such as "high functioning" or "low functioning" are both problematic and ineffective in describing the nuances of an individual's experience with a developmental and/or intellectual disability; instead, specify the individual's strengths and weaknesses. As with other diverse groups, insiders in disability culture may use negative and condescending terms with one another—it is not appropriate for an outsider (nondisabled person) to use these terms.

Avoid euphemisms that are condescending when describing individuals with disabilities (e.g., "special needs," "physically challenged," "handi-capable"). Many people with disabilities consider these terms patronizing and inappropriate. When writing about populations or participants with disabilities, emphasize both capabilities and concerns to avoid reducing them to a "bundle of deficiencies" (Rappaport, 1977). Refer to individuals with disabilities as "patients" (or "clients") within the context of a health care setting (see Section 3.6).

3.5 Gender

Gender offers an added layer of specificity when interpreting patterns or phenomena of human behavior. However, the terms related to gender and sex are often conflated, making precision essential to writing about gender and/or sex without bias. The language related to gender identity and sexual orientation has also evolved rapidly, and it is important to use the terms people use to describe themselves (Singh, 2017; for how to determine appropriate terms, see Section 3.2; for a list of terms and definitions, see APA, n.d.).

Gender Versus Sex. *Gender* refers to the attitudes, feelings, and behaviors that a given culture associates with a person's biological sex (APA, 2012a). Gender is a social construct and a social identity. Use the term "gender" when referring to people as social groups. For example, when reporting the genders of participants in the Method section, write something like this: "Approximately 60% of participants identified as cisgender women, 35% as cisgender men, 3% as transgender women, 1% as transgender men, and 1% as nonbinary." *Sex* refers to biological sex assignment; use the term "sex" when the biological distinction of sex assignment (e.g., sex assigned at birth) is predominant. Using "gender" instead of "sex" also avoids ambiguity over whether "sex" means "sexual behavior." In some cases, there may not be a clear distinction between biological and acculturative factors, so a discussion of both sex and gender would be appropriate. For example, in the study of sexual orientation (see Section 3.8), researchers continue to examine the extent to which sexuality or sexual orientation—attraction to sex, gender, or some combination of both—is a biological and/or acculturative phenomenon.

Gender Identity. *Gender identity* is a component of gender that describes a person's psychological sense of their gender. Many people describe gender identity as a deeply felt, inherent sense of being a boy, a man, or male; a girl, a woman, or female; or a nonbinary gender (e.g., genderqueer, gender-nonconforming, gender-neutral, agender, gender-fluid) that may or may not correspond to a person's sex assigned at birth, presumed gender based on sex assignment, or primary or secondary sex characteristics (APA, 2015a). Gender identity applies to all individuals and is not a characteristic only of transgender or gender-nonconforming individuals. Gender identity is distinct from sexual orientation (see Section 3.8); thus, the two must not be conflated (e.g., a gay transgender man has a masculine gender identity and a gay sexual orientation, a straight cisgender woman has a feminine gender identity and a straight sexual orientation).

Reporting of Gender. Authors are strongly encouraged to explicitly designate information about the gender identities of the participants making up their samples (e.g., whether participants are transgender, cisgender, or other gender identities) rather than assuming cisgender identities. *Cisgender* refers to individuals whose sex assigned at birth aligns with their gender identity (APA, 2015a). *Cisgenderism* or *cissexism* refers to the belief that being cisgender is normative, as indicated by the assumption that individuals are cisgender unless otherwise specified (both terms are in use). *Genderism* refers to the belief that there are only two genders and that gender is automatically linked to an individual's sex assigned at birth (American Psychological Association of Graduate Students, 2015).

Transgender and Gender-Nonconforming People. *Transgender* is used as an adjective to refer to persons whose gender identity, expression, and/or role does not conform to what is culturally associated with their sex assigned at birth. Some transgender people hold a binary gender, such as man or woman, but others have a gender outside of this binary, such as gender-fluid or nonbinary. Individuals whose gender varies from presumptions based on their sex assigned at birth may use terms other than "transgender" to describe their gender, including "gender-nonconforming," "genderqueer," "gender-nonbinary," "gender-creative," "agender," or "two-spirit," to name a few. (Note that "two-spirit" is a term specific to Indigenous and Native American communities.) *Transprejudice* and *transnegativity* denote discriminatory attitudes toward individuals who are transgender. Diverse identity terms are used by transgender and gender-nonconforming (TGNC) people, and "TGNC" is a generally agreed-upon umbrella term. These terms are generally used in an identity-first way (e.g., "transgender people," "TGNC people"). However, there is some variation in the field; for example, clinicians often refer to individuals according to identity (self-identified) or describe *gender variance*, *gender expansiveness*, or *gender diversity* rather than *gender nonconformity* or *nonbinary gender*. Be sure to use identity labels that are in accordance with the stated identities of the people you are describing, and clearly define how you are using such identity labels within your writing.

Sex Assignment. The terms "birth sex," "natal sex," "tranny," and "transvestite" are considered disparaging by scholars in TGNC psychological research; by many individuals identifying as transgender, gender-nonconforming, or nonbinary; and by people exhibiting gender diversity. Thus, these disparaging terms should be avoided. Additionally, "birth sex" and "natal sex" imply that sex is an immutable characteristic without sociocultural influence. It is more appropriate to use "assigned sex" or "sex assigned at birth," as this functionally describes the assignment of a sex term (frequently binary male or female; however, intersex is an accurate assignment for some) predicated on observation of genitalia and/or determination of chromosomes and anatomical structures of the body at birth, which necessarily is interpreted within a sociocultural context. The term "transsexual" is largely outdated, but some people identify with it; this term should be used only for an individual who specifically claims it.

Gender and Noun Usage. Refer to all people, including transgender people, by the name they use to refer to themselves, which may be different from their legal name or the name on their birth certificate, keeping in mind provisions for respecting confidentiality (more information on protecting participant confidentiality in quantitative and qualitative research can be found in Sections 1.15, 1.18, and 1.19 of the *Publication Manual*). Likewise, to reduce the possibility of stereotypic bias and avoid ambiguity, use specific nouns to identify people or groups of people (e.g., women, men, transgender men, trans men, transgender women, trans women, cisgender women, cisgender men, gender-fluid people). Use "male" and "female" as adjectives (e.g., a male participant, a female experimenter) when appropriate and relevant. Use "male" and "female" as nouns only when the age range is broad or ambiguous or to identify a transgender person's sex assignment at birth (e.g., "person assigned female at birth" is correct, not "person assigned girl at birth"). Otherwise, avoid using "male" and "female" as nouns and instead use the specific nouns for people of different ages (e.g., women) as described in Section 3.3.

To refer to all human beings, use terms like "individuals," "people," or "persons" rather than "man" or "mankind" to be accurate and inclusive. Avoid gendered endings such as "man" in occupational titles (e.g., use "police officer" instead of "policeman"), as these can be ambiguous and may imply incorrectly that all persons in the group self-identify as one gender. Instead, use a nongendered term if possible (e.g., "homemaker" instead of "housewife"). If you use sources that include the generic "man," generic "he," or dated occupational titles, clarify the historical context in which these terms were used (for more details, see the APA Style website at https://apastyle.apa.org).

Gender and Pronoun Usage. Pronoun usage requires specificity and care on the author's part. Do not refer to the pronouns that transgender and gender-nonconforming people use as "preferred pronouns" because this implies a choice about one's gender. Use the terms "identified pronouns," "self-identified pronouns," or "pronouns" instead. When writing about a known individual, use that person's identified pronouns. Some individuals use "they" as a singular pronoun; some use alternative pronouns such as "ze," "xe," "hir," "per," "ve," "ey," and "hen" (Swedish gender-neutral pronoun), among others. Some individuals may alternate between "he" and "she" or between "he and/or she" and "they," whereas others use no pronouns at all and use their name in place of pronouns. Refer to a transgender person using language appropriate to the person's gender, regardless of sex assigned at birth—for example, use the pronouns "he," "him," and "his" in reference to a transgender man who indicates use of these pronouns.

When referring to individuals whose identified pronouns are not known or when the gender of a generic or hypothetical person is irrelevant within the context, use the singular "they" to avoid making assumptions about an individual's gender. Use the forms "they," "them," "theirs," and so forth. Sexist bias can occur when pronouns are used carelessly, as when the pronoun "he" is used to refer to all people, when a gendered pronoun is used exclusively to define roles by sex (e.g., "the nurse . . . she"), or when "he" and "she" are alternated as though these terms are generic. Pronouns associated with a specific gender have been found to induce readers to think of individuals of that gender even when the pronoun use is intended to be generic (Gastil, 1990; Moulton et al., 1978). In addition, exposure to gender-specific language in a professional context has been linked with a lower sense of belonging, reduced motivation, and professional disidentification for individuals who do not identify with that gender (Stout & Dasgupta, 2011). When writers use the singular "they," it reduces bias in the way that readers perceive the individuals referred to in the text and thereby helps ensure that readers do not feel ostracized by that text.

Avoid using combinations such as "he or she," "she or he," "he/she," and "(s)he" as alternatives to the singular "they" because such constructions imply an exclusively binary nature of gender and exclude individuals who do not use these pronouns. These forms can also appear awkward and distracting, especially with repetition. However, the combinations "he or she" or "she or he" (but not the combinations with slashes or parentheses) can be used sparingly if all people being referred to by the pronouns use these terms. For further guidance on and examples of how to use the singular "they," see Section 2.18.

Terms That Imply Binaries. Avoid referring to one sex or gender as the "opposite sex" or "opposite gender"; appropriate wording may be "another sex" or "another gender." The word "opposite" implies strong differences between two sexes or genders; however, there are more similarities than differences among people of different genders or sexes (see, e.g., Zell et al., 2015). As noted previously, some individuals do not identify with either binary gender, and these phrases ignore the existence of individuals who have disorders or differences of sex development or who are intersex (for more information, see Accord Alliance, n.d.; APA, 2015a; Blackless et al., 2000; Intersex Society of North America, n.d.). To describe members of a relationship (e.g., romantic couples, people in polyamorous relationships), use the phrases "mixed gender" or "mixed sex" when the partners have different genders or sexes, rather than "opposite gender" or "opposite sex"; use the phrases "same gender" or "same sex" when the partners have the same gender or sex.

3.6 Participation in Research

People participate in research in a variety of settings, including laboratories, homes, schools, businesses, clinics, and hospitals. Specific terms are used in certain contexts. When writing about people who participate in research, descriptive terms such as "college students," "children," or "respondents" as well as the more general terms "participants" and "subjects" are acceptable. "Subjects" and "sample" are also customary when discussing established statistical terms and experimental designs (e.g., "within-subjects design," "between-subjects design," "sample-size-adjusted Bayesian information criterion," "between-samples estimate of the variance").

Use the term "patient" to describe an individual diagnosed with a mental health, behavioral health, and/or medical disease, disorder, or problem who is receiving services from a health care provider (e.g., psychologist, physician, nurse, or other provider). This language is consistent with the language used in the health care system and promotes psychologists as being perceived as a part of, and consistently integrated into, the culture of interprofessional, integrated health care. However, in academic, business, school, or other settings, the term "client" (or some other term) might be preferred instead of "patient." Within all contexts, respect the individual and/or cultural preferences expressed by recipients of psychological services and their families when you choose language to describe those individuals, families, or populations. (For further information, see *Resolution for the Use of the Term* Patient; APA, 2018.)

It is also important to recognize the difference between a *case*, which is an occurrence of a disorder or illness, and a *person* who is affected by the disorder or illness and is receiving care from a health care professional. For instance, "manic–depressive cases were treated" is problematic; revising the sentence to read "the people with bipolar disorder were treated" differentiates the people from the disorder. Likewise, in the medical context, avoid the terms "patient management" and "patient placement." In most cases, the treatment, not the patient, is managed; some alternatives are "coordination of care," "supportive services," and "assistance."

Broad clinical terms such as "borderline" and "at risk" should be properly explained when used. Avoid using these terms in a broad sense (e.g., "the diagnosis was borderline," "at-risk students") because such usage obscures the specific clinical or psychometric meaning of the terms. For example, "the diagnosis was borderline" in a neuropsychology and psychometric testing context may be clarified to specify a score on a specific test or instrument (e.g., "standard scores between 70 and 80 are considered psychometrically borderline, or between the low average and mildly impaired ranges, indicating a risk for a diagnosis of X"), whereas in a diagnostic context, "the diagnosis was borderline" may be clarified to specify a diagnosis (e.g., borderline personality disorder). When using the term "at risk," specify who is at risk and the nature of that risk (e.g., "adolescents who use substances are at risk for early school dropout").

Across contexts, write about the people who participated in your work in a way that acknowledges their contributions and agency. Sentence structure plays a key role in this acknowledgment, as does using professional language (see Section 2.7). Use the active voice to describe your actions and the actions of participants (see Section 2.13); the passive voice suggests individuals are acted upon instead of being actors (e.g., "the subjects completed the trial" and "we collected data from the participants" are preferable to "the trial was completed by the subjects" and "the participants were run"). Avoid the term "failed," as in "eight participants failed to complete the Rorschach test," because it can imply a personal shortcoming instead of a research result; "did not complete" is a more neutral choice (Knatterud, 1991). These choices will help ensure that you convey respect for the people about whom you are writing.

3.7 Racial and Ethnic Identity

Terms used to refer to racial and ethnic groups continue to change over time. One reason for this is simply personal preference; preferred designations are as varied as the people they name. Another reason is that designations can become dated over time and may hold negative connotations. When describing racial and ethnic groups, be appropriately specific and sensitive to issues of labeling (see Sections 3.1–3.2).

Race refers to physical differences that groups and cultures consider socially significant. For example, people might identify their race as Aboriginal, African American or Black, Asian, European American or White, Native American, Native Hawaiian or Pacific Islander, Māori, or some other race. *Ethnicity* refers to shared cultural characteristics such as language, ancestry, practices, and beliefs. For example, people might identify as Latino or another ethnicity. Be clear about whether you are referring to a racial group or to an ethnic group. Race is a social construct that is not universal, so one must be careful not to impose racial labels on ethnic groups. Whenever possible, use the racial and/or ethnic terms that your participants themselves use. Be sure that the racial and ethnic categories you use are as clear and specific as possible. For example, instead of categorizing participants as Asian American or Hispanic American, you could use more specific labels that identify their nation or region of origin, such as Japanese American or Cuban American. Use commonly accepted designations (e.g., census categories) while being sensitive to participants' preferred designation.

Spelling and Capitalization of Racial and Ethnic Terms. Racial and ethnic groups are designated by proper nouns and are capitalized. Therefore, use "Black" and "White" instead of "black" and "white" (do not use colors to refer to other human groups; doing so is considered pejorative). Likewise, capitalize terms such as "Native American," "Hispanic," and so on. Capitalize "Indigenous" and "Aboriginal" whenever they are used. Capitalize "Indigenous People" or "Aboriginal People" when referring to a specific group (e.g., the Indigenous Peoples of Canada), but lowercase "people" when describing persons who are Indigenous or Aboriginal (e.g., "the authors were all Indigenous people but belonged to different nations").

Do not use hyphens in multiword names, even if the names act as unit modifiers (e.g., write "Asian American participants," not "Asian-American participants"). If people belong to multiple racial or ethnic groups, the names of the specific groups are capitalized, but the terms such as "multiracial," "biracial," and "multiethnic" are lowercase.

Terms for Specific Groups. Designations for specific ethnic and racial groups are described next. These groups frequently are included in studies published in APA journals; the examples provided are far from exhaustive but illustrate some of the complexities of labeling.

People of African Origin. When writing about people of African ancestry, several factors inform the appropriate terms to use. People of African descent have widely varied cultural backgrounds, family histories, and family experiences. Some will be from Caribbean islands, Latin America, various regions in the United States, countries in Africa, or elsewhere. Some American people of African ancestry prefer "Black," and others prefer "African American"; both terms are acceptable. However, "African American" should not be used as an umbrella term for people of African ancestry worldwide because it obscures other ethnicities or national origins, such as Nigerian, Kenyan, Jamaican, or Bahamian; in these cases use "Black." The terms "Negro" and "Afro-American" are outdated; therefore, their use is generally inappropriate.

People of Asian Origin. When writing about people of Asian ancestry from Asia, the term "Asian" is appropriate; for people of Asian descent from the United States or Canada, the appropriate term is "Asian American" or "Asian Canadian," respectively. It is problematic to group "Asian" and "Asian American" as if they are synonymous. This usage reinforces the idea that Asian Americans are perpetual foreigners. "Asian" refers to Asians in Asia, not in the United States, and should not be used to refer to Asian Americans. The older term "Oriental" is primarily used to refer to cultural objects such as carpets and is pejorative when used to refer to people. To provide more specificity, "Asian origin" may be divided regionally, for example, into South Asia (including most of India and countries such as Afghanistan, Pakistan, Bangladesh, and Nepal), Southeast Asia (including the eastern parts of India and countries such as Vietnam, Cambodia, Thailand, Indonesia, and the Philippines), and East Asia (including countries such as China, Vietnam, Japan, South Korea and North Korea, and Taiwan). The corresponding terms (e.g., East Asian) can be used; however, refer to the specific nation or region of origin when possible.

People of European Origin. When writing about people of European ancestry, the terms "White" and "European American" are acceptable. Adjust the latter term as needed for location, for example, "European," "European American," and "European Australian" for people of European descent living in Europe, the United States, and Australia, respectively. The use of the term "Caucasian" as an alternative to "White" or "European" is discouraged because it originated as a way of classifying White people as a race to be favorably compared with other races. As with all discussions of race and ethnicity, it is preferable to be more specific about regional (e.g., Scandinavian, Southern European) or national (e.g., Italian, Irish, Swedish, French, Polish) origin when possible.

Indigenous Peoples Around the World. When writing about Indigenous Peoples, use the names that they call themselves. In general, refer to an Indigenous group as a "people" or "nation" rather than as a "tribe."

- In North America, the collective terms "Native American" and "Native North American" are acceptable (and may be preferred to "American Indian"). "Indian" usually refers to people from India. Specify the nation or people if possible (e.g., Cherokee, Navajo, Sioux).

- Hawaiian Natives may identify as "Native American," "Hawaiian Native," "Indigenous Peoples of the Hawaiian Islands," and/or "Pacific Islander."

- In Canada, refer to the Indigenous Peoples collectively as "Indigenous Peoples" or "Aboriginal Peoples" (*International Journal of*

Indigenous Health, n.d.); specify the nation or people if possible (e.g., People of the First Nations of Canada, People of the First Nations, or First Nations People; Métis; Inuit).

- In Alaska, the Indigenous People may identify as "Alaska Natives." The Indigenous Peoples in Alaska, Canada, Siberia, and Greenland may identify as a specific nation (e.g., Inuit, Iñupiat). Avoid the term "Eskimo" because it may be considered pejorative.

- In Latin America and the Caribbean, refer to the Indigenous Peoples collectively as "Indigenous Peoples" and by name if possible (e.g., Quechua, Aymara, Taíno, Nahuatl).

- In Australia, the Indigenous Peoples may identify as "Aboriginal People" or "Aboriginal Australians" and "Torres Strait Islander People" or "Torres Strait Island Australians." Refer to specific groups when people use these terms to refer to themselves (e.g., Anangu Pitjantjatjara, Arrernte).

- In New Zealand, the Indigenous People may identify as "Māori" or the "Māori people" (the proper spelling includes the diacritical macron over the "a").

For information on citing the Traditional Knowledge or Oral Traditions of Indigenous Peoples as well as the capitalization of terms related to Indigenous Peoples, see Section 8.9 of the *Publication Manual*.

People of Middle Eastern Origin. When writing about people of Middle Eastern and North African (MENA) descent, state the nation of origin (e.g., Iran, Iraq, Egypt, Lebanon, Israel) when possible. In some cases, people of MENA descent who claim Arab ancestry and reside in the United States may be referred to as "Arab Americans." In all cases, it is best to allow individuals to self-identify.

People of Hispanic or Latinx Ethnicity. When writing about people who identify as Hispanic, Latino (or Latinx, etc.), Chicano, or another related designation, authors should consult with their participants to determine the appropriate choice. Note that "Hispanic" is not necessarily an all-encompassing term, and the labels "Hispanic" and "Latino" have different connotations. The term "Latino" (and its related forms) might be preferred by those originating from Latin America, including Brazil. Some use the word "Hispanic" to refer to those who speak Spanish; however, not every group in Latin America speaks Spanish (e.g., in Brazil, the official language is Portuguese). The word "Latino" is gendered (i.e., "Latino" is masculine and "Latina" is feminine); the use of the word "Latin@" to mean both Latino and Latina is now widely accepted. "Latinx" can also be used as a gender-neutral or nonbinary term inclusive of all genders. There are compelling reasons to use any of the terms "Latino," "Latina," "Latino/a," "Latin@," and/or "Latinx" (see de Onís, 2017), and various groups advocate for the use of different forms.

Use the term(s) your participants or population uses; if you are not working directly with this population but it is a focus of your research, it may be helpful to explain why you chose the term you used or to choose a more inclusive term like "Latinx." In general, naming a nation or region of origin is preferred (e.g., Bolivian, Salvadoran, or Costa Rican is more specific than Latino, Latinx, Latin American, or Hispanic).

Parallel Comparisons Among Groups. Nonparallel designations (e.g., "African Americans and Whites," "Asian Americans and Black Americans") should be avoided because one group is described by color, whereas the other group is not. Instead, use "Blacks and Whites" or "African Americans and European Americans" for the former example and "Asian Americans and African Americans" for the latter example. Do not use the phrase "White Americans and racial minorities"; the rich diversity within racial minorities is minimized when it is compared with the term "White Americans."

Avoiding Essentialism. Language that essentializes or reifies race is strongly discouraged and is generally considered inappropriate. For example, phrases such as "the Black race" and "the White race" are essentialist in nature, portray human groups monolithically, and often perpetuate stereotypes.

Writing About "Minorities." To refer to non-White racial and ethnic groups collectively, use terms such as "people of color" or "underrepresented groups" rather than "minorities." The use of "minority" may be viewed pejoratively because it is usually equated with being less than, oppressed, or deficient in comparison with the majority (i.e., White people). Rather, a *minority group* is a population subgroup with ethnic, racial, social, religious, or other characteristics different from those of the majority of the population, though the relevance of this term is changing as the demographics of the population change (APA, 2015a). If a distinction is needed between the dominant racial group and nondominant racial groups, use a modifier (e.g., "ethnic," "racial") when using the word "minority" (e.g., ethnic minority, racial minority, racial-ethnic minority). When possible, use the specific name of the group or groups to which you are referring.

Do not assume that members of minority groups are underprivileged; *underprivileged* means having less money, education, resources, and so forth than the other people in a society and may refer to individuals or subgroups in any racial or ethnic group. Terms such as "economically marginalized" and "economically exploited" may also be used rather than "underprivileged." Whenever possible, use more specific terms (e.g., schools with majority Black populations that are underfunded) or refer to discrimination or systematic oppression as a whole.

3.8 Sexual Orientation

Sexual orientation is a part of individual identity that includes "a person's sexual and emotional attraction to another person and the behavior and/or social affiliation that may result from this attraction" (APA, 2015a, p. 862). Use the term "sexual orientation" rather than "sexual preference," "sexual identity," or "sexual orientation identity." All people choose their partners regardless of their sexual orientation; however, the orientation itself is not a choice.

Sexual orientation can be conceptualized first by the degree to which a person feels sexual and emotional attraction; some parallel terms are "sexual," "demisexual" (or "gray-asexual" or "gray-A"), and "asexual" (see The Asexual Visibility & Education Network, n.d.). A person who identifies as sexual feels sexual and emotional attraction toward some or all types of people, a person who identifies as demisexual feels sexually attracted only within the context of a strong emotional connection with another person, and a person who identifies as asexual does not experience sexual attraction or has little interest in sexual behavior (see APA, 2015b).

Second, sexual orientation can be conceptualized as having a direction. For people who identify as sexual or demisexual, their attraction then may be directed toward people who are similarly gendered, differently gendered, and so on. That is, sexual orientation indicates the gendered directionality of attraction, even if that directionality is very inclusive (e.g., nonbinary). Thus, a person might be attracted to men, women, both, neither, masculinity, femininity, and/or to people who have other gender identities such as genderqueer or androgynous, or a person may have an attraction that is not predicated on a perceived or known gender identity.

Terms for Sexual Orientation. Some examples of sexual orientation are lesbian, gay, heterosexual, straight, asexual, bisexual, queer, polysexual, and pansexual (also called multisexual and omnisexual). For example, a person who identifies as lesbian might describe herself as a woman (gender identity) who is attracted to women (sexual orientation)—the sexual orientation label of "lesbian" is predicated on a perceived or known gender identity of the other person. However, someone who identifies as pansexual might describe their attraction to people as being inclusive of gender identity but not determined or delineated by gender identity. Note that these definitions are evolving and that self-identification is best when possible.

Use the umbrella term "sexual and gender minorities" to refer to multiple sexual and/or gender minority groups, or write about "sexual orientation and gender diversity" (these terms are used by the Office on Sexual Orientation and Gender Diversity at APA and the Sexual & Gender Minority Research Office at the National Institutes of Health). Abbreviations such as LGBTQ, LGBTQ+, LGBTQIA, and LGBTQIA+ may also be used to refer to multiple groups. The form "LGBT" is considered outdated, but there is not consensus about which abbreviation including or beyond LGBTQ to use. If you use the abbreviation LGBTQ (or a related one), define it (see Section 5.13) and ensure that it is representative of the groups about which you are writing. Be specific about the groups to which you refer (e.g., do not use LGBTQ and related abbreviations to write about legislation that primarily affects transgender people; instead, specify the impacted group). However, if in doubt, use one of the umbrella terms rather than a potentially inaccurate abbreviation.

When using specific terms for orientations, define them if there is ambiguity. For example, the adjective "gay" can be interpreted broadly, to include all genders, or more narrowly, to include only men, so define "gay" when you use it in your paper, or use the phrase "gay men" to clarify the usage. By convention, the term "lesbians" is appropriate to use interchangeably with "lesbian women," but "gay men" or "gay people" should be used, not "gays."

Inaccurate or Pejorative Terms. Avoid the terms "homosexual" and "homosexuality." Instead, use specific, identity-first terms to describe people's sexual orientation (e.g., bisexual people, queer people). These specific terms refer primarily to identities and to the culture and communities that have developed among people who share those identities. It is inaccurate to collapse these communities into the term "homosexual." Furthermore, the term "homosexuality" has been and continues to be associated with negative stereotypes, pathology, and the reduction of people's identities to their sexual behavior. *Homoprejudice, biprejudice, homonegativity,* and similar terms are used to denote prejudicial and discriminatory attitudes toward lesbians, gay men, bisexual individuals, or other sexual minorities. *Heterosexism* refers to the belief that heterosexuality is normative, as indicated in the assumption that individuals are heterosexual unless otherwise specified (American Psychological Association of Graduate Students, 2015). The terms "straight" and "heterosexual" are both acceptable to use when referring to people who are attracted to individuals of another gender; the term "straight" may help move the lexicon away from a dichotomy of heterosexual and homosexual. For more information regarding sexual orientation, see "Guidelines for Psychological Practice With Transgender and Gender Nonconforming People" (APA, 2015a).

3.9 Socioeconomic Status

Socioeconomic status (SES) encompasses not only income but also educational attainment, occupational prestige, and subjective perceptions of social status and social class. SES encompasses quality of life attributes and opportunities afforded to people within society and is a consistent predictor of a vast array of psychological outcomes. Thus, SES should be reported as part of the description of participants in the Method section. Because SES is complex, it is not indexed similarly in all studies; therefore, precise terminology that appropriately describes a level of specificity and sensitivity is essential to minimize bias in language around SES (for a discussion, see Diemer et al., 2013).

Reporting SES. When reporting SES, provide as much detailed information as possible about people's income, education, and occupations or employment circumstances. For example, when referring to "low-income participants" or "high-income participants," classify whether reported incomes take into account household size, or provide information about the relation between household incomes and federal poverty guidelines. Additionally, SES can be described by providing information related to specific contextual and environmental conditions such as participants' housing arrangement (e.g., renting a home, owning a home, residing in subsidized housing) and neighborhood characteristics such as median household income, percentage of unemployed people, or proportion of students who qualify for free or reduced-price lunch in local schools.

Pejorative or Stereotyping Terms. Avoid using broad, pejorative, and generalizing terms to discuss SES. Specifically, negative connotations are associated with terms such as "the homeless," "inner-city," "ghetto," "the projects," "poverty stricken," and "welfare reliant." Instead, use specific, person-first language such as "mothers who receive TANF benefits" rather than "welfare mothers" ("TANF" stands for "Temporary Assistance for Needy Families" and is the proper term for the current welfare program in the United States). When discussing people without a fixed, regular, or adequate nighttime residence, use specific language that addresses the quality or lack of housing or length of time without housing, not whether the people consider their residence a home. That is, use language like "people experiencing homelessness," "people who are homeless," "people in emergency shelter," or "people in transitional housing" rather than calling people "the homeless."

It is important to note that SES terms such as "low income" and "poor" have historically served as implicit descriptors for racial and/or ethnic minority people. Thus, it is critical that authors include racial and/or ethnic descriptors within SES categories—for example, "This sample includes low-income and middle-income Puerto Rican fathers." Implicit biases around economic and occupational status can result in deficit-based language that blames individuals for their occupational, educational, or economic situation (e.g., "attendant economic deficits") rather than recognizing a broader societal context that influences individual circumstances. Deficit-based language also focuses on what people lack rather than on what they possess. Instead of labeling people as "high school dropouts," "being poorly educated," or "having little education," provide more sensitive and specific descriptors such as "people who do not have a high school diploma or equivalent." Alternatively, by adopting a strengths-based perspective, authors can write about "people who have a grade school education." Likewise, instead of writing about an "achievement gap," write about an "opportunity gap" to emphasize how the context in which people live affects their outcomes or opportunities.

3.10 Intersectionality

When authors write about personal characteristics, they should be sensitive to *intersectionality*—that is, to the way in which individuals are shaped by and identify with a vast array of cultural, structural, sociobiological, economic, and social contexts (Howard & Renfrow, 2014). Intersectionality is a paradigm that addresses the multiple dimensions of identity and social systems as they intersect with one another and relate to inequality, such as racism, genderism, heterosexism, ageism, and classism, among other variables (APA, 2017). Thus, individuals are located within a range of social groups whose structural inequalities can result in marginalized identities.

Because people are unique, many identities are possible. As one example of a group with an intersectional identity, Black lesbian women may have similarities to and differences from other oppressed groups in the meanings that are assigned to their multiple positionalities. Black women may identify with the oppressive and discriminatory experiences of White women as well as with those of Black men. At the same time, Black lesbian women's experiences may not be equivalent to those of these other groups. They may experience discrimination as a response to their race, gender, and/ or sexual orientation. Thus, their experience does not necessarily reflect the sum of oppressions of racism, sexism, and heteronormativity (i.e., race + sex + heterosexism) but rather is informed by their unique identities and social locations as Black lesbian women that are not based in or driven by the perspectives of White women or of Black men (Bowleg, 2008; Crenshaw, 1989). That is, for example, even though Black women and White women are both women, and Black women and Black men are both Black, this does not mean that the perspectives and experiences of White women or Black men are the same as or related to those of Black lesbian women.

Intersectional identities also include experiences of privileged contexts that intersect with those of oppression. For example, a Laotian immigrant woman with a disability may experience a sense of safety and privilege because of her legal immigration status in the United States, but she may experience discrimination and a lack of access to appropriate resources within and outside of her family and ethnic community on the basis of her disability status. A Jewish American adolescent may experience privilege as a result of being perceived as White but may be the target of anti-Semitic slurs at school and in social media because of their religious beliefs. These examples illustrate how perspectives are shaped by the multiplicity of identities and contexts to which an individual belongs, some oppressed and some privileged. Aspects of identity such as race, gender, and class can be oppressed or privileged, in ways that may differ across contexts, and can result in differing experiences that interact dynamically to shape an individual's experiences, advantages, and disadvantages across time and space. The intersections of multiple identities transform the oppressed and privileged aspects of each person's layered, interlocking identities.

INTERSECTIONALITY

To address intersectionality in a paper, identify individuals' relevant characteristics and group memberships (e.g., ability and/or disability status, age, gender, gender identity, generation, historical as well as ongoing experiences of marginalization, immigrant status, language, national origin, race and/or ethnicity, religion or spirituality, sex, sexual orientation, social class, and SES, among other variables), and describe how their characteristics and group memberships intersect in ways that are relevant to the study. Report participant data for each group using specific terms as described in Sections 3.3 to 3.9. For example, when describing participants in terms of their race and gender, write "20 participants were African American women, 15 participants were European American women, 23 participants were African American men, and 18 participants were European American men (all participants were cisgender)" rather than "35 participants were women and 41 were men; 43 were African American and 33 were European American." Reporting participant characteristics in this way helps readers understand how many groups are composed of individuals with the same characteristics. Likewise, when reporting and interpreting the results, note the impact of any intersections on the findings rather than assuming that one characteristic is responsible for what you found. For more discussion of intersectionality, see the *Multicultural Guidelines: An Ecological Approach to Context, Identity, and Intersectionality* (APA, 2017).

4

PUNCTUATION, LISTS, AND ITALICS

Style refers to guidelines for ensuring clear, consistent presentation in written works. APA Style provides guidelines for writing and formatting scholarly papers. Instructors often require students to follow specific style guidelines to avoid inconsistencies among and within their academic papers and assignments. These guidelines include the use of punctuation, which help clarify your meaning for readers; lettered, numbered, and bulleted lists, which help organize your key points; and italics, which help distinguish elements and words from surrounding text.

This chapter provides APA Style guidelines for punctuation, lists, and italics in scholarly writing. We start by listing correct and incorrect ways to use specific punctuation marks, followed by guidelines for organizing lists and using italics in APA Style.

Punctuation

Punctuation establishes the cadence of a sentence, telling readers where to pause (comma, semicolon, and colon), stop (period and question mark), or take a detour (dash, parentheses, and square brackets). Punctuation of a sentence usually denotes a pause in thought; different kinds of punctuation indicate different kinds and lengths of pauses.

4.1 Spacing After Punctuation Marks

Insert one space after the following:

- periods or other punctuation marks at the end of a sentence
- commas, colons, and semicolons
- periods that separate parts of a reference list entry (see Section 9.5)
- periods following initials in names (M. P. Clark)

Do not insert a space in the following cases:

- after internal periods in abbreviations (e.g., a.m., i.e., U.S.)
- after periods in identity-concealing labels for study participants (F.I.M.)
- around colons in ratios (1:4)

> *Note:* We recommend using one space after the period or other punctuation mark at the end of a sentence; however, follow the guidelines of your instructor if they have different requirements.

4.2 Period

Use a period or periods in the following cases:

- to end a complete sentence
- with initials in names (Bazerman, M. H.)
- in the abbreviations for "United States" and "United Kingdom" when they are used as adjectives (U.S. Navy; it is not required to abbreviate these terms)
- in identity-concealing labels for study participants (F.I.M.)
- in Latin abbreviations (a.m., cf., e.g., i.e., p.m., vs.)
- in reference abbreviations (Vol. 1, 2nd ed., p. 6, paras. 11–12, F. Supp.)
- in era designations (B.C.E., C.E., B.C., A.D.; see Section 9.41)
- to end each element within a reference (except DOIs and URLs; see Section 9.5)

Do not use periods in the following cases:

- in abbreviations of state, province, or territory names (NY; CA; Washington, DC; BC; ON; NSW)

- in capital letter abbreviations and acronyms (APA, NIMH, NDA, IQ)
- in abbreviations for academic degrees (PhD, PsyD, EdD, MD, MA, RN, MSW, LCSW; see Section 1.8)
- in abbreviations for routes of administration (icv, im, ip, iv, sc)
- in metric and nonmetric measurement abbreviations (cm, hr, kg, min, ml, s)

> *Note:* Use a period with the abbreviation for "inch" or "inches" (in.) because otherwise it could be misread.

- after URLs in the text (see Section 8.22); instead, place URLs in the middle of the sentence or in parentheses to avoid ending a sentence with a URL
- after DOIs or URLs in the reference list (see Section 9.35)

4.3 Comma

Use a comma in the following cases:

- between elements in a series of three or more items, including before the final item (see also Section 4.11); this last comma is called a *serial comma* or *Oxford comma*

  Correct: height, width, and depth
  Incorrect: height, width and depth

- after an introductory phrase (if the introductory phrase is short, the comma after it is optional)

  After the nurses administered the medication, patients rated their pain.
  in this section, we discuss

  or

  in this section we discuss

- to set off a nonessential or nonrestrictive clause (see Section 2.21)—that is, a clause that embellishes a sentence but if removed would leave the grammatical structure and meaning of the sentence intact

  Strong fearful faces, which are rarely seen in everyday life, convey intense expression of negative emotions.

- to set off statistics in the text that already contain parentheses, to avoid nested parentheses

  Sleep amount was not significantly different between the three groups (nap: $M = 7.48$ hr, $SD = 1.99$; wake: $M = 8.13$ hr, $SD = 1.22$; nap + wake: $M = 7.25$ hr, $SD = 0.76$), $F(2, 71) = 2.32$, $p = .11$.

  There was a main effect of group on corrected recognition, $F(2, 71) = 3.38$, $p < .04$, $\eta_p^2 = .087$.

- to separate two independent clauses joined by a conjunction

  Facial expressions were presented, and different photo models were chosen randomly.

- to set off the year in exact dates in the text or in a retrieval date (see Section 9.16); however, when only a month and year appear in the text, do not use a comma

  Retrieved April 24, 2020, from

  in April 2020

- to set off the year in parenthetical in-text citations

  (Bergen-Abramoff, 2018)

  (Horowitz, 2019, discovered . . .)

- to separate groups of three digits in most numbers of 1,000 or more (see Section 6.7 for exceptions)

Do not use a comma in the following cases:

- before an essential or restrictive clause (see Section 2.21) because removing such a clause from the sentence would alter the intended meaning

  Adolescents who spent a small amount of time on electronic communication activities were happier than those who spent no time on such activities.

- between the two parts of a compound predicate

  Correct: Participants rated the items and completed a demographic questionnaire.

  Incorrect: Participants rated the items, and completed a demographic questionnaire.

- to separate parts of measurement

  7 years 4 months

  2 min 35 s

  5 ft 10 in.

4.4 Semicolon

Use a semicolon in the following cases:

- to separate two independent clauses that are not joined by a conjunction

  Students received course credit for participation; community members received $10.

- to separate two independent clauses joined by a conjunctive adverb such as "however," "therefore," or "nevertheless"

  The children studied the vocabulary words; however, they had difficulties with recall.

- to separate items in a list that already contain commas (see Section 4.11)

  The color groups were red, yellow, and blue; orange, green, and purple; or black, gray, and brown.

- to separate multiple parenthetical citations (see Section 8.12)

  (Gaddis, 2018; Lai et al., 2016; Williams & Peng, 2019)

- to separate different types of information in the same set of parentheses, to avoid back-to-back parentheses

  (n = 33; Fu & Ginsburg, 2020)

- to separate sets of statistics that already contain commas

  (age, M = 34.5 years, 95% CI [29.4, 39.6]; years of education, M = 10.4 [8.7, 12.1]; and weekly income, M = $612 [522, 702]).

4.5 Colon

Use a colon in the following cases:

- between a grammatically complete introductory clause (one that could stand alone as a sentence, including an imperative statement) and a final phrase or clause that illustrates, extends, or amplifies the preceding thought (if the clause following the colon is a complete sentence, begin it with a capital letter; see Section 5.3)

  There are three main patterns of mother–infant attachment: secure, avoidant, and resistant/ambivalent (Ainsworth et al., 1978).

  Yag et al. (2019) confirmed the finding: Test performance depended on preparation.

- in ratios and proportions

  The proportion of salt to water was 1:8.

Do not use a colon in the following case:

- after an introduction that is not an independent clause or complete sentence

  The formula is $r_i = a_i + e$.

  Target behaviors included eating, sleeping, and socializing.

  The participants were asked to

  - rank the 15 items,
  - explain their choices, and
  - close their notebooks when finished.

4.6 Dash

Two dash forms are used in APA Style: the *em dash* (long dash) and the *en dash* (midsized dash). These dashes are different from hyphens (see Section 5.2) and minus signs (see Section 6.11).

Em Dash. Use an em dash to set off an element added to amplify or digress from the main clause. Overuse of the em dash weakens the flow of material, so use it carefully. Do not insert a space before or after an em dash. Word-processing programs can be set to automatically convert two back-to-back hyphens to an em dash. (See Section 5.7 for capitalization following em dashes in titles.)

  Social adjustment—but not academic adjustment—was associated with extraversion.

En Dash. An en dash is longer and thinner than a hyphen but shorter than an em dash. Use an en dash between words of equal weight in a compound adjective and to indicate a numerical range, such as a page or date range. Do not insert a space before or after an en dash. Word-processing programs have options for inserting an en dash.

  author–date citation

  Sydney–Los Angeles flight

  pp. 4–7

  50%–60%

A hyphen rather than an en dash is generally used in an abbreviation that contains dashes, such as the abbreviation for a test or scale (e.g., MMPI-2) or a diagnostic manual (*DSM-5*, *ICD-11*; see Section 5.13).

4.7 Quotation Marks

This section addresses how to use quotation marks other than with direct quotations (see Sections 8.25–8.34). Quotation marks often appear with other punctuation marks. Place commas and periods inside closing quotation marks. Place other punctuation marks (e.g., colons, semicolons, ellipses) outside closing quotation marks.

Use double quotation marks in the following cases:

- to refer to a letter, word, phrase, or sentence as a linguistic example or as itself

  the letter "m"

  the singular "they"

  answered "yes" or "no"

  Instead of referring to someone as a "defective child," talk about a "child with a congenital disability" or a "child with a birth impairment."

  Students wrote "I promise to uphold the honor code" at the top of the test page.

- to present stimuli in the text (long lists of stimuli may be better presented in a table, where quotation marks are not needed)

  The stimulus words were "garden," "laundry," "briefcase," and "salary."

- to reproduce material from a test item or verbatim instructions to participants (if instructions are long, present them in an appendix or set them off from text in block quote format without quotation marks; see Sections 1.14 and 8.27)

  The first item was "How tired do you feel after a long day at work?"

  Participants read, "You can write as much as you like when answering the questions."

- to introduce a word or phrase used as an ironic comment, as slang, or as an invented or coined expression; use quotation marks only for the first occurrence of the word or phrase, not for subsequent occurrences

First occurrence:	Subsequent occurrence:
considered "normal" behavior	normal behavior
called a "friendly link"	a friendly link

- to introduce a label; after the label has been used once, do not use quotation marks for subsequent occurrences

  The image label changed from "spiderweb" to "dartboard." The spiderweb and dartboard labels . . .

- to set off the title of a periodical article or book chapter when the title is used in the text or in a copyright attribution (do not use quotation marks around the article or book chapter title in the reference list entry)

In text:

Oerlemans and Bakker's (2018) article, "Motivating Job Characteristics and Happiness at Work: A Multilevel Perspective," described . . .

In the reference list:

Oerlemans, W. G. M., & Bakker, A. B. (2018). Motivating job characteristics and happiness at work: A multilevel perspective. *Journal of Applied Psychology*, *103*(11), 1230–1241. https://doi.org/10.1037/apl0000318

In a copyright attribution:

Adapted from "Motivating Job Characteristics and Happiness at Work: A Multilevel Perspective," by W. G. M. Oerlemans and A. B. Bakker, 2018, *Journal of Applied Psychology*, *103*(11), p. 1236 (https://doi.org/10.1037/apl0000318). Copyright 2018 by the American Psychological Association.

Do not use double quotation marks in the following cases:

- to highlight a key term or phrase (e.g., around a term for which you are going to provide a definition); instead, use italics (see Section 4.15)

- to identify the anchors of a scale; instead, use italics (see Section 4.15)

- to refer to a numeral as itself because the meaning is sufficiently clear without quotation marks

The numeral 2 was displayed onscreen.

- to hedge or downplay meaning (do not use any punctuation with these expressions)

Correct: The teacher rewarded the class with tokens.

Incorrect: The teacher "rewarded" the class with tokens.

4.8 Parentheses

Use parentheses in the following cases:

- to set off structurally independent elements

The patterns were statistically significant (see Figure 5).

- to set off in-text citations (see Section 8.11)

  Barnes and Spreitzer (2019) described
  (Proctor & Hoffmann, 2016)

- to introduce an abbreviation in the text (see also Section 5.13)

  galvanic skin response (GSR)
  Child Report of Parental Behavior Inventory (CRPBI; Schaefer, 1965)

- to set off letters that identify items in a list within a sentence or paragraph (see also Section 4.12)

  The subject areas included (a) synonyms associated with cultural interactions, (b) descriptors for ethnic group membership, and (c) psychological symptoms and outcomes associated with bicultural adaptation.

- to enclose statistical values that do not already contain parentheses

  was statistically significant (p = .031)

- to enclose degrees of freedom

  $t(75)$ = 2.19 $F(2, 116)$ = 3.71

> *Note:* (When a complete sentence is enclosed in parentheses, like this, place the end punctuation inside the parentheses.) If only part of a sentence is enclosed in parentheses, place punctuation outside the parentheses (like this).

Do not use parentheses in the following cases:

- to enclose text within other parentheses; instead, use square brackets to avoid nested parentheses

  (Beck Depression Inventory [BDI]; Beck et al., 1996)

- to enclose statistics that already contain parentheses; instead, use a comma before the statistics to avoid nested parentheses

  were significantly different, $F(4, 132)$ = 13.62, p < .001

- to enclose back-to-back parenthetical information; instead, put the information in one set of parentheses, separated with a semicolon

  Correct: (e.g., flow; Csikszentmihalyi, 2014)
  Incorrect: (e.g., flow) (Csikszentmihalyi, 2014)

4.9 Square Brackets

Use square brackets in the following cases:

- to enclose parenthetical material that is already in parentheses

  (The results for the control group [*n* = 8] are also presented in Figure 2.)

- to enclose abbreviations when the abbreviated term appears in parentheses

  (Minnesota Multiphasic Personality Inventory–2 [MMPI-2]; Butcher et al., 2001)

- to enclose values that are the limits of a confidence interval

  95% CIs [–7.2, 4.3], [9.2, 12.4], and [–1.2, –0.5]

- to enclose material inserted in a quotation by someone other than the original author (see also Section 8.31)

  Schofield et al. (2016) found that "these types of [warm and accepting] parenting behaviors are positively associated with healthy child and adolescent adjustment" (p. 615).

- to enclose a description of form for some works (e.g., those outside the typical peer-reviewed academic literature; see Section 9.21) in a reference list entry

Do not use square brackets in the following cases:

- to set off statistics that already include parentheses

  Correct: in the first study, $F(1, 32) = 4.37$, $p = .045$.
  Incorrect: in the first study ($F[1, 32] = 4.37$, $p = .045$).
  Incorrect: in the first study [$F(1, 32) = 4.37$, $p = .045$].

> *Note:* In mathematical material, the placement of brackets and parentheses is reversed; that is, parentheses appear within brackets (see Section 6.12).

- around the year in a narrative citation when the sentence containing the narrative citation appears in parentheses; instead, use commas (see Section 8.11)

  Correct: (as Gregory, 2020, concluded . . .)
  Incorrect: (as Gregory [2020] concluded . . .)

4.10 Slash

Use a slash in the following cases:

- to clarify a comparison in a compound adjective, especially when one of the elements is a hyphenated compound (alternatively, use an en dash; see Section 4.6)

  the classification/similarity-judgment condition

  hits/false-alarms comparison

  test/retest reliability or test–retest reliability

- to specify either of two possibilities

  and/or (use sparingly)

  Latino/a

- to separate a numerator from a denominator

  X/Y

- to separate units of measurement accompanied by a numeric value (see Section 5.15); if no numeric value appears with the unit of measurement, spell out the word "per"

  0.5 deg/s

  7.4 mg/kg

  cost per square meter

- to set off phonemes

  /o/

- in citations of translated, reprinted, reissued, or republished works in the text (see Sections 9.39–9.40)

  Freud (1923/1961)

Do not use a slash when a phrase would be clearer.

> **Correct:** Each child handed the toy to their parent or guardian.
>
> **Incorrect:** Each child handed the toy to their parent/guardian.

Lists

4.11 List Guidelines

Just as heading structure alerts readers to the order of ideas in a paper, *seriation*—that is, lists—helps readers understand a related set of key points within a sentence or paragraph. In a series, all items should be syntactically and conceptually parallel (see Section 2.24 for a more detailed discussion of parallelism).

When a list within a sentence contains three or more items, use a serial comma before the final item (see also Section 4.3).

> Participants were similar with respect to age, gender, and ethnicity.

However, if any item in a list of three or more items already contains commas, use semicolons instead of commas between the items (see Section 4.4).

> We were interested in how students describe their gender identities and expressions; their perceptions of emotional and physical safety on campus, including whether and how such perceptions impact their gender expression; and their perceptions of trans-affirming versus trans-negative reactions among fellow students and faculty.

4.12 Lettered Lists

Within a sentence or paragraph narrative, identify elements in a series with lowercase letters in parentheses when doing so will help readers understand the separate, parallel items in a complex list. Lettered lists may also be used to draw attention to the items—but not as much attention as a numbered or bulleted list. Use commas or semicolons between items as described in Section 4.11.

> Our sample organization used a waterfall model that featured the following sequential stages: (a) requirements analysis, (b) specification, (c) architecture, (d) design, and (e) deployment.
>
> We tested three groups of (a) low scorers, who scored fewer than 20 points; (b) moderate scorers, who scored between 20 and 50 points; and (c) high scorers, who scored more than 50 points.

4.13 Numbered Lists

Use a numbered list to display complete sentences or paragraphs in a series (e.g., itemized conclusions, steps in a procedure). Use a lettered or bulleted list rather than a numbered list if the items are phrases. Use the numbered list function of your word-processing program to create the numbered list; this will automatically indent the list as well. Select the option for an Arabic numeral followed by a period but not enclosed in or followed by parentheses. Capitalize the first word after the number (and the first word in any subsequent sentence), and end each sentence with a period or other punctuation as appropriate.

We addressed the following research questions:

1. What research methodologies are used to examine the effects of cultural competency training?
2. How are psychologists trained to be culturally competent?
3. How are training outcomes assessed?
4. What are the outcomes of cultural competency training?

4.14 Bulleted Lists

The use of a numbered list may connote an unwanted or unwarranted ordinal position (e.g., chronology, importance, priority) among the items. To achieve the same effect without the implication of ordinality, use bullets to identify the items in the series. Use the bulleted list function of your word-processing program to create the bulleted list; this will automatically indent the list as well. Symbols such as small circles, squares, dashes, and so forth may be used for the bullets.

Items That Are Complete Sentences. If bulleted list items are complete sentences, begin each sentence with a capital letter and finish it with a period or other end punctuation.

There are several ways in which psychologists could apply social-media-driven methods to improve their work:

- Social psychologists could use these methods to improve research on emotional experiences.
- Community psychologists could use these methods to improve population assessment at the city level.
- Clinical psychologists could use these methods to improve assessment or treatment.

Items That Are Phrases. If bulleted list items are phrases or sentence fragments (i.e., not full sentences), begin each bulleted item with a lowercase letter (for exceptions, such as proper nouns, see Sections 5.4–5.11). There are two options for punctuating a bulleted list in which the items are phrases or fragments.

Phrases Without End Punctuation. The first option is to use no punctuation after the bulleted items (including the final one), which may be better when the items are shorter and simpler.

Some strategies used by faculty of color in the United States for survival and success on the tenure track include the following:

- learning the rules of the game
- being aware of who possesses power

- working doubly hard
- emphasizing one's strengths and establishing some authority
- finding White allies (Lutz et al., 2013; Turner et al., 2011)

Phrases With End Punctuation. The second option is to insert punctuation after the bulleted items as though the bullets were not there, following the guidelines in Sections 4.3 and 4.4 for comma and semicolon usage; this option may be better when the items are longer or more complex.

Adolescents may crave the opportunities for peer connection that social media affords because it allows them to

- communicate privately with individuals or publicly with a larger audience,
- seek affirmation by posting pictures or commentary and receiving likes or comments,
- see how their numbers of friends and followers compare with those of their peers, and
- monitor who is doing what with whom by seeing how many peers like and comment on their posts and comparing the feedback they get with what others received (Underwood & Ehrenreich, 2017).

Items That Contain Both Phrases and Sentences. When bulleted items contain both phrases and sentences (as with a list of definitions in a glossary), various formats are possible, but the presentation should be consistent and logical. One approach is to lowercase the word or phrase at the beginning of the bullet in bold, followed by a colon. If what follows the colon is a sentence fragment, lowercase the first word after the colon.

creativity: the ability to produce or develop original work, theories, techniques, or thoughts.

Use a period after a sentence fragment when an additional sentence follows the fragment; otherwise, the punctuation after the fragment is optional.

goal: the end state toward which a human or nonhuman animal is striving. It can be identified by observing that an organism ceases or changes its behavior upon attaining this state.

If what follows the colon is a complete sentence, capitalize the first word after the colon and end the sentence with a period or other end punctuation.

problem solving: Individuals use problem solving to attempt to overcome difficulties, achieve plans that move them from a starting situation to a desired goal, or reach conclusions through the use of higher mental functions, such as reasoning and creative thinking.

Italics

4.15 Use of Italics

Use italics for the following:

- key terms or phrases, often accompanied by a definition

  Mindfulness is defined as "the act of noticing new things, a process that pro-motes flexible responding to the demands of the environment" (Pagnini et al., 2016, p. 91).

  > *Note:* Use italics for a term or phrase only once, when it is most appropriate to draw readers' attention to the term or phrase; else-where, the term should be in standard (nonitalic) type. For example, if a word is used in a heading and then defined in the text that follows, italicize the term as part of the definition rather than in the heading.

- titles of books, reports, webpages, and other stand-alone works (see Section 9.19)

  Multicultural Feminist Therapy: Helping Adolescent Girls of Color to Thrive

- titles of periodicals (see Section 9.25)

  Cultural Diversity & Ethnic Minority Psychology

- genera, species, and varieties

  Cebus apella

- letters used as statistical symbols or algebraic variables

  Cohen's d = 0.084

  $a/b = c/d$

  MSE

- periodical volume numbers in reference lists

  Neuropsychology, 30(5), 525–531.

- anchors of a scale (but not the associated number)

  ranged from 1 (*poor*) to 5 (*excellent*)

  rated using a Likert scale (1 = *strongly disagree* to 5 = *strongly agree*)

- the first use of a word, phrase, or abbreviation from another language when readers may not be familiar with it; however, if the term appears in a dictionary for the language in which you are writing (see Section 5.1), do not use italics

ITALICS

Do not use italics for the following:

- titles of book series (e.g., the Harry Potter series)
- the punctuation mark after an italicized word or phrase

  What is *plurality*?

> *Note:* Italicize a punctuation mark that is part of an italic element, such as a colon, comma, or question mark within a book title, periodical title, or heading.
>
> Miles and Sweet's (2017) book *Chicken or Egg: Who Comes First?* addressed . . .

- punctuation between elements of a reference list entry (e.g., the comma after a volume and issue number, the period after a book title)
- words, phrases, and abbreviations of foreign origin that appear in a dictionary for the language in which you are writing (see Section 5.1)

a posteriori	et al.	a priori	per se
ad lib	vis-à-vis	fait accompli	mens rea
force majeure	zeitgeist		

- Greek letters

  β, α, χ^2

- letters used as abbreviations

  reaction time (RT)

- mere emphasis

  Incorrect: It is important to bear in mind that *this* process is *not* proposed as a *stage* theory of development.

> *Note:* Italics for emphasis are acceptable if emphasis might otherwise be lost or the material misread; in general, however, use syntax to provide emphasis. See Section 8.31 for how to add emphasis in quoted material. Italics and bold may be used for emphasis in tables (e.g., to show factor loadings of a particular size), unless your instructor says otherwise.

4.16 Reverse Italics

When words that would normally be italicized appear within text that is already italicized, those words should be set in standard (nonitalic) type, referred to as *reverse italicization*. For example, when the title of a book contains the title of another book, use standard type for the title within the title. In the text, use title case for both titles; in the reference list entry, use sentence case for both titles. In the following example, Marinelli and Mayer wrote a book about Freud's book *The Interpretation of Dreams*; Marinelli and Mayer's book title is italicized, and Freud's book title within it is written in standard type.

In text:

In *Dreaming by the Book: Freud's* The Interpretation of Dreams *and the History of the Psychoanalytic Movement*, Marinelli and Mayer (2003) explored . . .

In the reference list:

Marinelli, L., & Mayer, A. (2003). *Dreaming by the book: Freud's* The interpretation of dreams *and the history of the psychoanalytic movement*. Other Press.

ITALICS

5

SPELLING, CAPITALIZATION, AND ABBREVIATIONS

Style guidelines ensure consistency in the presentation of words and abbreviations and help clarify your main points and improve your writing. For example, without style guidelines, writers might use the spellings "health-care," "health care," and "healthcare" interchangeably in the same paper. Although the meaning of these terms is the same and the choice of one style over the other may seem arbitrary (in this case, "health care," with a space and no hyphen, is APA Style), such variations in style can distract or confuse instructors or other readers. Likewise, the inconsistent use of capitalization can be distracting for readers, and overuse and underuse of abbreviations can lead to writing that is unclear. Style guidelines help readers focus on your ideas and key points and help you communicate more clearly.

This chapter provides APA Style guidelines for spelling, capitalization, and abbreviations in scholarly writing. We address which dictionaries to consult for preferred spellings and common questions writers have with regard to capitalizing terms, titles, and headings. Last, we address abbreviation use and demonstrate how to use abbreviations for common cases such as measurement, time, and chemical compounds.

Spelling

5.1 Preferred Spelling

Spelling in APA Style papers should conform to *Merriam-Webster.com Dictionary* (https://www.merriam-webster.com). Spellings of psychological terms should conform to the *APA Dictionary of Psychology* (https://dictionary.apa.org). If a word appears differently in these two dictionaries, follow the spelling in the *APA Dictionary of Psychology*. If a word is not in either of these dictionaries, consult an unabridged edition of *Webster's* dictionary (https://unabridged.merriam-webster.com) or another dictionary used in your field or language. If the dictionary offers a choice of spellings, select one and use it consistently throughout your paper.

The plural forms of some words of Latin or Greek origin can be troublesome (particularly those that end in the letter "a"). A list of preferred spellings of some of the more common words follows.

Singular:	appendix	criterion	curriculum	datum	phenomenon
Plural:	appendices	criteria	curricula	data	phenomena

Remember that plural nouns take plural verbs.

Correct: The data indicate

Incorrect: The data indicates

Form the possessive of a singular name by adding an apostrophe and an "s" (e.g., "Milner's theory"). This guideline also applies when a name ends in "s" (e.g., "Descartes's philosophy," "James's work").

The spellings of terms related to technology evolve over time. Use the following spellings for common technology words in APA Style papers:

email	ebook	ereader	database
data set	smartphone	internet	intranet
Wi-Fi	website	webpage	the web
home page	username	login page (but "log in" when used as a verb)	emoji (for the plural, either "emoji" or "emojis")

5.2 Hyphenation

Compound words—words composed of two or more words—take many forms; they may be written as (a) two separate words (open), (b) one hyphenated word, or (c) one solid word. Compound words are often introduced into the language as separate or hyphenated words; as they become more commonplace, they tend to fuse into a solid word. For example, "data base" has become "database," and "e-mail" has become "email." The dictionary is an excellent guide for choosing the proper form: When a compound appears in the dictionary, its usage is established, and it is considered a permanent compound (e.g., "health care," "self-esteem," "caregiver"). In general, follow the hyphenation shown in the dictionary for permanent compounds (e.g., write "health care" without a hyphen, even in a phrase like "health care setting"); adjust hyphenation only to prevent misreading. Dictionaries do not always agree on the way a compound should be written (open, hyphenated, or solid); Section 5.1 specifies the dictionaries to use for APA Style papers.

Another form of compound—the temporary compound—is made up of two or more words that occur together, perhaps only in a particular paper, to express a thought. Temporary compounds are not usually listed in the dictionary. To determine how to hyphenate temporary compounds, follow these guidelines:

- If a temporary compound can be misread or expresses a single thought, use a hyphen, especially when the temporary compound appears as an adjective before the noun. When in doubt, use a hyphen for clarity. For example, "Adolescents resided in two parent homes" may mean that two homes served as residences or that each adolescent lived with two parents; a hyphen in "two-parent homes" specifies the latter meaning.

- If the compound appears after the noun it modifies, do not use a hyphen because, in almost all cases, the phrase is sufficiently clear without one. See Table 5.1 for further examples of hyphen use in temporary compounds.

t-test results	*but*	results of t tests
same-sex children	*but*	children of the same sex

- Write most words formed with prefixes and suffixes as one word without a hyphen. See Table 5.2 for examples of prefixes and suffixes that do not require hyphens; see Table 5.3 for examples of

Table 5.1 Guide to Hyphenating Temporary Compound Terms

Grammar guideline	Example
Hyphenate	
A compound with a participle when it precedes the term it modifies	decision-making behavior water-deprived animals Canadian-born actor
A phrase used as an adjective when it precedes the term it modifies	trial-by-trial analysis to-be-recalled items one-on-one interviews
An adjective-and-noun compound when it precedes the term it modifies	high-anxiety group middle-class families low-frequency words
A compound with a number as the first element when the compound precedes the term it modifies	six-trial problem 12th-grade students 16-min interval
A fraction used as an adjective	two-thirds majority
Do not hyphenate	
A compound that follows the term it modifies	behavior related to decision making students in the 12th grade a majority of two thirds
A compound including an adverb ending in "-ly"	widely used test relatively homogeneous sample randomly assigned participants
A compound including a comparative or superlative adjective	better written paper less informed interviewers higher order learning highest scoring students
Chemical terms	sodium chloride solution amino acid compound
Latin phrases used as adjectives or adverbs	a posteriori test post hoc comparisons were fed ad lib (but hyphenate the adjectival form: ad-lib feeding)
A modifier including a letter or numeral as the second element	Group B participants Type II error Trial 1 performance
Fractions used as nouns	one third of the participants

Table 5.2 Prefixes and Suffixes That Do Not Require Hyphens

Prefix or suffix	Example	Prefix or suffix	Example
able	retrievable	mid	midterm
after	aftercare	mini	minisession
anti	antisocial	multi	multimethod
bi	bilingual	non	nonsignificant
cede/sede/ceed	intercede	over	oversampling
co	covariate	phobia	agoraphobia
cyber	cyberwarfare	post	posttest
equi	equimax	pre	preexperimental
extra	extracurricular	pseudo	pseudoscience
gram	cardiogram	quasi	quasiperiodic
infra	infrared	re	reevaluate
inter	intersex	semi	semidarkness
like	wavelike	socio	socioeconomic
macro	macrocosm	sub	subtest
mega	megawatt	super	superordinate
meta	metaethics	supra	supraliminal
meter	nanometer	un	unbiased
micro	microcosm	under	underdeveloped

Note. However, use a hyphen in "meta-analysis" and "quasi-experimental."

Table 5.3 Compound Words That Require Hyphens

Occurrence	Example
Compounds in which the base word is • capitalized	pro-Freudian Likert-type Stroop-like
• a number	post-1977
• an abbreviation	pre-UCS trial
• more than one word	non-achievement-oriented students
All "self-" compounds, whether adjectives or nouns [a]	self-report technique the test was self-paced self-esteem
Words that could be misunderstood	re-pair (pair again) re-form (form again) un-ionized (not ionized)
Words in which the prefix ends and the base word begins with "a," "i," or "o" [b]	meta-analysis anti-intellectual co-occur

[a] *But* "self psychology."
[b] "Pre" and "re" compounds are not hyphenated with base words beginning with "e" (e.g., "preexisting," "reexamine").

prefixed and suffixed words that do require hyphens. The same suffix may be hyphenated in some cases and not in others (e.g., "nationwide" and "worldwide" vs. "industry-wide").

- When two or more compound modifiers have a common base, that base is sometimes omitted in all except the last modifier, but the hyphens are retained. Leave a space after the hyphen when the base has been omitted, unless punctuation follows the hyphen.

long- and short-term memory
2-, 3-, and 10-min trials

Capitalization

APA Style is a "down" style, meaning that words are lowercase unless there is specific guidance to capitalize them.

5.3 Words Beginning a Sentence

Capitalize the following:

- the first word in a complete sentence
- the first word after a colon if what follows the colon is a complete sentence

The statement was emphatic: Further research is needed.

Do not capitalize the following:

- a personal name that begins with a lowercase letter when the name begins a sentence; alternatively, reword the sentence

. . . after the test. van de Vijver et al. (2019) concluded

- a proper noun (other than a personal name) that begins with a lowercase letter (e.g., iPad, eBay) or a lowercase statistical term (e.g., t test, p value) when it begins a sentence (see Section 5.14); instead, reword the sentence to avoid beginning with a lowercase letter

5.4 Proper Nouns and Trade Names

Capitalize the following:

- proper nouns and proper adjectives
- names of racial and ethnic groups (see also Section 3.7)

We interviewed 25 Black women living in rural Louisiana.

- names of specific university departments, academic institutions, and academic courses

Capitalize	Do not capitalize
Department of Psychology, San Francisco State University	a psychology department, a university
Psychology 101	a psychology course
Science of Nursing Practice	a nursing course

- trade and brand names (in general, do not include the copyright or trademark symbol after a trade or brand name used in an academic paper; however, such symbols may be included in business and marketing materials)

Capitalize	Do not capitalize
APA Style	a writing style
Zoloft	sertraline (generic name for Zoloft)
iPhone, Android phone	smartphone
Wi-Fi	wireless, hotspot

Do not capitalize the following:

- proper adjectives that have a common meaning (consult a dictionary for guidance; see Section 5.1), except for personal names within these terms

eustachian tube

cesarean section

but

Freudian slip

Wilks's lambda

Euclidean geometry

5.5 Job Titles and Positions

Capitalize a job title or position when the title precedes a name (titles are not used in bylines; see Section 1.8):

President Lincoln was elected in 1860.

Executive Director of Marketing Carolina Espinoza led the meeting.

Dr. Aisha Singh, Dr. Singh

Registered Nurse Paul T. Lo, Nurse Lo

Do not capitalize a job title or position when the title follows the name or refers to a position in general:

> Abraham Lincoln was president of the United States.
>
> Carolina Espinoza, executive director of marketing, led the meeting.
>
> president, vice president, chief executive officer, executive director, manager
>
> professor, instructor, faculty, dean
>
> psychologist, psychiatrist, counselor, social worker
>
> physician, doctor, physician assistant
>
> nurse, registered nurse, advanced practice nurse, nurse practitioner

5.6 Diseases, Disorders, Therapies, Theories, and Related Terms

Do not capitalize the names of the following:

- diseases or disorders

autism spectrum disorder	diabetes
major depression	leukemia

- therapies and treatments

cognitive behavior therapy	immunotherapy
applied behavior analysis	cataract surgery

- theories, concepts, hypotheses, principles, models, and statistical procedures

object permanence	theory of mind
associative learning model	law of effect
psychoanalytic theory	two-group t test

However, capitalize personal names that appear within the names of diseases, disorders, therapies, treatments, theories, hypotheses, concepts, principles, models, and statistical procedures.

Alzheimer's disease	Down syndrome
non-Hodgkin's lymphoma	Maslow's hierarchy of needs
Freudian theory	Pavlovian conditioning

5.7 Titles of Works and Headings Within Works

APA Style uses two types of capitalization for titles of works and headings within works: title case and sentence case. In *title case*, major words are capitalized. In *sentence case*, most words are lower-cased. Nouns, verbs (including linking verbs), adjectives, adverbs, pronouns, and all words of four letters or more are considered major words. Short (i.e., three letters or fewer) conjunctions, short prepositions, and all articles are considered minor words.

Title Case. In title case, capitalize the following words in a title or heading:

- the first word, even a minor word such as "The"
- the first word of a subtitle, even if it is a minor word
- the first word after a colon, em dash, or end punctuation in a heading, even if it is a minor word
- major words, including the second part of hyphenated major words (e.g., "Self-Report," not "Self-report")
- words of four letters or more (e.g., "With," "Between," "From")

Lowercase only minor words that are three letters or fewer in a title or heading (except the first word in a title or subtitle or the first word after a colon, em dash, or end punctuation in a heading):

- short conjunctions (e.g., "and," "as," "but," "for," "if," "nor," "or," "so," "yet")
- articles ("a," "an," "the")
- short prepositions (e.g., "as," "at," "by," "for," "in," "of," "off," "on," "per," "to," "up," "via")

When to Use Title Case. Use title case for the following:

- titles of articles, books, reports, and other works appearing in text

  In the book *Bilingualism Across the Lifespan: Factors Moderating Language Proficiency*

  In the article "Media Influences on Self-Stigma of Seeking Psychological Services: The Importance of Media Portrayals and Person Perception"

- titles of tests or measures, including subscales (see Section 5.8)

  Wechsler Adult Intelligence Scale

  WAIS-IV Verbal Comprehension Index

- all headings within a work (Levels 1–5; see Section 1.26)
- the title of your paper and of named sections within it

  the Data Analyses section

- titles of periodicals (these are also italicized)

  Journal of Experimental Psychology: Learning, Memory, and Cognition
  The Washington Post
- table titles (these are also italicized; see Section 7.11)
- figure titles (these are also italicized), axis labels, and legends (see Sections 7.25–7.27)

Sentence Case. In sentence case, lowercase most words in the title or heading. Capitalize only the following words:

- the first word of the title or heading
- the first word of a subtitle
- the first word after a colon, em dash, or end punctuation in a heading
- nouns followed by numerals or letters
- proper nouns

When to Use Sentence Case. Use sentence case for the following:

- titles of articles, books, reports, webpages, and other works in reference list entries, even if title case was used in the original work (see also Section 9.19)

  Golden, A. R., Griffin, C. B., Metzger, I. W., & Cooper, S. M. (2018). School racial climate and academic outcomes in African American adolescents: The protective role of peers. *Journal of Black Psychology*, 44(1), 47–73. https://doi.org /10.1177/ 0095798417736685

  Mena, J. A., & Quina, K. (Eds.). (2019). *Integrating multiculturalism and intersectionality into the psychology curriculum: Strategies for instructors.* American Psychological Association. https://doi.org/10.1037/0000137
- table column headings, entries, and notes (see Sections 7.12–7.14)
- figure notes (see Section 7.28)

> *Note:* Words in the image of a figure (see Section 7.26) may be in either title case or sentence case. Follow the same guidelines for capitalization in a figure image as used in the text.

5.8 Titles of Tests and Measures

Capitalize titles of published and unpublished tests and measures and their subscales. Do not capitalize words such as "test" and "scale" unless they are part of the test or subscale title. See Section 10.9 for more on use of italics with the titles of test and measures.

> Thematic Apperception Test
> Minnesota Multiphasic Personality Inventory–2
> MMPI-2 Depression scale
> Stroop Color–Word Interference Test
> the authors' Mood Adjective Checklist
> SF–36 Physical Functioning scale

Do not capitalize shortened, inexact, or generic titles of tests or measures.

> a vocabulary test
> Stroop-like color test

5.9 Nouns Followed by Numerals or Letters

Capitalize nouns followed by numerals or letters that denote a specific place in a series.

> Figure 3   Table 1, Row 2, Column 6
> Appendix B   Research Question 3
> Footnote 2   Chapter 8

Exception: Do not capitalize the words "page" or "paragraph" before a numeral, in accordance with long-standing practice.

> page 2
> paragraph 4

Do not capitalize the following:

- the words "numeral" or "letter" when referring to a numeral or letter as itself because the numeral or letter does not denote a place in a series beyond integers or the alphabet

> the numeral 7
> the letter "a"

- nouns that precede a variable

> trial *n* and item *x*
>   *but*
> Trial 3 and Item b (The number and letter are not variables.)

5.10 Names of Conditions or Groups in an Experiment

Do not capitalize names of conditions or groups in an experiment.

> the experimental and control groups
>
> participants were assigned to information and no-information conditions
>> *but*
> Conditions A and B (see Section 5.9)

5.11 Names of Factors, Variables, and Effects

Capitalize names of derived variables within a factor or principal components analysis. The words "factor" and "component" are not capitalized unless followed by a numeral (see Section 5.9).

> Big Five personality factors of Extraversion, Agreeableness, Openness to Experience, Conscientiousness, and Neuroticism
>
> Mealtime Behavior (Factor 4)

Do not capitalize effects or variables unless they appear with multiplication signs. (Be careful not to use the term "factor" when you mean "effect" or "variable," e.g., in an interaction or analysis of variance.)

> small age effect
>
> sex, age, and weight variables
>> *but*
> Sex x Age x Weight interaction
>
> 3 x 3 x 2 (Groups x Trials x Responses) design
>
> 2 (methods) x 2 (item types)

Abbreviations

5.12 Use of Abbreviations

An *abbreviation is* a shortened form of a word or phrase; abbreviations of phrases are often composed of the first letter of each word of the phrase (i.e., acronym). To maximize clarity, use abbreviations sparingly and consider readers' familiarity with the abbreviation.

Although abbreviations can be useful for long, technical terms in scholarly writing, communication is often garbled rather than clarified if an abbreviation is unfamiliar to readers. In general, use an abbreviation if (a) it is conventional and readers are likely to be more familiar with the abbreviation than with the complete form and (b) considerable space can be saved and cumbersome repetition avoided. For example, the abbreviations "L" for large and "S" for small in a paper describing different sequences of reward (LLSS or LSLS) would be effective and readily understood shortcuts. In another paper, however, writing about the "L reward" and the "S reward" might be both unnecessary and confusing. In most instances, abbreviating experimental group names is ineffective because the abbreviations are not adequately informative or easily recognizable; some are more cumbersome than the full name.

Overuse. Sometimes the space saved by using abbreviations is not justified by the time necessary for readers to master the meaning, as in the following example:

> The advantage of the LH was clear from the RT data, which reflected high FP and FN rates for the RH.

Without abbreviations, the previous passage reads as follows:

> The advantage of the left hand was clear from the reaction time data, which reflected high false-positive and false-negative rates for the right hand.

Although there is no absolute limit for the use of abbreviations, writing is generally easier to understand when most words are written out rather than when overflowing with abbreviations.

Underuse. In general, if you abbreviate a term, use the abbreviation at least three times in a paper. If you use the abbreviation only one or two times, readers may have difficulty remembering what it means, so writing the term out each time aids comprehension. However, a standard abbreviation for a long, familiar term is clearer and more concise even if it is used fewer than three times.

5.13 Definition of Abbreviations

In APA Style papers, do not define abbreviations that are listed as terms in the dictionary (e.g., AIDS, IQ). Also do not define measurement abbreviations (see Section 5.15), time abbreviations (see Section 5.16), Latin abbreviations (see Section 5.17), or many statistical abbreviations (see Section 6.10). Define all other abbreviations, even those that may be familiar to your readers (e.g., "RT" for reaction time or "ANOVA" for analysis of variance; see also Section 5.12). After you define an abbreviation, use only the abbreviation; do not alternate between spelling out the term and abbreviating it.

Definition in the Text. When you first use a term that you want to abbreviate in the text, present both the full version of the term and the abbreviation.

- When the full version of a term appears for the first time in a heading, do not define the abbreviation in the heading; instead, define the abbreviation when the full version next appears. Use abbreviations in headings only if the abbreviations have been previously defined in the text or if they are listed as terms in the dictionary.

- When the full version of a term first appears in a sentence in the text, place the abbreviation in parentheses after it.

  attention-deficit/hyperactivity disorder (ADHD)

- When the full version of a term first appears in parenthetical text, place the abbreviation in square brackets after it. Do not use nested parentheses.

  (i.e., attention-deficit/hyperactivity disorder [ADHD])

- If a citation accompanies an abbreviation, include the citation after the abbreviation, separated with a semicolon. Do not use nested or back-to-back parentheses.

  Beck Depression Inventory–II (BDI-II; Beck et al., 1996)

  (Beck Depression Inventory–II [BDI-II]; Beck et al., 1996)

Definition in Tables and Figures. Define abbreviations used in tables and figures within each table and figure, even if the abbreviations have already been defined in the text. The abbreviation can appear in parentheses after first use of the term within the table or figure, including in the table or figure title, or the definition can appear in a table or figure general note or a figure legend. If an abbreviation is used in multiple tables and figures, define it in each table or figure. Do not define abbreviations that do not appear in a table or figure. Do not define or write out standard abbreviations for units of measurement and statistics in a table or figure (see Sections 6.10 and 7.15).

5.14 Format of Abbreviations

Plural Forms. To form the plural of most abbreviations and statistical symbols, add a lowercase "s" alone, without an apostrophe.

  IQs   DOIs   URLs   Eds.   vols.   *M*s   *p*s   *n*s   ESs

Note: To form the plural of the reference abbreviation for "page" (p.), write "pp." Do not add an "s" to make abbreviations for units of measurement plural.

    3 cm (not 3 cms)   24 hr (not 24 hrs)

Abbreviations Beginning a Sentence. Never begin a sentence with a lowercase abbreviation (e.g., lb) or with a stand-alone symbol (e.g., α). Begin a sentence with a symbol connected to a word (e.g., β-Endorphins) only when necessary to avoid indirect or awkward phrasing.

5.15 Unit of Measurement Abbreviations

Metrication. Use the metric system when writing in APA Style. When reporting nonmetric units (e.g., feet, pounds), also provide the established metric equivalent in parentheses.

Measurement in metric units:
The rods were spaced 19 mm apart.

Measurement in nonmetric units with the rounded metric equivalent:
The rod was 3 ft (0.91 m) long.

Presentation. Write out the full names of units of measurement that are not accompanied by numeric values.

several kilograms   age in years   duration of hours   centimeters

Use abbreviations and symbols for units of measurement that are accompanied by numeric values; do not make symbols or abbreviations of units plural.

4 cm   30 kg   12 min   18 hr   22 °C

Also use the abbreviation or symbol in column and row headings of tables to conserve space, even when the term appears without a numeric value.

lag in ms

Do not define or spell out unit of measurement abbreviations, even the first time they are used. See Table 5.4 for a list of abbreviations for common units of measurement (for statistical symbols and abbreviations, including percentages and money symbols, see Section 6.10).

Capitalization and Spelling. In most cases, use lowercase letters for symbols (e.g., kg), even in capitalized material. However, the following are exceptions:

- Symbols derived from the name of a person usually include uppercase letters (e.g., Gy).

- Symbols for prefixes that represent powers of 10 are usually written in uppercase letters: exa (E), peta (P), tera (T), giga (G), and mega (M).

- Use the symbol "L" for liter when it stands alone (e.g., 5 L, 0.3 mg/L) because a lowercase "l" may be misread as the numeral 1 (use lowercase "l" for fractions of a liter: 5 ml, 9 ng/dl).

Do not use a period after a symbol, except at the end of a sentence. An exception is to include a period after the abbreviation for "inch" (in.), which could be misread without the period.

Use a space between a symbol and the number to which it refers (e.g., degrees, minutes, and seconds). An exception is the measure of angles, in which case the symbol is written without a space after the measurement.

4.5 m   6 hr   12 °C   *but*   45° angle

Repeated Units of Measurement. Do not repeat abbreviated units of measurement when expressing multiple amounts.

16–30 kHz   0.3, 1.5, and 3.0 mg/dl

When reporting related statistics, such as means and standard deviations, report the unit with the main statistic but do not repeat it for the related statistic(s) when the unit remains the same.

Correct: (M = 8.7 years, SD = 2.3)

Incorrect: (M = 8.7 years, SD = 2.3 years)

5.16 Time Abbreviations

To prevent misreading, do not abbreviate the words "day," "week," "month," and "year," even when they are accompanied by numeric values. Do abbreviate the words "hour," "minute," "second," "millisecond," "nanosecond," and any other division of the second when they are accompanied by numeric values.

Term	Abbreviation	Example
hour	hr	6 hr
minute	min	30 min
second	s	5 s
millisecond	ms	2.65 ms
nanosecond	ns	90 ns

Table 5.4 Abbreviations for Common Units of Measurement

Abbreviation	Unit of measurement	Abbreviation	Unit of measurement
AC	alternating current	µm	micrometer
°C	degrees Celsius	mA	milliampere
cc	cubic centimeter	mEq	milliequivalent
cm	centimeter	meV	million electron volts
cps	cycles per second	mg	milligram
dB	decibel (specify scale)	mi	mile [a]
DC	direct current	ml	milliliter
deg/s	degrees per second	mm	millimeter
dl	deciliter	mM	millimolar
F	farad	mmol	millimole
°F	degrees Fahrenheit [a]	mol	mole
ft	foot [a]	mol wt	molecular weight
g	gram	mph	miles per hour [a]
g	gravity	MΩ	megohm
Gy	gray	N	newton
Hz	hertz	ng	nanogram
in.	inch [a]	nmol	nanomole
IU	international unit	MΩ, Ω	megohm, ohm
J	joule	oz	ounce [a]
K	kelvin	Pa	pascal
kg	kilogram	ppm	parts per million
km	kilometer	psi	pounds per square inch [a]
km/h	kilometers per hour	rpm	revolutions per minute
kW	kilowatt	S	siemens
L	liter	Sv	sievert
lb	pound [a]	T	tesla
lm	lumen	V	volt
lx	lux	W	watt
m	meter	Wb	weber
µg	microgram	yd	yard [a]

Note. These abbreviations do not need to be defined when they are used in a paper.
[a] Include the metric unit equivalent in parentheses when using nonmetric units.

5.17 Latin Abbreviations

Use the following standard Latin abbreviations only in parenthetical material; in the narrative, use the translation of the Latin term. In both cases, punctuate as if the abbreviation were spelled out.

Latin abbreviation	Translation
cf.	compare
e.g.,	for example,
, etc.	, and so forth
i.e.,	that is,
viz.,	namely,
vs.	versus or against

Exceptions: Use the abbreviation "v." (for "versus") in the title or name of a court case in the reference list and in all in-text citations (see Section 10.15). Use the Latin abbreviation "et al." (which means "and others") in both narrative and parenthetical citations (see Section 8.17). (The abbreviation "ibid." is not used in APA Style.)

5.18 Chemical Compound Abbreviations

Chemical compounds may be expressed by the common name or the chemical name. If you prefer to use the common name, provide the chemical name in parentheses on first mention. Avoid expressing compounds with chemical formulas because these are usually less informative to readers and have a high likelihood of being typed or typeset incorrectly (e.g., "aspirin" or "salicylic acid," not "$C_9H_8O_4$"). If names of compounds include Greek letters, retain the letters as symbols and do not write them out (e.g., "β carotene," not "beta carotene"). If a compound name containing a Greek letter appears at the beginning of a sentence, capitalize the first letter of the word to which the symbol is connected (see Section 5.14).

Long names of organic compounds are often abbreviated. If the abbreviation is listed as a term in a dictionary (see Section 5.13; e.g., "NADP" for "nicotinamide adenine dinucleotide phosphate"), you do not need to write it out in full on first use.

Concentrations. If you express a solution as a percentage concentration instead of as a molar concentration, specify the percentage as a weight-per-volume ratio (wt/vol), a volume ratio (vol/vol), or a weight ratio (wt/wt) of solute to solvent. The higher the concentration, the more ambiguous the expression is as a percentage. Specifying the ratio is especially necessary for concentrations of alcohol, glucose, and sucrose. Specifying the salt form is also essential for precise reporting of *d*-amphetamine HCl or *d*-amphetamine SO$_4$ (expression of a chemical name in combination with a formula is acceptable in this case).

12% (vol/vol) ethyl alcohol solution

1% (wt/vol) saccharin solution

Routes of Administration. Abbreviate a route of administration when it is paired with a number-and-unit combination. Do not use periods with abbreviations for routes of administration: icv = intracerebral ventricular, im = intramuscular, ip = intraperitoneal, iv = intravenous, sc = subcutaneous, and so forth.

anesthetized with sodium pentobarbital (90 mg/kg ip)

two subcutaneous injections (*not* sc injections)

NUMBERS AND STATISTICS

Writing a scholarly work often involves the need to report numbers, statistics, and other mathematical terms. Presenting numbers and statistics in a consistent style helps make your paper easier for instructors and readers to follow and understand.

This chapter describes APA Style guidelines for presenting numbers and statistics in scholarly writing, including exceptions and special usages of numbers. General guidance on presenting statistics and equations includes sections on statistical symbols and abbreviations as well as spacing, alignment, and punctuation within statistics.

Numbers

In general, use numerals to express numbers 10 and above and words to express numbers below 10. Consider on a case-by-case basis whether to follow the general guideline or if an exception applies.

6.1 Numbers Expressed in Numerals

Use numerals to express the following:

- numbers 10 and above throughout the paper, including in the abstract (for exceptions, see Sections 6.2–6.3) and both cardinal and ordinal numbers (see Section 6.4)

15th trial	200 participants
13 lists	10th-grade students
12 models	105 stimulus words

- numbers that immediately precede a unit of measurement

  a 5-mg dose   with 10.5 cm of

- numbers that represent statistical or mathematical functions, fractional or decimal quantities, percentages, ratios, and percentiles and quartiles

multiplied by 5	3 times as many
0.33 of the sample	more than 5%
a ratio of 16:1	the 5th percentile

- numbers that represent time, dates (including approximations of days, months, and years), ages, scores and points on a scale, exact sums of money, and numerals as numerals

5 days	about 8 months
4 decades	was 2 years old
12:30 a.m.	scored 4 on a 7-point scale
1 hr 34 min	the numeral 6 on the keyboard
2-year-olds	approximately 3 years ago
ages 65–70 years	received $5 in compensation

- numbers that denote a specific place in a numbered series and parts of books and tables (the noun before the number is also capitalized when it denotes a specific place in a series; see Section 5.9); however, when the number precedes the noun, the usual guidelines for number use apply

Number after a noun	Number before a noun
Year 1	the 1st year
Grade 4, Grade 10	the fourth grade, the 10th grade
Items 3 and 5	the third and fifth items
Question 2	the second question
Table 2, Figure 5	the second table, the fifth figure
Column 8, Row 7	the eighth column, the seventh row
Chapter 1, Chapter 12	the first chapter, the 12th chapter

Exceptions: Do not capitalize the abbreviations for page(s) or paragraph(s), even when they are followed by a numeral (e.g., p. 3, pp. 2–5, para. 9, paras. 1–4).

6.2 Numbers Expressed in Words

Use words to express the following:

- numbers zero through nine (except as described in Sections 6.1 and 6.3) in the text, including in the abstract

- any number that begins a sentence, title, or heading (when possible, reword the sentence to avoid beginning with a number)

  Forty-eight percent of the sample showed an increase; 2% showed no change.

  Twelve students improved, and 12 students did not improve.

- common fractions

  one fifth of the class   two-thirds majority

- universally accepted usage

  Twelve Apostles   Five Pillars of Islam

6.3 Combining Numerals and Words to Express Numbers

Use a combination of numerals and words to express back-to-back numerical modifiers.

  2 two-way interactions   ten 7-point scales

However, if this makes the text more difficult for readers, consider rewording the sentence.

6.4 Ordinal Numbers

Treat ordinal numbers as you would cardinal numbers.

Ordinal	Cardinal base
second-order factor	two orders
fourth grade, 10th grade	four grades, 10 grades
first item of the 75th trial	one item, 75 trials
first and third groups	one group, three groups
3rd year	3 years

The suffixes of ordinal numbers can be presented with or without a superscript (e.g., either 4th or 4th), but be consistent in presentation throughout your paper.

NUMBERS

6.5 Decimal Fractions

Use a zero before the decimal point in numbers that are less than 1 when the statistic can exceed 1.

$t(20) = 0.86$ $F(1, 27) = 0.57$

Cohen's $d = 0.70$ 0.48 cm

Do not use a zero before a decimal fraction when the statistic cannot be greater than 1 (e.g., correlations, proportions, levels of statistical significance).

$r(24) = -.43, p = .028$

The number of decimal places to use in reporting the results of experiments and data-analytic manipulations should be governed by the following principle: Round as much as possible while considering how the data will be used and their statistical precision. As a general rule, fewer decimal digits are easier to comprehend than are more digits; therefore, it is usually better to round to two decimal places or to rescale the measurement (in which case effect sizes should be presented in the same metric). For instance, a difference in distances that must be carried to four decimals to be seen when scaled in meters can be more effectively illustrated in millimeters, which would require only a few decimal digits to illustrate the same difference.

When properly scaled, most data can be effectively presented with two decimal digits of accuracy. Report correlations, proportions, and inferential statistics such as t, F, and chi-square to two decimals. When reporting data measured on integer scales (as with many questionnaires), report means and standard deviations to one decimal place (as group measures, they are more stable than individual scores). Report exact p values (e.g., $p = .031$) to two or three decimal places. However, report p values less than .001 as $p < .001$. In tables, the "$p <$" notation may be necessary for clarity (see Section 7.14).

6.6 Roman Numerals

If Roman numerals are part of an established terminology, do not change them to Arabic numerals. For example, use "Type II error," not "Type 2 error." Use Arabic numerals for routine seriation (e.g., Step 1, Experiment 2, Study 3).

6.7 Commas in Numbers

Use commas between groups of three digits in most figures of 1,000 or more. Some exceptions are as follows:

Category	Example of exception
page numbers	page 1029
binary digits	00110010
serial numbers	290466960
degrees of temperature	3414 °C
acoustic frequency designations	2000 Hz
degrees of freedom	$F(24, 1000)$

6.8 Plurals of Numbers

To form the plurals of numbers, whether expressed as numerals or as words, add "s" or "es" alone, without an apostrophe.

twos and sixes   the 1960s   30s and 40s

Statistics and Equations

6.9 Presentation of Statistics

When presenting statistics, consider how to optimize readers' understanding of the data. In general, follow these guidelines:

- If you need to present three or fewer numbers, first try using a sentence.

- If you need to present four to 20 numbers, first try using a table.

- If you need to present more than 20 numbers, first try using a figure.

Note that APA Style addresses standards for presentation only; it does not provide guidance on how to choose statistics, conduct analyses, or interpret results. Consult a statistics reference work or a statistician for help if needed. For guidance on the types of statistics to report in your paper, see the reporting standards for quantitative methods and results found in Sections 3.6 and 3.7 of the *Publication Manual*.

When reporting inferential statistics (e.g., t tests, F tests, chi-square tests, and associated effect sizes and confidence intervals), include sufficient information to allow readers to fully understand the analyses conducted. The data supplied, preferably in the text but possibly in an appendix depending on the magnitude of the data arrays and assignment instructions, should allow readers to confirm the basic reported analyses (e.g., cell means, standard deviations, sample sizes, correlations). What constitutes sufficient information depends on the analytic approach reported.

F *ratios:*
For immediate recognition, the omnibus test of the main effect of sentence format was significant, $F(2, 177) = 6.30$, $p = .002$, est $\omega^2 = .07$.

t *values:*
The one-degree-of-freedom contrast of primary interest was significant at the specified $p < .05$ level, $t(177) = 3.51$, $p < .001$, $d = 0.65$, 95% CI [0.35, 0.95].

Hierarchical and other sequential regression statistics:
High school GPA predicted college mathematics performance, $R^2 = .12$, $F(1, 148) = 20.18$, $p < .001$, 95% CI [.02, .22].

If you present descriptive statistics in a table or figure, do not repeat them in the text, although you should (a) mention the table in which the statistics can be found in the text and (b) emphasize particular data in the text when they aid in the interpretation of the findings.

When listing a series of similar statistics, be certain that the relation between the statistics and their referents is clear. Words such as "respectively" and "in order" can clarify this relationship.

Means (with standard deviations in parentheses) for Trials 1–4 were 2.43 (0.50), 2.59 (1.21), 2.68 (0.39), and 2.86 (0.12), respectively.

When reporting confidence intervals, use the format 95% CI [*LL*, *UL*], where *LL* is the lower limit of the confidence interval and *UL* is the upper limit. Every report of a confidence interval must clearly state the level of confidence. However, when confidence intervals are repeated in a series or within the same paragraph, the level of confidence (e.g., 95%) has remained unchanged, and the meaning is clear, do not repeat "95% CI."

95% CIs [5.62, 8.31], [–2.43, 4.31], and [–4.29, –3.11], respectively

When a confidence interval follows the report of a point estimate, do not repeat the units of measurement.

$M = 30.5$ cm, 99% CI [18.0, 43.0]

6.10 Statistical Symbols and Abbreviations

Symbols and abbreviations are often used for statistics (e.g., "mean" is abbreviated "*M*"). Table 6.1 contains common statistical abbreviations and symbols.

- Do not define symbols or abbreviations that represent statistics (e.g., *M*, *SD*, *F*, *t*, *df*, *p*, *N*, *n*, *OR*, *r*) or any abbreviations or symbols composed of Greek letters (e.g., α, β, χ^2) in Table 6.1.

- However, define the other abbreviations shown in Table 6.1 (e.g., ANOVA, CI, SEM) when they are used anywhere in your paper (see Sections 5.13 and 7.14–7.15).

Some terms are used as both abbreviations and symbols. Use the abbreviation when referring to the concept and the symbol when specifying a numeric value. The symbol form will usually be either a non-English letter or an italicized English letter. Most abbreviations can be turned into symbols (for use when reporting numerical estimates) by simply italicizing the abbreviation. Carefully examine all mathematical and statistical material to ensure there are no errors.

Table 6.1 Statistical Abbreviations and Symbols

Abbreviation or symbol	Definition
English character set	
ANCOVA	analysis of covariance
ANOVA	analysis of variance
CFA	confirmatory factor analysis
CI	confidence interval
d	Cohen's measure of sample effect size for comparing two sample means
df	degrees of freedom
EFA	exploratory factor analysis
ES	effect size
f	frequency
f_e	expected frequency
f_o	observed frequency
F	*F* distribution; Fisher's *F* ratio
F_{crit}	critical value for statistical significance in an *F* test
g	Hedges's measure of effect size
H_0	null hypothesis, hypothesis under test
H_1 (or H_a)	alternative hypothesis
HLM	hierarchical linear model(ing)

Table 6.1 Statistical Abbreviations and Symbols (*continued*)

Abbreviation or symbol	Definition
HSD	Tukey's honestly significant difference
LL	lower limit (as of a CI)
LR	likelihood ratio
M (or $\overline{X}$)	sample mean; arithmetic average
MANOVA	multivariate analysis of variance
MANCOVA	multivariate analysis of covariance
Mdn	median
MLM	multilevel model(ing)
MS	mean square
MSE	mean square error
n	number of cases (generally in a subsample)
N	total number of cases
ns	not statistically significant
OR	odds ratio
p	probability; probability of a success in a binary trial
r	estimate of the Pearson product–moment correlation coefficient
r^2	coefficient of determination; measure of strength of relationship; estimate of the Pearson product–moment correlation squared
r_s	Spearman rank-order correlation
R	multiple correlation
R^2	multiple correlation squared; measure of strength of association
SD	standard deviation
SE	standard error
SEM	standard error of measurement; standard error of the mean
SEM	structural equation model(ing)
SS	sum of squares
t	Student's *t* distribution; a statistical test based on the Student *t* distribution; the sample value of the *t*-test statistic
UL	upper limit (as of a CI)
z	a standardized score; the value of a statistic divided by its standard error

STATISTICS

Table 6.1 Statistical Abbreviations and Symbols (*continued*)

Abbreviation or symbol	Definition
Greek character set	
α (alpha)	in statistical hypothesis testing, the probability of making a Type I error; Cronbach's index of internal consistency (a form of reliability)
β (beta)	in statistical hypothesis testing, the probability of making a Type II error ($1 - \beta$ denotes statistical power); population values of regression coefficients (with appropriate subscripts as needed)
Δ (capital delta)	increment of change
ε^2 (epsilon-squared)	measure of strength of relationship in analysis of variance
η^2 (eta-squared)	measure of strength of relationship
θ_k (theta k)	generic effect size in meta-analysis
κ (kappa)	Cohen's measure of agreement corrected for chance agreement
μ (mu)	population mean; expected value
ν (nu)	degrees of freedom
ρ (rho)	population product–moment correlation
ρ^I (rho I)	population intraclass correlation
σ (sigma)	population standard deviation
σ^2 (sigma-squared)	population variance
Σ (capital sigma)	population variance–covariance matrix
χ^2 (chi-squared)	the chi-square distribution; a statistical test based on the chi-square distribution; the sample value of the chi-square test statistic
ω^2 (omega-squared)	strength of a statistical relationship
Mathematical symbols	
$|a|$	absolute value of a
Σ (capital sigma)	summation

Note. It is acceptable to use the form est(θ) or $\hat{\theta}$ to indicate an estimator or estimate of the parameter θ.

STATISTICS

Symbols Versus Words. When using a statistical term in narrative text, use the term, not the symbol. For example, state "the means were," not "the *M*s were." When using a statistical term in conjunction with a mathematical operator, use the symbol or abbreviation. For example, write "(M = 7.74)," not "(*mean* = 7.74)."

Symbols for Population Versus Sample Statistics. Population parameters are usually represented by Greek letters. Most estimators are represented by italicized Latin letters. For example, the population correlation would be represented as ρ, and the estimator would be represented as r; est(ρ) and $\hat{\rho}$ are also acceptable. Some test statistics are represented by italicized Latin letters (e.g., t and F), and a few are represented by Greek letters (e.g., α, κ).

Symbols for Number of Subjects. Use an uppercase, italicized N to designate the number of members in the total sample (e.g., N = 135). Use a lowercase, italicized n to designate the number of members in a limited portion or subsample of the total sample (e.g., n = 80 in the treatment group).

Symbols for Percentage and Currency. Use the percent symbol and currency symbols only when they are accompanied by a numeral; also use them in table headings and in figure labels and legends to conserve space. Use the word "percentage" or the name of the currency when a number is not given. Repeat the symbol for a range of percentages or quantities of currency.

18%–20%

determined the percentage

$10.50, £10, €9.95, ¥100–¥500

in Australian dollars, in U.S. dollars

Standard, Bold, and Italic Type. Statistical symbols and mathematical information in papers are prepared with three different type styles: standard (roman), **bold**, and *italic*. The same type style is used in text, tables, and figures.

- Use standard type for Greek letters, for subscripts and superscripts that function as identifiers (i.e., are not variables, as in the subscript "girls" in the example that follows), and for abbreviations that are not variables (e.g., log, GLM, WLS).

  μ_{girls}, α, β_i

- Use bold type for symbols for vectors and matrices.

  V, **Σ**

- Use italic type for all other statistical symbols.

  N, M$_x$*, df, MSE, t, F*

On occasion, an element may serve as both an abbreviation and a symbol (e.g., *SD*); in this case, use the type style that reflects the function of the element (see Table 6.1).

6.11 Spacing, Alignment, and Punctuation for Statistics

Space mathematical copy as you would space words: $a+b=c$ is as difficult to read as *wordswithoutspacing*. Instead, type $a + b = c$. For a minus sign indicating subtraction, use a space on each side of the sign (e.g., $z - y = x$); for a minus sign indicating a negative value, use a space before but not after the sign (e.g., –8.25).

> *Note:* A minus sign is a different typographical character from a hyphen (it is longer and slightly higher); your word-processing program has options for inserting a minus sign in your paper.

Align signs and symbols carefully. Use the subscript and superscript functions of your word-processing program. In most cases, type subscripts first and then superscripts (x_a^2). However, place a subscript or superscript such as the symbol for prime right next to its letter or symbol (x'_a).

6.12 Presentation of Equations

Place short and simple equations, such as $a = [(1 + b)/x]^{1/2}$, in the line of text. To present fractions in the line of text, use a slash (/). To make the order of operations in an equation visually unambiguous, use parentheses, square brackets, and braces (together referred to as "fences"). Use parentheses first to enclose material; use square brackets to enclose material already in parentheses; and use braces (curly brackets) to enclose material already in square brackets and parentheses: first ( ), then [( )], and finally {[( )]}.

Equations in the line of text should not project above or below the line; for example, the equation at the beginning of this section would be difficult to set in the line of text if it were in this form:

$$a = \sqrt{\frac{1 + b}{x}}.$$

Instead, such equations are displayed on their own line. Punctuate all equations, whether they are in the line of text or displayed (i.e., typed on a separate line), to conform to their place in the syntax of the sentence.

STATISTICS

7 ∾

TABLES AND FIGURES

Tables and figures help writers present a large amount of information efficiently and make their data more comprehensible. A table usually shows numerical values (e.g., means and standard deviations) or textual information (e.g., lists of stimulus words, responses from participants) arranged in columns and rows. A figure may be a chart, graph, photograph, drawing, or any other illustration. At times, the distinction between tables and figures may be unclear; in general, tables are characterized by a row–column structure, whereas any type of illustration or image other than a table is considered a figure.

This chapter provides essential guidelines for creating and formatting tables and figures in APA Style. We start by outlining the purpose of tables and figures and presenting general guidelines for creating tables and figures including how to design, prepare, format, place, and reproduce them. The second section is devoted to tables, including table construction, table components, and abbreviations within tables. The third section presents general principles of figure construction, including descriptions of figure components, labeling, and notes. Both tables and figures sections end with a checklist and a variety of samples.

General Guidelines for Tables and Figures

7.1 Purpose of Tables and Figures

The primary purpose of any table or figure is to facilitate readers' understanding of the work. For example, tables and figures can be used to summarize information (e.g., a theoretical model) or to present the results of data analyses (e.g., an analysis of variance [ANOVA]). Although tables and figures attract attention, they should not be used for mere decoration in an academic paper. Instead, every table and figure should serve a purpose.

7.2 Design and Preparation of Tables and Figures

When preparing a table or figure, first determine the purpose of the display; then, select a format that supports that purpose (see Sections 7.21 and 7.32 for sample tables and figures, respectively). For example, if the purpose is to illustrate a theoretical model, a chart is most likely the best option. Sometimes, multiple approaches are possible; for example, if your goal is to present group scores, a table would allow readers to see each group's exact scores, whereas a figure would emphasize similarities or differences between groups. When possible, use a standard, or *canonical*, form for a table or figure (examples are shown in Sections 7.21 and 7.32).

Design tables and figures with readers in mind. Communicate findings clearly while also creating attractive visual displays. Prepare tables and figures with the same care as the text of the paper; changes in text often demand changes in tables and figures, and a mismatch between data discussed in the text and data presented in tables and figures may result in a lower grade for student assignments if the error is not corrected before submission. Use the following principles when designing tables and figures:

- Label all columns in tables.
- Label all elements in figure images (e.g., label the axes of a graph).
- Place items that are to be compared next to each other.
- Place labels next to the elements they are labeling.
- In figure images, use sans serif fonts that are large enough to be read without magnification.
- Design the table or figure so it can be understood on its own (meaning readers do not have to refer to the text to understand it). Define abbreviations used in the table or figure even if they are also defined in the text (see Section 7.15 for some exceptions).
- Avoid decorative flourishes, which are distracting and can interfere with readers' comprehension; instead, ensure that every element supports the goal of effective communication.

7.3 Graphical Versus Textual Presentation

Be selective in choosing how many tables and figures to include in your paper. Readers may lose track of your message if there are a large number of tables and figures but only a small amount of text. Moreover, graphical presentation is not always optimal for effective communication. For example, the results of a single statistical significance test or a few group means and standard deviations can be presented in text.

The one-way ANOVA, $F(1, 136) = 4.86$, $MSE = 3.97$, $p = .029$, $\eta^2 = .03$, demonstrated . . .

Scores on the insomnia measure ($M = 4.08$, $SD = 0.22$) were . . .

A table or figure is an effective choice to present the results of multiple statistical tests or many descriptive statistics (e.g., when reporting the results of numerous ANOVAs or summarizing participant demographic data). It may also be possible to combine several smaller tables or figures with similar content into one larger table or figure. Consider how the table or figure augments or supplements the text. For example, when the components of a theoretical model are discussed in the text, a figure may help summarize the model; the value of the figure is the visual summary. However, tables or figures that are redundant with the text may be unnecessary. Most important is how you can best communicate your data in an understandable and meaningful manner.

7.4 Formatting Tables and Figures

Tables and figures follow the same structure: They have a table or figure number, a table or figure title, a body (for tables) or an image (for figures), and table or figure notes as needed.

Use the tables function of your word-processing program to create tables. If you copy and paste tables from another program (e.g., SPSS, Excel) into your word-processing program, you may need to adjust the formatting to comply with APA Style guidelines. Do not use the tab key or space bar to manually create the look of a table; this approach is prone to alignment errors.

Figures can be created in various ways using many programs, including Excel, PowerPoint, Photoshop, Illustrator, MATLAB, Inkscape, and others. Check with your assigning instructor or institution for any requirements or restrictions on acceptable programs for designing your figures. Regardless of the program used to create the figure, the output should be of sufficient resolution to produce high-quality images. File formats such as JPG, PNG, TIFF, and EPS are acceptable for classroom assignments. Some types of figures require higher resolution than others; for example, line art requires finer detail than a photograph. Ensure that the format used supports the resolution needed for clear presentation of the image.

7.5 Referring to Tables and Figures in the Text

In the text, refer to every table and figure by its number—known as a *callout* (see Sections 7.10 and 7.24, respectively, for how to assign numbers for tables and figures that accompany the main text; see Section 1.14 for how to assign numbers for tables and figures that appear in appendices). When you call out a table or figure, also tell readers what to look for in that table or figure.

> As shown in Table 1, the demographic characteristics . . .
>
> Figure 2 shows the model . . .
>
> . . . of the results of the testing (see Table 3).
>
> . . . of the comparisons (see Figures 4 and 7).

Do not write "the table above" (or "below") or "the figure on page 32." Page numbers often shift during the writing process, which can lead to errors. Referring to tables and figures by number rather than by location on the page also helps readers who access a work using assistive technologies such as screen readers.

7.6 Placement of Tables and Figures

There are two options for the placement of tables and figures in a paper. The first option is to place all tables and figures on separate pages after the reference list (with each table on a separate page followed by each figure on a separate page). The second option is to embed each table and figure within the text after its first callout. Your instructor may specify which option to use; either approach is acceptable if your instructor does not specify.

Align all tables and figures with the left margin regardless of where they appear in the paper. When embedding a table or figure within the text, position it after a full paragraph, ideally the paragraph where it is first called out. Place the table or figure so that it fits on one page if possible (see Section 7.18 for tables that are longer or wider than a page). If text appears on the same page as a table or figure, add a double-spaced blank line between the text and the table or figure so that the separation between the text and table or figure is easier to see. Put a short table or small figure at the beginning or end of a page rather than in the middle.

Tables and figures that support but are not essential to the text may be placed in one or more appendices. Tables and figures may appear within an appendix that also contains text, or a table or figure may constitute a whole appendix by itself (see Section 1.14).

7.7 Reprinting or Adapting Tables and Figures

If you reprint or adapt a table or figure from another source in your paper (e.g., a table from a journal article, an image you found on the internet), you must include a copyright attribution in the table note or figure note indicating the origin of the reprinted or adapted material in addition to a reference list entry for the work. You may also need to obtain permission from the copyright holder to reprint or adapt the table or figure. Figures 7.3 and 7.8 in Section 7.32 show copyright attributions for a reprinted figure when permission is not necessary and a reprinted figure in the public domain. See Sections 8.35 to 8.39 for information on copyright and permission and for copyright attribution formats and examples.

Tables

7.8 Principles of Table Construction

Tables should be integral to the text but designed so that they are concise and can be understood in isolation. The principle of conciseness is relevant not only for tables included with the main text but also for tables to be placed in appendices. All tables are meant to show something specific. Often, the same data can be arranged in different ways to emphasize different features of the data, and which arrangement is better depends on your purpose. Above all, table layout should be logical and easily grasped by readers. Table entries that are to be compared should be next to one another. In general, different indices (e.g., means, sample sizes) should be presented in different rows or columns. Place variable and condition labels close to their values to facilitate comparison. See the sample tables (Section 7.21) for examples of effective layouts.

7.9 Table Components

The basic components of a prototypical table are shown in Table 7.1 and are summarized as follows:

- **number:** The table number (e.g., Table 1) appears above the table in bold font (see Section 7.10).
- **title:** The table title appears one double-spaced line below the table number in italic title case (see Sections 5.7 and 7.11).

- **headings:** Tables may include a variety of headings depending on the nature and arrangement of the data. All tables should include column headings, including a stub heading (heading for the leftmost column). Some tables also include column spanners, decked heads, and table spanners (see Section 7.12).

- **body:** The table body includes all the rows and columns of a table (see Section 7.13). A *cell* is the point of intersection between a row and a column. The body may be single-spaced, one-and-a-half-spaced, or double-spaced.

- **notes:** Three types of notes (general, specific, and probability) appear below the table as needed to describe contents of the table that cannot be understood from the table title or body alone (e.g., definitions of abbreviations, copyright attribution). Not all tables include table notes (see Section 7.14).

See Section 7.21 for sample tables.

7.10 Table Numbers

Number all tables that are part of the main text (i.e., not part of an appendix) using Arabic numerals—for example, Table 1, Table 2, and Table 3. Assign the numbers in the order in which each table is first mentioned in the text, regardless of whether a more detailed discussion of the table occurs elsewhere in the paper. Write the word "Table" and the number in bold and flush left (i.e., not indented or centered). Tables that appear in appendices follow a different numbering scheme (see Section 1.14).

7.11 Table Titles

Give every table a brief but clear and explanatory title. Write the table title in italic title case below the table number and double-space the table number and title. Avoid overly general and overly detailed table titles.

Title quality	Example title	Rationale
Too general	*Relation Between College Majors and Performance*	It is unclear what data are presented in the table.
Too detailed	*Mean Performance Scores on Test A, Test B, and Test C of Students With Psychology, Physics, English, and Engineering Majors*	The title duplicates information in the headings of the table.
Effective	*Mean Performance Scores of Students With Different College Majors*	The title is specific but not redundant with headings.

Table 7.1 Basic Components of a Table

column spanner: heading that describes the entries in two or more columns in the table body

table number

table title

stub heading: heading that describes the leftmost column

table spanner: heading that covers the entire width of the table body, allowing for further divisions

stub column or stub: leftmost column of the table; usually lists the major independent or predictor variables

decked heads: headings that are stacked, often to avoid repetition in column heads

column heading: heading that identifies the entries in just one column in the table body

cell: point of intersection between a row and a column

table body: rows and columns of cells containing the primary data of the table

table notes: explanations to supplement or clarify information in the table body

Table 1

Numbers of Children With and Without Proof of Parental Citizenship

Grade	Girls		Boys	
	With	Without	With	Without
Wave 1				
3	280[a]	240[b]	281	232
4	297	251	290	264
5	301	260	306	221
Total	878	751	877	717
Wave 2				
3	201	189	210	199
4	214	194	236	210
5	221	216	239	213
Total	636	599	685*	622

table spanner → Wave 2

Note. This table demonstrates the elements of a prototypical table. A *general note* to a table appears first and contains information needed to understand the table, including definitions of abbreviations (see Sections 7.14–7.15) and the copyright attribution for a reprinted or adapted table (see Section 7.7).

[a] A *specific note* appears in a separate paragraph below the general note.
[b] Subsequent specific notes follow in the same paragraph (see Section 7.14).

*A *probability note* (for *p* values) appears as a separate paragraph below any specific notes; subsequent probability notes follow in the same paragraph (see Section 7.14).

Abbreviations that appear in the headings or the body of a table may be parenthetically explained in the table title.

Hit and False-Alarm (FA) Proportions in Experiment 2

Abbreviations may also be defined in a general note to the table (see Section 7.14). Do not use a specific note to clarify an element of the title.

7.12 Table Headings

Headings establish the organization of information in the table and identify what is in each column. Column headings describe the entries below them. Table headings should be brief; if possible, each heading should be not much wider than the information in the column below it. Provide a heading for every column in a table, including the *stub column* or *stub*, which is the leftmost column of the table (see Table 7.1 for an illustration).

The stub column usually lists the major independent or predictor variables. In Table 7.1, for instance, the stub column lists the grades. For the stub column, the heading "Variable" is often used when no other heading is suitable. Write the entries in the stub column in parallel form (see Section 2.24 for guidance on parallel construction). Number entries in the stub column only in a correlation matrix (see Table 7.8 in Section 7.21) or when they are referred to by number in the text. To show subordination within the stub column, use indentation rather than creating an additional column (see, e.g., Table 7.2 in Section 7.21, in which "Single," "Married/Partnered," etc. are indented under the heading "Marital Status").[1] Set indentation using the paragraph-formatting feature of your word-processing program rather than by using the tab key; use paragraph indentation of 0.15 in. or insert an em space from the special characters menu of your word-processing program.

The headings above the columns to the right of the stub column identify what is in each column. A *column heading* applies to just one column; a *column spanner* is a heading that covers two or more columns, each with its own column heading. Headings stacked in this way are called *decked heads*. Often, decked heads can be used to avoid repetition of words in column headings (see Table 7.1). If possible, do not use more than two levels of decked heads. More complex tables may require *table spanners*, which are headings within the body of the table that cover the entire width of the table, allowing for further divisions within the table when the column headings remain the same (see Table 7.1). Table spanners can also be used to combine two tables, provided they have identical column headings.

Any item within a column should be syntactically as well as conceptually comparable with the other items in that column, and all items should be described by the column heading. For example, a column with the heading "%" would contain only percentages; numbers in that column would not be followed by the percent

---

[1] Table stub entries and column headings are written in sentence case in a table but in title case if they are referred to in the text.

symbol because the symbol is already in the heading (see Table 7.2 in Section 7.21).

Use sentence case for all headings in a table (see Section 5.7). Center all table headings above their column(s). Stub headings, column headings, and column spanners should be singular (e.g., Measure, Item) unless they refer to a group (e.g., Children, Women), but table spanners may be singular or plural.

7.13 Table Body

The main part of the table, the *table body*, contains information organized in cells. Information in a table body may be in the form of numbers, words, or a mixture of both. The body of the table (including table headings) may be single-spaced, one-and-a-half-spaced, or double-spaced, depending on which presentation most effectively conveys information to readers (e.g., single spacing may allow a table to fit on one page). If entries are longer than one line, use a hanging indent of 0.15 in. or one em space. In the stub column of the table, center the stub heading and align the entries flush left beneath it. If entries in this column are significantly shorter than the stub heading, it is permissible to center them beneath the stub heading (e.g., single-digit numbers in the stub column; see the partial table later in this section for an example). The entries in all other cells of the table should be centered (however, aligning them flush left is acceptable if doing so improves the readability of longer entries). Use sentence case for all word entries in the table body (see Section 5.7). Numbers that appear in the table body should be written as words or numerals according to the guidelines in Sections 6.1 to 6.8; however, it is permissible to use numerals for all numbers in tables if this would be clearer or save space.

Decimal Values. Express numerical values to the number of decimal places that the precision of measurement justifies (see Section 6.5). If possible, carry all comparable values to the same number of decimal places. Numerical values should be centered in the column and may also be aligned on the decimal if desired.

Empty Cells. If a cell cannot be filled because data are not applicable, leave the cell blank. Use a general or specific table note if you need to explain why the cell is blank or the element is inapplicable (see Section 7.14). If a cell cannot be filled because data were not obtained or are not reported, insert a dash in that cell and explain the use of the dash in the general note to the table (see Section 7.14). By convention, a dash in the main diagonal position of a correlation matrix (see Table 7.8 in Section 7.21) indicates the correlation of an item with itself; because this correlation must be 1.00, it is simply replaced by the dash with no explanation needed.

Conciseness. Be selective in your presentation. Do not include columns of data that can be calculated easily from other columns. For example, the following partial table is redundant because it shows both the number of responses per trial and the total number of responses; instead, show only whichever is more important to the discussion.

Participant	No. of responses		Total responses
	First trial	Second trial	
1	5	7	12
2	6	4	10

Citations in Tables. If a table contains citations to other works, follow the formats described in Section 8.11. Use an ampersand (&) for the word "and" in all citations in tables to conserve space.

7.14 Table Notes

Tables may have three kinds of notes, which are placed below the body of the table: general notes, specific notes, and probability notes. Table notes apply only to a specific table and not to any other table. If information in one table note is true for another table, repeat the information in the notes for both tables so that the tables can be understood on their own. Some tables do not require table notes at all.

General Note. A *general note* qualifies, explains, or provides information relating to the table as a whole and explains any abbreviations; symbols; special use of italics, bold, or parentheses; and the like. The general note also includes any acknowledgments that a table is reprinted or adapted from another source (see Section 7.7). General notes are designated by the word "*Note*" (italicized) followed by a period (see Table 7.1 and the sample tables in Section 7.21 for examples). Explanations of abbreviations and copyright attributions for reprinted or adapted tables appear at the end of the general note, in that order.

Note. Factor loadings greater than .45 are shown in bold. M = match process; N = nonmatch process.

Specific Note. A *specific note* refers to a particular column, row, or cell. Specific notes are indicated by superscript lowercase letters (e.g., [a], [b], [c]). Do not add specific notes to a table title; instead, use a general note. Within each table that has specific notes, order the superscripts from left to right and from top to bottom, starting at the top left and beginning with the letter "a" (see, e.g., Tables 7.2, 7.8, and 7.10 in Section 7.21). The corresponding specific note below the table begins with the same superscript letter. Place a superscript space before the superscript letter in the table body (e.g., Group [a]). Place a superscript space after the superscript letter in the specific note. This space prevents specific notes from getting caught by spell-check and improves readability.

[a] $n = 25$. [b] This participant did not complete the trials.

Probability Note. A *probability note* describes how asterisks and other symbols are used in a table to indicate p values and thus the significance of the results of statistical hypothesis testing. To report the results of significance testing, it is best to provide the exact probabilities to two or three decimal places (e.g., $p = .023$; see, e.g., Tables 7.6–7.7 in Section 7.21; see also Section 6.5). However, when p values are less than .001, it is acceptable to write the values as "<.001" in the table (see, e.g., Tables 7.4 and 7.11 in Section 7.21).

It may sometimes be difficult to report exact p values in a table because doing so would make the table difficult to read. An alternative to reporting exact p values in a table is to use the "$p <$" notation. Use this notation only in tables and figures (see Section 7.28 for more on figure notes), not in the text. In the "$p <$" notation, asterisks or daggers appear after table entries to indicate that the entries have reached the established threshold for significance; definitions of the asterisks and/or daggers appear in a corresponding probability note. Use the same number of asterisks to indicate the same p values across tables (or figures) within your paper, such as $^*p < .05$, $^{**}p < .01$, and $^{***}p < .001$ (see, e.g., Table 7.8 in Section 7.21). In general, do not use any p value smaller than .001. Daggers are sometimes used to indicate nonsignificant trends based on the threshold established for your study (e.g., $^\dagger p < .10$) or to distinguish between one-tailed and two-tailed tests. Use superscript formatting for asterisks and daggers. In a table body (or a figure), position asterisks and daggers immediately after the entries they belong to, with no space in between (e.g., .02[*]). In the probability note, place asterisks and daggers immediately before the p, with no space in between (e.g., $^*p < .002$).

One-Tailed Versus Two-Tailed Tests. If you need to distinguish between one-tailed and two-tailed tests in the same table, use an asterisk for the two-tailed p values and an alternate symbol (e.g., dagger) for the one-tailed p values, and specify the convention in the probability note.

> *$p < .05$, two-tailed. **$p < .01$, two-tailed. †$p < .05$, one-tailed. ††$p < .01$, one-tailed.

Indicating Significant Differences Between Values. To indicate statistically significant differences between two or more table values—for example, when comparing values with post hoc tests such as Tukey's honestly significant difference (HSD) test—use lowercase subscript letters (see Table 7.7 in Section 7.21 for an example). Explain the use of the subscripts in the table's general note, as in the following example:

> *Note.* Means sharing a common subscript are not significantly different at $\alpha = .01$ according to Tukey's honestly significant difference procedure.

Formatting of Notes. Begin each kind of note on a new line below the table body. A general note appears first. A specific note begins on a new line under a general note; subsequent specific notes begin on the same line. A probability note begins on a new line under any general or specific notes; subsequent probability notes begin on the same line. Multiple specific or probability notes are separated from each other by a period and a space. Lengthy specific notes may be presented on separate lines if this improves readability. Double-space all table notes, and align all notes flush left (i.e., with no paragraph indentation).

> *Note.* The responses were gathered in the laboratory.
> [a]$n = 25$. [b]$n = 42$.
> *$p < .05$. **$p < .01$. ***$p < .001$.

Use of Notes to Eliminate Repetition. Table notes can be useful for eliminating repetition from the body of a table. Certain types of information are appropriate either in the table body or in a note. To determine the placement of such material, remember that clearly and efficiently organized data enable readers to focus on those data. Thus, if probability values or subsample sizes are numerous, use a column rather than many notes. Conversely, if a row or column contains few entries (or the same entry), eliminate the column by adding a note to the table, as shown in the following partial tables.

Repetitive	
Group	*n*
Anxious	15
Depressed	15
Control	15

Concise
Group [a]
Anxious
Depressed
Control

[a] *n* = 15 for each group.

7.15 Standard Abbreviations in Tables and Figures

Use standard abbreviations and symbols for all statistics (e.g., M, SD, SE, F, df, n, p), Greek letters (e.g., α, χ^2), and units of measurement (see Table 6.1) in tables without defining them in a note. This guidance also applies to statistics, Greek letters, and units of measurement appearing in figures (see Section 7.28 for more on figure notes). The abbreviation "no." (for "number") and the symbol "%" (for "percent") may also be used without providing a definition. Other abbreviations used in a table or figure should be defined in the table or figure title, body, or note, even if the abbreviations are also defined in the paper (see Section 6.10). Except where it makes sense to group similar abbreviations, define the abbreviations in the order that they appear in the table, starting at the top left and moving left to right, top to bottom.

7.16 Confidence Intervals in Tables

When a table includes point estimates—for example, means, correlations, or regression slopes—it should also, when possible, include confidence intervals. Report confidence intervals in tables either by using square brackets, as in the text (see Section 4.9), or by giving lower and upper limits in separate columns, as in Table 7.11 in Section 7.21. In every table that includes confidence intervals, state the confidence level (e.g., 95% or 99%). It is usually best to use the same confidence level throughout a paper.

7.17 Table Borders and Shading

Limit the use of borders or lines in a table to those needed for clarity. In general, use a border at the top and bottom of the table, beneath column headings (including decked heads), and above column spanners. You may also use a border to separate a row containing totals or other summary information from other rows in the table (see

Table 7.1 for an example). Do not use vertical borders to separate data, and do not use borders around every cell in a table. Use spacing between columns and rows and strict alignment to clarify relations among the elements in a table.

Avoid the use of shading in tables. Do not use shading for mere decoration. To emphasize the content of a particular cell or cells, use a specific or probability note; italics or bold may also be used with explanation in the table's general note. Instead of using shading, add white space or borders between rows and columns to help readers distinguish them. If shading is necessary, explain its purpose in the table's general note.

7.18 Long or Wide Tables

If a table is longer than one page, repeat the heading row on each subsequent page of the table. It is best to use the automated table-formatting tools of your word-processing program rather than manually retyping the headings.

Wide tables may be presented in landscape orientation (it is not important if landscape orientation affects the position of the page header). If a table in landscape format is still too wide to fit on one page, repeat the stub column (left column) on each subsequent page. If a table is too wide and too long to fit on one page, create separate tables.

7.19 Relation Between Tables

Consider combining tables that repeat data. Ordinarily, identical columns or rows of data should not appear in two or more tables. Be consistent in the presentation of all tables within a paper to facilitate comparisons. Use similar formats, titles, and headings and the same terminology across tables whenever possible (e.g., do not use "response time" in one table and "reaction time" in another table to refer to the same concept). If multiple tables contain similar data but cannot be combined, number these tables separately (e.g., Table 1 and Table 2); do not use letters to indicate subtables (i.e., do not label two tables Table 1A and Table 1B).

7.20 Table Checklist

The table checklist will help ensure that the data in your table are effectively presented and that the table conforms to the style guidelines presented in this chapter.

Table Checklist

☐ Is the table necessary?

☐ Are all comparable tables in the paper consistent in presentation?

☐ Are all tables numbered consecutively with Arabic numerals in the order in which they are first mentioned in the text? Is the table number bold and flush left?

☐ Are all tables called out or referred to in the text?

☐ Is the table title brief but explanatory? Is it written in italic title case and flush left?

☐ Does every column have a column heading, including the leftmost (stub) column? Are all column headings centered?

☐ Are all abbreviations explained (with exceptions as noted in Section 7.15), as well as the special use of italics, bold, parentheses, dashes, and symbols?

☐ Are the table notes, if needed, in the order of general note, specific note, and probability note? Are the notes double-spaced and flush left and in the same font as the text of the paper?

☐ Are table borders correctly applied (at the top and bottom of the table, beneath column headings, above table spanners)?

☐ Is the line spacing of the table correctly applied (double-spacing for the table number, title, and notes; single-spacing, one-and-a-half-spacing, or double-spacing for the table body)?

☐ Are entries in the left column flush left beneath the centered stub heading? Are all other column headings and cell entries centered (except when aligning entries to the left would improve readability)?

☐ Are confidence intervals reported for all major point estimates? Is the confidence level—for example, 95%—stated, and is the same level of confidence used for all tables and throughout the paper?

☐ If the results of statistical significance testing are included in the table, are all p values correctly identified? Are exact p values provided? Is the "$p <$" notation used only when needed? When the "$p <$" notation is used, are asterisks or daggers attached to the appropriate table entries and defined? Are asterisks or daggers used consistently to indicate the same p value in all tables in the same paper?

☐ If all or part of a table is reprinted or adapted, is there a copyright attribution? If permission was necessary to reproduce the table, have you received written permission for its reuse (in print and electronic forms) from the copyright holder and sent a copy of that written permission with the final version of your paper?

7.21 Sample Tables

Some tables have certain standard, or *canonical*, forms (e.g., a correlation table). When possible, use a standard form rather than designing your own form. The advantage of using the canonical form is that readers generally already know where to look in the table for certain kinds of information. In some situations, you may want to use a form other than the canonical table form to make a specific point or to stress certain relationships. When using nonstandard forms, make certain that labeling is clear.

Sample tables are presented next; follow these samples to design basic tables. The exact contents and structure of your table will vary from the sample tables depending on the nature of the information being presented. For variations not addressed in this chapter, consult similar published articles to see examples of current standards and practices.

- **demographic characteristics of study participants** (Table 7.2): Demographic data can help readers understand the generalizability of the results. The demographic data you report will depend on the nature of the study.

- **properties of study variables** (Table 7.3): Describe the properties of study variables (e.g., means, standard deviations). If reporting psychometric information, clearly state the index of reliability (or other psychometric property) being used and the sample on which the reliability was based (if different from the study sample).

- **descriptive statistics for study measures** (Table 7.4): Descriptive statistics include means and standard deviations. The exact statistics you should provide will depend on the nature and purpose of the analyses.

- **chi-square results** (Table 7.5): The results of individual chi-square tests are usually reported in the text only (see Section 6.9). The results of multiple chi-square tests may be summarized in a table, which typically also includes frequencies, *p* values, and any other relevant statistics such as effect sizes.

- ***t*-test results** (Table 7.6): When there is only one *t* test to report, the results should be incorporated into the text (see Section 6.9). Use a table to report the results of multiple *t* tests.

- **a priori or post hoc comparisons** (Table 7.7): A priori and post hoc tests (e.g., Tukey's HSD test, Bonferroni procedure, Scheffé method, Fisher's least significant difference, Duncan's new multiple range test) are used to compare specific group means in studies in which the independent variables have more than two levels. Although these results are often presented in the text rather than in a table, a table can be used to summarize comparisons. This table is similar to the table for presenting descriptive statistics (Table 7.6) with the addition of subscripts to note significantly different means.

- **correlations** (Table 7.8): A correlation table presents correlations between study variables and may also incorporate descriptive statistics, alpha values, or other relevant statistics. The perfect correlation along the diagonal is indicated by an em dash. The variables in a correlation table should be numbered and named in the stub column, with corresponding numbers alone in the column headings to avoid repeating the variable names in the column headings.

- **analysis of variance** (Table 7.9): The results of a single one-way ANOVA are typically reported in the text only. The results of multiple ANOVAs can be reported in a table; various presentations are possible. For example, degrees of freedom may be presented in the column heading when they are the same for all tests.

- **multiple regression** (Tables 7.10–7.11): The results of multiple regression, including mediation and moderation analyses, can be presented in a variety of ways depending on the purpose of the table and the need for detail. Clearly label the regression type (e.g., hierarchical) and the type of regression coefficients (raw or standardized) being reported. For hierarchical and other sequential regressions, be sure to provide the increments of change (see Section 6.9). Two options are shown in the sample tables: regression coefficients without confidence intervals (Table 7.10) and a moderator analysis with confidence intervals in separate columns (Table 7.11).

- **qualitative tables** (Table 7.12): Qualitative data can be presented in tabular form in an innumerable variety of ways depending on the purpose of the table. Qualitative tables might include descriptions of variables, referenced studies, test items, or quotations from research participants. Quantitative data may be incorporated alongside the qualitative data (e.g., quotations might be presented alongside response frequencies, as in the sample table).

- **mixed methods tables** (Table 7.13): The procedures or findings of mixed methods research can be presented in tabular form in various ways depending on the purpose of the table.

Table 7.2 Sample Demographic Characteristics Table

Table 1

Sociodemographic Characteristics of Participants at Baseline

Baseline characteristic	Guided self-help		Unguided self-help		Wait-list control		Full sample	
	n	%	*n*	%	*n*	%	*n*	%
Gender								
Female	25	50	20	40	23	46	68	45.3
Male	25	50	30	60	27	54	82	54.7
Marital status								
Single	13	26	11	22	17	34	41	27.3
Married/partnered	35	70	38	76	28	56	101	67.3
Divorced/widowed	1	2	1	2	4	8	6	4.0
Other	1	1	0	0	1	2	2	1.3
Children[a]	26	52	26	52	22	44	74	49.3
Cohabitating	37	74	36	72	26	52	99	66.0
Highest educational level								
Middle school	0	0	1	2	1	2	2	1.3
High school/some college	22	44	17	34	13	26	52	34.7
University or post-graduate degree	27	54	30	60	32	64	89	59.3
Employment								
Unemployed	3	6	5	10	2	4	10	6.7
Student	8	16	7	14	3	6	18	12.0
Employed	30	60	29	58	40	80	99	66.0
Self-employed	9	18	7	14	5	10	21	14.0
Retired	0	0	2	4	0	0	2	1.3
Previous psychological treatment[a]	17	34	18	36	24	48	59	39.3
Previous psychotropic medication[a]	6	12	13	26	11	22	30	20.0

use of specific note → (pointing to "Previous psychological treatment")

Note. N = 150 (*n* = 50 for each condition). Participants were on average 39.5 years old (*SD* = 10.1), and participant age did not differ by condition.

[a] Reflects the number and percentage of participants answering "yes" to this question.

Table 7.3 Sample Properties of Study Variables Table

Table 1

Psychometric Properties for DLOPFQ Scales and Subscales

Scale	M	SD	Range	Cronbach's α
Identity total score	86.6	28.0	28–155	.94
Work Identity	41.6	13.3	16–76	.88
Social Identity	45.0	15.7	14–84	.91
Self-Directedness total score	91.2	26.5	34–151	.92
Work Self-Directedness	44.9	13.5	16–76	.85
Social Self-Directedness	46.3	14.3	17–80	.86
Empathy total score	101.8	15.8	48–139	.84
Work Empathy	49.9	8.2	20–72	.72
Social Empathy	51.9	8.6	28–76	.77
Intimacy total score	122.9	28.6	56–189	.91
Work Intimacy	61.7	14.3	28–94	.82
Social Intimacy	61.2	15.4	24–96	.86

Note. The *Diagnostic and Statistical Manual of Mental Disorders* (5th ed.) Levels of Personality Functioning Questionnaire (DLOPFQ) we developed had four scales (Identity, Self-Directedness, Empathy, and Intimacy), each with subscales for the work and social domains.

Table 7.4 Sample Descriptive Statistics for Study Measures Table

Table 1

Means and Standard Deviations of Scores on Baseline Measures

Scale	High BAS group	Moderate BAS group	p
BAS-T	46.17 (2.87)	37.99 (1.32)	<.001
SR	17.94 (1.88)	11.52 (1.84)	<.001
BDI	7.11 (6.50)	6.18 (6.09)	.254
ASRM	6.46 (4.01)	5.63 (3.69)	.109
M-SRM	11.05 (3.36)	11.76 (2.75)	.078

Parenthetical values in a short table are easily read. In most tables, different indices should be presented in different rows or columns.

Note. Standard deviations are presented in parentheses. BAS = Behavioral Activation System; BAS-T = Behavioral Activation System–Total scores from the Behavioral Inhibition System/Behavioral Activation System Scales; SR = Sensitivity to Reward scores from the Sensitivity to Punishment and Sensitivity to Reward Questionnaire; BDI = Beck Depression Inventory scores; ASRM = Altman Self-Rating Mania Scale scores; M-SRM = Modified Social Rhythm Metric Regularity scores.

Table 7.5 Sample Chi-Square Analysis Table

Table 1

Frequencies and Chi-Square Results for Belief Perseverance in Attitudes Toward Celebrities (N = 201)

Source	Do not believe		Unsure		Believe		$\chi^2(2)$
	n	%	n	%	n	%	
Media reports	17	8.46	140	69.65	44	21.89	124.75*
Family reports	47	23.38	106	52.74	48	23.88	34.06*
Friends' reports	42	20.90	112	55.72	47	23.38	45.52*
Caught by media	19	9.45	82	40.80	100	49.75	54.00*
Celebrity display of behavior	12	5.97	61	30.35	128	63.68	101.22*

*$p < .001$.

Table 7.6 Sample Results of Several *t* Tests Table

Table 2

Results of Curve-Fitting Analysis Examining the Time Course of Fixations to the Target

exact *p* values

Logistic parameter	9-year-olds		16-year-olds		$t(40)$	p	Cohen's d
	M	SD	M	SD			
Maximum asymptote, proportion	.843	.135	.877	.082	0.951	.347	0.302
Crossover, in ms	759	87	694	42	2.877	.006	0.840
Slope, as change in proportion per ms	.001	.0002	.002	.0002	2.635	.012	2.078

Note. For each participant, the logistic function was fit to target fixations separately. The maximum asymptote is the asymptotic degree of looking at the end of the time course of fixations. The crossover is the point in time when the function crosses the midway point between peak and baseline. The slope represents the rate of change in the function measured at the crossover. Mean parameter values for each of the analyses are shown for the 9-year-olds (n = 24) and the 16-year-olds (n = 18), as well as the results of t tests (assuming unequal variance) comparing the parameter estimates between the two ages.

Table 7.7 Sample a Priori or Post Hoc Comparisons Table

Table 3

Analyses for the Interaction of Professor Type and Timing of Response on Perceptions of Professor Traits

Professor trait	End of semester professor type		Start of semester professor type		F ratio	p	η^2
	Typical	Effective	Typical	Effective			
Dedicated	4.706$_b$	4.789$_b$	4.154$_c$	5.000$_a$	19.26	.001	.15
Easy to understand	3.059$_c$	4.895$_a$	3.231$_c$	4.429$_b$	5.01	.028	.03
Fair	4.000$_b$	4.263$_b$	3.731$_c$	4.667$_a$	5.75	.019	.06
Manipulative	1.471$_a$	1.632$_a$	1.731$_a$	1.238$_a$	3.92	.051	.05
Insensitive	2.059$_b$	1.526$_c$	2.538$_a$	1.143$_c$	8.12	.006	.06

Note. Means with different subscripts differ at the $p = .05$ level by Duncan's new multiple range test.

(annotation: exact p values →)

Table 7.8 Sample Correlation Table

Table 1

Descriptive Statistics and Correlations for Study Variables

Variable	n	M	SD	1	2	3	4	5	6	7
1. Internal–external status [a]	3,697	0.43	0.49	—						
2. Manager job performance	2,134	3.14	0.62	−.08**	—					
3. Starting salary [b]	3,697	1.01	0.27	.45**	−.01	—				
4. Subsequent promotion	3,697	0.33	0.47	.08**	−.07**	.04*	—			
5. Organizational tenure	3,697	6.45	6.62	−.29**	.09**	.01	.09**	—		
6. Unit service performance [c]	3,505	85.00	6.98	−.25**	−.39**	.24**	.08**	.01	—	
7. Unit financial performance [c]	694	42.61	5.86	.00	−.03	.12*	−.07	−.02	.16**	—

(annotation: use of specific note →)

(annotation: asterisks for p values →)

[a] 0 = internal hires and 1 = external hires. [b] A linear transformation was performed on the starting salary values to maintain pay practice confidentiality. The standard deviation (0.27) can be interpreted as 27% of the average starting salary for all managers. Thus, ±1 SD includes a range of starting salaries from 73% (i.e., 1.00 − 0.27) to 127% (i.e., 1.00 + 0.27) of the average starting salaries for all managers. [c] Values reflect the average across 3 years of data.

*$p < .05$. **$p < .01$.

Table 7.9 Sample Analysis of Variance Table

Table 1

Means, Standard Deviations, and One-Way Analyses of Variance in Psychological and Social Resources and Cognitive Appraisals

Measure	Urban		Rural		$F(1, 294)$	η^2
	M	SD	M	SD		
Self-esteem	2.91	0.49	3.35	0.35	68.87***	.19
Social support	4.22	1.50	5.56	1.20	62.60***	.17
Cognitive appraisals						
Threat	2.78	0.87	1.99	0.88	56.35***	.20
Challenge	2.48	0.88	2.83	1.20	7.87***	.03
Self-efficacy	2.65	0.79	3.53	0.92	56.35***	.16

***$p < .001$.

Table 7.10 Sample Regression Table, Without Confidence Intervals

Table 2

Regression Coefficients of Leader Sleep on Charismatic Leadership

Variable	Model 1			Model 2		
	B	β	SE	B	β	SE
Constant	2.65**		.31	2.76		
Leader gender [a]	−.11	−.07	.16	−.09	−.06	.15
Leader sleep condition [b]				−.36**	−.24	.15
R^2	.09				.14	
ΔR^2		use of specific notes			.05*	

Note. $N = 88$. We examined the impact of leader sleep condition (control vs. sleep deprived) on ratings of charismatic leadership. In Model 1, we entered the control variables of gender and video length to predict leader charisma. In Model 2, we entered sleep condition as a predictor.

[a] Male = 1, female = 2. [b] Control condition = 0, sleep-deprived condition = 1.

*$p < .05$. **$p < .01$.

Table 7.11 Sample Regression Table, With Confidence Intervals in Separate Columns

Table 3

Moderator Analysis: Types of Measurement and Study Year

Effect	Estimate	*SE*	95% CI		*p*
			LL	*UL*	
Fixed effects					
Intercept	.119	.040	.041	.198	.003
Creativity measurement[a]	.097	.028	.042	.153	.001
Academic achievement measurement[b]	−.039	.018	−.074	−.004	.03
Study year[c]	.0002	.001	−.001	.002	.76
Goal[d]	−.003	.029	−.060	.054	.91
Published[e]	.054	.030	−.005	.114	.07
Random effects					
Within-study variance	.009	.001	.008	.011	<.001
Between-study variance	.018	.003	.012	.023	<.001

Note. Number of studies = 120, number of effects = 782, total *N* = 52,578. CI = confidence interval; *LL* = lower limit; *UL* = upper limit.

[a] 0 = self-report, 1 = test. [b] 0 = test, 1 = grade point average. [c] Study year was grand centered.

[d] 0 = other, 1 = yes. [e] 0 = no, 1 = yes.

confidence intervals in separate columns

Table 7.12 Sample Qualitative Table Incorporating Quantitative Data

Table 1

Reasons Why Individuals Chose to Watch the Royal Wedding (N = 45)

Reason for interest	Example quote	Frequency, *n* (%)
Royal family and its history	"I love all things British. I studied abroad in the U.K. I also watched the weddings of Charles & Diana and Andrew & Fergie. I watched Diana's funeral. Watching William & Kate get married seemed like the natural thing to do."	16 (35.6)
	"I find the royal family and their practices and traditions fascinating. I am a big fan of tradition in any capacity (graduation ceremonies, weddings, etc.) and enjoy watching traditions older than our own country (the U.S.)."	
Fashion and pop culture	"When big pop culture things happen, I tend to want to watch so I'm 'in on it.' Also, when I was little my mom made us get up to watch Princess Diana get married, so it felt a little like tradition."	13 (28.9)
	"I was curious. Wanted to see her dress and how the other people who attended dressed. Like pomp and ceremony."	
Fairy tales and love stories	"I watched his mom and dad get married, watched him grow up. Plus I love a fairy tale that comes true. I believe in love and romance."	11 (24.4)
	"I am a romantic and think this is a great love story."	
To pass time/it was on TV	"I was at the airport and it was broadcasting on TV while I was waiting for my flight."	5 (11.1)
	"It was on CNN when I got up."	

Table 7.13 Sample Mixed Methods Table

Table 3

Integrated Results Matrix for the Effect of Topic Familiarity on Reliance on Author Expertise

Quantitative result	Qualitative result	Example quote
When the topic was more familiar (climate change) and cards were more relevant, participants placed less value on author expertise.	When an assertion was considered to be more familiar and to be general knowledge, participants perceived less need to rely on author expertise.	Participant 144: "I feel that I know more about climate, and there are several things on the climate cards that are obvious, and that if I sort of know it already, then the source is not so critical . . . whereas with nuclear energy, I don't know so much, so then I'm maybe more interested in who says what."
When the topic was less familiar (nuclear power) and cards were more relevant, participants placed more value on author expertise.	When an assertion was considered to be less familiar and not general knowledge, participants perceived more need to rely on author expertise.	Participant 3: "[Nuclear power], which I know much, much less about, I would back up my arguments more with what I trust from the professors."

Note. We integrated quantitative data (whether students selected a card about nuclear power or about climate change) and qualitative data (interviews with students) to provide a more comprehensive description of students' card selections between the two topics.

Figures

7.22 Principles of Figure Construction

All types of graphical displays other than tables are considered figures in APA Style. Ensure that all figures add substantively to readers' understanding and do not duplicate other elements of the paper. Also consider whether a figure is the best way to communicate the information. In some cases (particularly when quantitative information is being conveyed), a table may offer more precision than, say, a graph. If you focus on the principle of enhancing readers' understanding, other questions—for example, use of color, use of photographic images, or magnitude of cropping of a picture—should be relatively easy to resolve.

The standards for good figures are simplicity, clarity, continuity, and (of course) information value. A good figure

- augments rather than duplicates the text,
- conveys only essential information,
- omits visually distracting detail,
- is easy to read—its elements (e.g., type, lines, labels, symbols) are large enough to be seen and interpreted with ease,
- is easy to understand   its purpose is readily apparent,
- is carefully planned and prepared, and
- is consistent with and in the same style as similar figures in the same paper.

For figures of all types, check that

- images are clear,
- lines are smooth and sharp,
- font is simple and legible,
- units of measurement are provided,
- axes are clearly labeled, and
- elements within the figure are labeled or explained.

Be certain, for instance, to distinguish between error bars and confidence intervals. When using confidence intervals, clearly specify the size of the interval (e.g., 95%); when using error bars, provide the label for the error (e.g., standard error of the mean) in the figure image or note. In addition, check all figures to ensure that

- sufficient information is given in the legend and/or note to make the figure understandable on its own (i.e., apart from the text),
- symbols are easy to differentiate, and
- the graphic is large enough for its elements to be discernible.

Even when using high-quality graphics software to construct figures, examine figures carefully and make any necessary adjustments to follow these guidelines.

7.23 Figure Components

The basic components of a prototypical figure are shown in Figure 7.1 and are summarized as follows:

- **number:** The figure number (e.g., Figure 1) appears above the figure in bold (see Section 7.24).
- **title:** The figure title appears one double-spaced line below the figure number in italic title case (see Sections 5.7 and 7.25).
- **image:** The image portion of the figure is the chart, graph, photograph, drawing, or other illustration itself (see Section 7.26).
- **legend:** A figure legend, or key, if present, should be positioned within the borders of the figure and explains any symbols used in the figure image (see Section 7.27).
- **note:** Three types of notes (general, specific, and probability) can appear below the figure to describe contents of the figure that cannot be understood from the figure title, image, and/or legend alone (e.g., definitions of abbreviations, copyright attribution). Not all figures include figure notes (see Section 7.28).

See Section 7.32 for sample figures.

7.24 Figure Numbers

Number all figures that are part of the main text (i.e., not part of an appendix) using Arabic numerals—for example, Figure 1, Figure 2, and Figure 3. Assign the numbers in the order in which each figure is first mentioned in the text, regardless of whether a more detailed discussion of the figure occurs elsewhere in the paper. Write the word "Figure" and the number in bold and flush left (i.e., not indented or centered). Figures that appear in appendices follow a different numbering scheme (see Section 1.14).

Figure 7.1 Basic Components of a Figure

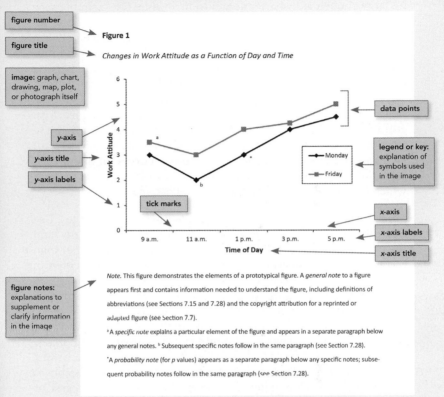

7.25 Figure Titles

Give every figure a brief but clear and explanatory title; the basic content of the figure should be easily inferred from the title. Write the figure title in italic title case below the figure number, and double-space the figure number and title. As with table titles, avoid overly general and overly detailed figure titles (see Section 7.11).

7.26 Figure Images

The image part of the figure (e.g., graph, chart, diagram) should be saved in a resolution sufficient to allow for clear printing or viewing (see Section 7.4). Consider the following considerations when creating images.

Size and Proportion of Elements. Each element in a figure must be large enough and sharp enough to be legible. Use a simple sans serif font (e.g., Arial, Calibri, Lucida Sans Unicode; see Section 1.18) within the image portion of the figure with enough space between letters to avoid crowding. Letters should be clear, sharp, and uniformly dark and should be sized consistently throughout the figure; the font size should be no smaller than 8 points and no larger than 14 points. As a general guideline, plot symbols should be about the size of lowercase letters that appear in a label within the figure. Also consider the weight (i.e., size, density) of each element in a figure in relation to that of every other element, and make the most important elements the most prominent. For example, curves on line graphs and outlines of bars on bar graphs should be bolder than axis labels, which should be bolder than the axes and tick marks.

Spelling, Capitalization, and Numbers Within Figure Images. Use title case for axis labels. Abbreviate the word "number" to "no." and the word "percentage" to "%." Words within figure images other than those on the axis labels or in the figure legend may be written in either title case or sentence case (see Section 5.7), depending on the contents of the figure. In general, labels, phrases, or words that serve as headings would be better set in title case, whereas other descriptive phrases, sentences, or paragraphs within a figure would be better set in sentence case. Numbers that appear in the image portion of a figure should be written as words or numerals according to the guidelines in Sections 6.1 to 6.8; however, it is permissible to use numerals for all numbers in a figure if this would be clearer or save space. Statistics, Greek letters, and units of measurement do not need to be defined in a figure note (see Section 7.15).

Shading. Limit the number of different shadings used in a single graphic. If different shadings are used to distinguish bars or segments of a graph, choose shadings that are distinct; for example, the best option to distinguish two sets of bars is no shading ("open") and black or gray ("solid"). If more than two shadings are needed, use patterns, again making sure that the patterns are distinct—for example, use no (open) shading, solid black or gray, and stripes for three shadings. If error bars or other information overlaps with shaded areas (e.g., double-sided error bars in a bar graph), ensure that the overlapping information can be clearly distinguished from the shading.

Color. Color can serve both communicative and decorative purposes in figures. Students preparing a figure for a course assignment may use color provided that the assignment will be delivered in a format that supports it (e.g., submitted through an online learning management system).

When selecting colors for a figure, ensure that there is plenty of contrast so that people with a color-vision deficiency (often referred to as "color blindness") or people who do not see color in a typical way can understand the information and tell the colors apart. Use a contrast checker such as the free Colour Contrast Analyser (https://developer.paciellogroup.com/resources/contrastanalyser) to evaluate the contrast ratio and confirm that your content passes the standards for WCAG 2.0 AA or later.[2] Adequate contrast ratios ensure that the figure is not only accessible to readers with color-deficient vision but also understandable by all readers if the figure is printed or photocopied in grayscale. Another strategy to achieve adequate contrast is to use a pattern in combination with color so that the differentiation of elements does not rely on color alone (e.g., in a line graph, different lines may be in different colors and also of different styles, such as solid, dashed, and dotted). When many colors must be used and it is not possible to achieve high contrast among all of them, label colored areas directly in the image or use lines to connect the object to its label rather than placing the label in a legend, if possible, so that readers do not have to match colors in the figure to colors in the legend. See the APA Style website (https://apastyle.apa.org) for an example of how people with certain color-vision deficiencies see color and how the colors used in figures can be adjusted to accommodate them.

Gridlines and 3-D Effects. Avoid the use of gridlines in figures unless the gridlines will substantially aid readers in understanding the content, such as when many data points need to be compared across the x-axis. Likewise, avoid including 3-D effects for mere decoration (e.g., 3-D bar graphs) because they may make the figure more difficult to read. However, 3-D effects can be used to convey essential information (e.g., 3-D representations of stimuli).

Panels. The decision of whether to divide a figure into panels or create a separate figure for each panel will depend on the nature of the information being presented. Although panels help readers directly compare information, they also increase the density of the information being presented on the page; as always, prioritize clear

---

[2] WCAG 2.0 refers to the Web Content Accessibility Guidelines, Version 2.0 (Web Accessibility Initiative, 2018).

communication when constructing any figure. If the figure includes multiple panels, it is optional to label them. If panels are unlabeled, refer to panels by their position (e.g., "the top panel," "the left panel," "the middle panel"). To label panels, assign each one a capital letter (e.g., A, B) and place the label at the top left of the panel. Refer to the panels as "Panel A," "Panel B," and so forth. In the main text, refer to a panel as "Figure 5A" or "Panel A of Figure 5." In the figure general note, explain each panel.

Citations in Figures. If a figure contains citations to other works, follow the formats described in Section 8.11. Use an ampersand (&) for the word "and" in all citations in figures to conserve space.

7.27 Figure Legends

A *legend* (also called a *key*) explains any symbols, line styles, or shading or pattern variants used in the image portion of the figure (see Figures 7.2–7.3 in Section 7.32 for examples). The legend is an integral part of the figure; therefore, its lettering should be the same style and proportion as the lettering in the rest of the figure. Use title case in the legend (see Section 5.7). Only figures that have symbols, line styles, or shadings needing definition should include legends. When possible, place legends within or below the image instead of to the side to avoid having empty space around the legend.

7.28 Figure Notes

Figure notes contain information needed to clarify the contents of the figure for readers. As with tables, figures may have three kinds of notes: general, specific, and probability.

A general note should explain units of measurement, symbols, and abbreviations that are not included in the legend or defined elsewhere in the figure (see Section 7.15 for information on abbreviations and symbols that do not require definitions). Make certain that the symbols, abbreviations, and terminology in the note and legend match the symbols, abbreviations, and terminology in the figure, in other figures in the paper, and in the text. Explain the use of shading, color, and any other design element that carries meaning. Provide individual descriptions of panels for multipanel figures. If a graph includes error bars, explain in the image or general note whether they represent standard deviations, standard errors, confidence limits, or ranges; it is also helpful to provide sample sizes. Also include within the general note any acknowledgment that a figure is reprinted or adapted from another source (see Section 7.7). Place

explanations of abbreviations and copyright attributions for reproduced figures last in the general note.

Position any superscripts for specific notes near the element
being identified. It is preferable to report exact *p* values; however, if
statistically significant values are marked with asterisks or daggers in
the figure, explain them in a probability note (see Section 7.14). For
guidelines on formatting figure notes, see Section 7.14.

7.29 Relation Between Figures

Similar figures or figures of equal importance should be of equal size
and scale. Combine figures that are alike to facilitate comparisons
between their content. For example, two line graphs with identical
axes might be combined horizontally into a single figure, or multiple
figures might be combined into one figure with multiple panels (see
Section 7.26).

7.30 Photographs

Photographs are a type of figure with special considerations. Photographs in most student papers can be in color and saved in any
widely available photo format (see Section 7.26 for more information on the use of color in figures). Because reproduction softens
contrast and detail in photographs, starting with rich contrast and
sharp detail will improve the final version of the image. The cam-
era view and the lighting should highlight the subject and provide
high contrast; a light or dark background can provide even more
contrast. Photographs usually benefit from cropping to, for example, eliminate extraneous detail or center the image. However, when
a photographic image has been altered in a manner beyond simple cropping and/or adjustment for light levels, clearly indicate in
a general note how the image has been altered. Ethical principles
of publication forbid any intentional misrepresentation of images,
just as fraudulent data manipulation is forbidden. See Figure 7.10 in
Section 7.32 for an example of a photograph as a figure.

If you photograph an identifiable person, obtain a signed release
from that person to use the photograph in your paper (see Section 8.38);
if the person is not identifiable, a release is not needed. If you took a
photograph yourself, no citation or copyright attribution is required
in the figure note. If you want to reprint or adapt a photograph from
another source, you may need to obtain permission to use it in your
paper because professional photographs are usually the property of
the photographer. See Sections 8.35 to 8.39 for further information on
reprinting or adapting photographs from other sources.

7.31 Figure Checklist

The figure checklist will help to ensure that the data in your figure are effectively communicated and that the figure conforms to the style guidelines presented in this chapter.

Figure Checklist

☐ Is the figure necessary?

☐ Is the figure in high resolution and in an acceptable file format?

☐ Are figures of equally important concepts prepared according to the same size and scale?

☐ Are all figures numbered consecutively with Arabic numerals in the order in which they are first mentioned in the text? Is the figure number bold and flush left?

☐ Are all figures called out or referred to in the text?

☐ Is the figure title brief but explanatory? Is it written in italic title case and flush left?

☐ Is the figure image simple, clear, and free of extraneous detail?

☐ Are all elements of the image clearly labeled?

☐ Are the magnitude, scale, and direction of grid elements clearly labeled?

☐ Has the figure been formatted properly? Is the font sans serif within the image portion of the figure and between 8 and 14 points in size?

☐ Are all abbreviations explained (with exceptions as noted in Section 7.15), as well as the use of special symbols?

☐ If the figure includes a legend to define symbols, line styles, or shading variants, does the legend appear within or below the image? Are words in the legend written in title case?

☐ Have all substantive modifications to photographic images been disclosed?

☐ Are the figure notes, if needed, in the order of general note, specific note, and probability note? Are the notes double-spaced and flush left and in the same font as the text of the paper?

☐ If all or part of a figure is reprinted or adapted, is there a copyright attribution? If permission was necessary to reproduce the figure, have you received written permission for reuse (in print and electronic forms) from the copyright holder and sent a copy of that written permission with the final version of your paper?

7.32 Sample Figures

Many types of figures can be used to present data to readers. The more common types of figures used in qualitative, quantitative, and mixed methods research are presented next. There are many variations and versions of each, and the distinctions among many of them are not clear. For situations not addressed here, consult similar published articles to see examples of current standards and practices and follow those examples.

- **graphs** (Figures 7.2–7.3): Graphs typically display the relationship between two quantitative indices or between a continuous quantitative variable (usually displayed on the y-axis) and groups of participants or subjects (usually displayed on the x-axis). Bar graphs (Figure 7.2) and line graphs (Figure 7.3) are two examples of graphs.

- **charts** (Figures 7.4–7.6): Charts generally display nonquantitative information with the use of enclosed boxes, squares, or circles connected with straight or curved lines or arrows. They are used to
  - illustrate models—for example, conceptual or theoretical models (Figure 7.4) and
  - illustrate qualitative (Figure 7.5) and mixed methods (Figure 7.6) research designs or frameworks.

- **drawings** (Figure 7.7): Drawings show information pictorially and can be used to illustrate, for example, experimental stimuli.

- **maps** (Figure 7.8): Maps generally display spatial information—for example, geographic census information. This information often comes from government sources (e.g., the U.S. Census Bureau or the Centers for Disease Control and Prevention); to reprint or adapt tables or figures from these sources, see Section 8.37.

- **plots** (Figure 7.9): Plots present individual data points as a function of axis variables. For example, a scatterplot is used to explore the relationship between two variables (e.g., a linear relationship may be indicated if the data points are clustered along the diagonal).

- **photographs** (Figure 7.10): Photographs (see Section 7.30) contain direct visual representations of information. They are often used to present information that would be difficult to portray effectively with drawings, such as facial expressions or precise placement of stimuli in an environment.

Multipanel Figures. A multipanel figure may combine bar graphs, line graphs, histograms, and other figure types into one figure (see also Section 7.26). Whether it is advisable to combine panels into one figure or to present panels as separate figures will depend on the size of the figures and the nature of the information being presented.

Figure 7.2 Sample Bar Graph

Figure 1

Framing Scores for Different Reward Sizes

Note. Framing scores of adolescents and young adults are shown for low and high risks and for small, medium, and large rewards (error bars show standard errors).

Figure 7.3 Sample Line Graph

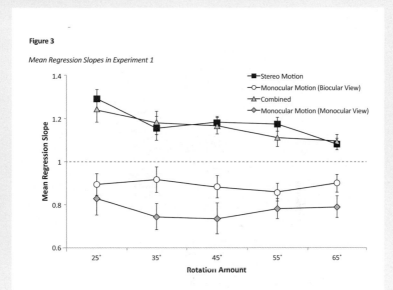

Figure 3

Mean Regression Slopes in Experiment 1

Note. Mean regression slopes in Experiment 1 are shown for the stereo motion, biocularly viewed monocular motion, combined, and monocularly viewed monocular motion conditions, plotted by rotation amount. Error bars represent standard errors. From "Large Continuous Perspective Change With Noncoplanar Points Enables Accurate Slant Perception," by X. M. Wang, M. Lind, and G. P. Bingham, 2018, *Journal of Experimental Psychology: Human Perception and Performance, 44*(10), p. 1513 (https://doi.org/10.1037/xhp0000553). Copyright 2018 by the American Psychological Association.

example copyright attribution for a reprinted figure when permission is not necessary

Figure 7.4 Sample Conceptual Model

Figure 2

Integrated Child and Youth Behavioral Health System

Note. This model shows that the integrated child and youth behavioral health system is centered on the child or youth and family and includes promotion; prevention; screening; and treatment, ongoing support, and monitoring both in the health sector and in other community systems. This structure is supported by information systems, policy and service system coordination, and financing, which are shown in rectangles beneath the ovals to illustrate this support.

Figure 7.5 Sample Qualitative Research Figure

Figure 1

Organizational Framework for Racial Microaggressions in the Workplace

Figure 7.6 Sample Mixed Methods Research Figure

Figure 1

A Multistage Paradigm for Integrative Mixed Methods Research

Note. Items are numbered in the order presented in the text. All modeled correlations and path coefficients are significant ($p < .05$).

Figure 7.7 Sample Illustration of Experimental Stimuli

Figure 4

Examples of Stimuli Used in Experiment 1

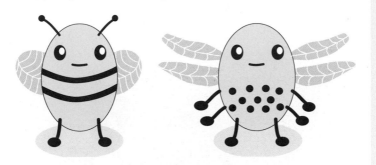

Note. Stimuli were computer-generated cartoon bees that varied on four binary dimensions, for a total of 16 unique stimuli. They had two or six legs, a striped or spotted body, single or double wings, and antennae or no antennae. The two stimuli shown here demonstrate the use of opposite values on all four binary dimensions.

Figure 7.8 Sample Map

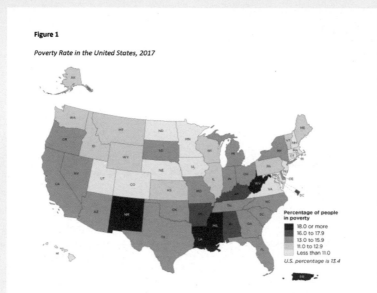

Figure 1

Poverty Rate in the United States, 2017

Note. The U.S. percentage does not include data for Puerto Rico. Adapted from 2017 *Poverty Rate in the United States*, by U.S. Census Bureau, 2017 (https://www.census.gov/library/visualizations /2018/comm/acs-poverty-map.html). In the public domain.

example copyright attribution for an adapted figure in the public domain

Figure 7.9 Sample Scatterplot

Figure 2

Association Between Perceptual Speed and Empathic Pattern Accuracy for Happiness

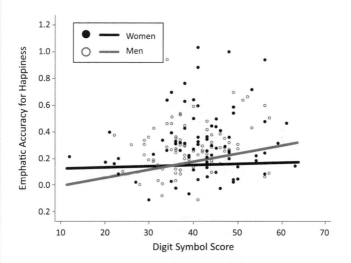

Note. Each dot represents an individual participant. Scores for empathic pattern accuracy for happiness were obtained in a zero-order multilevel model in which a target's self-reported happiness was the only predictor of a rater's perceptions (the estimate plotted on the y-axis is equivalent to β_{1j} in Equation 4). Among men, higher levels of digit symbol performance were associated with higher empathic pattern accuracy for happiness in daily life (gray line). Among women, the association was not significant (black line).

Figure 7.10 Sample Photograph

Figure 1

Example Scenes of Participant Response to Locations of Schema-Irrelevant Objects

Note. Top panel: A version of the kitchen scene using schema-irrelevant objects (walking boots, bath towel, and teapot) in unexpected locations (right side of the floor, rail beneath table, and stool, respectively). Middle panel: One of the possible test images (out of two) associated with the study image depicted in the top panel used in Study 1 (shift-to-expected condition). Bottom panel: Example participant response when the participant originally studied the image in the top panel in the recall task of Study 2. Schema-relevant objects in expected places at study are the metal pot and toaster; those in unexpected places are the microwave and teapot; those not present are the fruit bowl and paper towel roll.

8 ∽

WORKS CREDITED IN TEXT

Scientific knowledge represents the accomplishments of many researchers over time. A critical part of writing in APA Style is helping readers place your contribution in the context of this broader research base by citing the researchers who influenced you.

This chapter provides ground rules for acknowledging how others contributed to your work. In the first section we describe general guidelines for citation, including the appropriate level of citation and techniques to avoid plagiarism and self-plagiarism in your writing. Specific guidance for in-text citation follows, including the formats for interviews, classroom and intranet sources, and personal communications; in-text citations in general; and paraphrases and direct quotations. We end with guidance regarding copyright and permission that authors need to follow when reprinting or adapting certain kinds of content from other works (e.g., how to appropriately credit an image reproduced from the internet in a paper).

General Guidelines for Citation

8.1 Appropriate Level of Citation

Cite the work of those individuals whose ideas, theories, or research have directly influenced your work. The works you cite provide key background information, support or dispute your thesis, or offer critical definitions and data. Cite only works that you have read and ideas that you have incorporated into your writing. Cite primary sources when possible and secondary sources sparingly (see Section 8.6). In addition to crediting the ideas of others that you used to develop your thesis, provide documentation for all facts and figures that are not common knowledge. Both paraphrases (see Sections 8.23–8.24) and direct quotations (see Sections 8.25–8.34) require citations. If you reprint or adapt a table or figure (e.g., if you reproduce an image from the internet, even if it was free or in the Creative Commons) or reprint a long quotation or commercially copyrighted test item, you may also need to seek permission from the copyright holder and provide a copyright attribution (see Sections 8.35–8.39).

The number of sources you cite in your paper depends on the purpose of your work. For most papers, cite one or two of the most representative sources for each key point. Literature review papers, however, typically include a more exhaustive list of references, given that the purpose of the paper is to acquaint readers with everything that has been written on the topic.

Avoid both undercitation and overcitation. Undercitation can lead to plagiarism (see Section 8.2) and/or self-plagiarism (see Section 8.3). Even when sources cannot be retrieved (e.g., because they are personal communications; see Section 8.9), you still need to credit them in the text (however, avoid using online sources that are no longer recoverable; see Section 9.37). Overcitation can be distracting and is unnecessary. For example, it is considered overcitation to repeat the same citation in every sentence when the source and topic have not changed. Instead, when paraphrasing a key point in more than one sentence within a paragraph, cite the source in the first sentence in which it is relevant and do not repeat the citation in subsequent sentences as long as the source remains clear and unchanged (see Section 8.24). When the author's name appears in the narrative, the year can be omitted in repeated citations under certain circumstances (see Section 8.16). Figure 8.1 provides an example of an appropriate level of citation.

8.2 Plagiarism

Plagiarism is the act of presenting the words, ideas, or images of another as your own; it denies authors or creators of content the credit they are due. Whether deliberate or unintentional, plagiarism violates ethical standards in scholarship (see APA Ethics Code Standard 8.11, Plagiarism). Writers who plagiarize disrespect the efforts of original authors by failing to acknowledge their contributions, stifle further research by preventing readers from tracing ideas back to their

Figure 8.1 Example of an Appropriate Level of Citation

> Humor plays an important role in everyday life, from interacting with strangers to attracting mates (Bressler & Balshine, 2006; Earleywine, 2010; Tornquist & Chiappe, 2015). Some people, however, come up with funny and witty ideas much more easily than do others. In this study, we examined the role of cognitive abilities in humor production, a topic with a long past (e.g., Feingold & Mazzella, 1991; Galloway, 1994) that has recently attracted more attention (Greengross & Miller, 2011; Kellner & Benedek, 2016). Humor production ability is measured with open-ended tasks (Earleywine, 2010), the most common of which involves asking participants to write captions for single-panel cartoons (for a review, see Nusbaum & Silvia, 2017).

Note. The authors have provided citations to representative sources for each new idea in the text. Common knowledge (here, the idea that some people come up with funny ideas more easily than do others) does not require a citation.

original sources, and unfairly disregard those who exerted the effort to complete their own work. Professional writers who try to publish plagiarized work face rejection from publication and possible censure in their place of employment. Students who plagiarize may fail the assignment or course, be placed on academic probation, or be expelled from their institution.

To avoid plagiarism, provide appropriate credit to the source whenever you do the following:

- paraphrase (i.e., state in your own words) the ideas of others (see Sections 8.23–8.24)
- directly quote the words of others (see Sections 8.25–8.34)
- reprint or adapt a table or figure, even images from the internet that are free or licensed in the Creative Commons (see Sections 8.35–8.39)
- reprint a long text passage or commercially copyrighted test item (see Sections 8.35–8.39)

For most works, appropriate credit takes the form of an author–date citation (see Section 8.10). However, according to U.S. copyright law, authors who wish to reprint or adapt tables, figures, and images or to reprint long quotations or commercially copyrighted test items (see

Section 8.36) must provide more comprehensive credit in the form of a copyright attribution (see Section 8.39) and may need permission from the copyright holder to use the materials (see Section 8.38).

The necessity for credit extends to the ideas of others as well. For example, authors should credit the originators of theories they refer to in their paper. If authors model a study after one conducted by someone else, the author of the original study should be given credit. If the rationale for a study was suggested in someone else's article, that person should be given credit. Given the free exchange of ideas, which is important to the health of intellectual discourse, authors may not be able to pinpoint exactly where the idea for their study originated. They should make their best effort to find and acknowledge the source(s), including any personal communications (see Section 8.9).

Although many cases of plagiarism are straightforward (e.g., passages of text copied from another source without attribution), other cases are more challenging to evaluate. Usually, using incorrect citations (e.g., misspelling an author's name, forgetting or mistyping an element in a reference list entry, or citing a source in the text that does not have a corresponding reference list entry) is not considered plagiarism if the error is minor and attributable to an editorial oversight rather than an intentional attempt to steal someone's ideas or obfuscate the origin of the information (Cooper, 2016). However, such errors may still result in deductions on an academic assignment.

Instructors and publishers may use plagiarism-checking software (e.g., iThenticate, Turnitin) to identify cases in which entire papers have been copied, passages of specified lengths match, or a few words have been changed but content is largely the same (the latter is known as *patchwriting*; see Merriam-Webster, n.d.-a). However, human review is often necessary to determine whether plagiarism has actually taken place. Take careful notes as you research and write to keep track of and accurately cite your sources. Check your work carefully to ensure that you acknowledge the words and ideas of others with citations in the text that have corresponding reference list entries.

Unethical writing practices other than plagiarism are also prohibited. For example, it is unethical to fabricate citations and/or reference list entries. This practice gives the appearance of properly credited sources, but the sources are fictitious or untraceable; the author may have made up the information as well as the sources, or the information may come from real works that have not been credited. Likewise, *contract cheating*, in which students hire another person to write a paper for them, is unethical. Even when the resulting work is original (i.e., not plagiarized), these students still take credit for work that they did not do themselves, which violates academic integrity policies, honor codes, and ethics codes.

8.3 Self-Plagiarism

Self-plagiarism is the use of your own previously published work as original; like plagiarism, self-plagiarism is unethical. Self-plagiarism deceives readers by making it appear that more information is available on a topic than really exists. It gives the impression that findings are more replicable than is the case or that particular conclusions are more strongly supported than is warranted by the evidence.

Some institutions may consider it self-plagiarism if a student submits a paper written for one class to complete an assignment for another class without permission from the current instructor; using the same paper in multiple classes may violate the academic integrity policy, honor code, or ethics code of the university. However, incorporating previous classwork into one's thesis or dissertation and building on one's own existing writing may be permissible; students who wish to do this should discuss their ideas with their instructor or advisor and follow their university's honor code, ethics code, or academic policies when reusing their previous work.

An exception to the prohibition against self-plagiarism is publishing a work of limited circulation in a venue of wider circulation. For example, doctoral dissertations or master's theses may be published in whole or in part in one or more journal articles. Seek clarification from the course instructor or journal editor if you are concerned about duplicate publication or self-plagiarism. For more information on self-plagiarism, including how to acceptably reuse previous work, see Sections 1.16 and 2.7 of the *Publication Manual*.

8.4 Correspondence Between Reference List and Text

APA Style uses the author–date citation system (see Section 8.10), in which a brief in-text citation directs readers to a full reference list entry. Each work cited in the text must appear in the reference list, and each work in the reference list must be cited in the text. Ensure that the spelling of author names and the publication dates in the reference list entries match the in-text citations. The date element of a reference list entry may include the month, season, and/or day in addition to the year; however, the corresponding in-text citation includes only the year (see, e.g., Chapter 10, Example 15).

There are a few exceptions to these guidelines:

- Personal communications, which are unrecoverable sources, are cited in the text only (see Section 8.9).

- General mentions of whole websites or periodicals (see Section 8.22) and common software and apps (see Section 10.8) in the text do not require a citation or reference list entry.

- The source of an epigraph does not usually appear in the reference list (see Section 8.34).

Additional exceptions include unrecorded Traditional Knowledge or Oral Traditions of Indigenous Peoples, quotations from research participants, and references in a meta-analysis (see Sections 8.9, 8.36, and 9.52 of the *Publication Manual*, respectively).

8.5 Use of the Published Version or Archival Version

Multiple versions of the same work might coexist on the internet, and you should cite the version of the work you used. Ideally, use and cite the final, published version of a work (see Chapter 10, Examples 1–3). However, if you used the advance online version (see Chapter 10, Example 7), the in-press version (see Chapter 10, Example 8), or the final peer-reviewed manuscript accepted for publication (but before it was typeset or copyedited; see Chapter 10, Example 65), cite that version. The final peer-reviewed manuscript as accepted for publication might be available from a variety of places, including a personal website, an employer's server, an institutional repository, a reference manager, or an author's social network.

Informally published works, such as those in a preprint archive (e.g., PsyArXiv) or an institutional repository or database (e.g., ERIC), can also be cited (see Chapter 10, Examples 65–66) when these are the version used. Publishers label advance online publications in various ways (e.g., "online first publication," "advance online publication," "epub ahead of print"); standardize this label to "advance online publication" for an APA Style reference list entry (see Chapter 10, Example 7). Draft manuscripts (unpublished, in preparation, or submitted) can be cited when the draft is the most current version of the work. When you cite a draft manuscript, in-press article, advance online publication, or informally published work in your paper, ensure you have the most up-to-date publication information for these works and update the reference list entry if necessary before you submit your paper. For more information on citing unpublished works, see Section 10.8 of the *Publication Manual*.

8.6 Primary and Secondary Sources

In scholarly work, a *primary source* reports original content, and a *secondary source* refers to content first reported in another source. Cite secondary sources sparingly—for instance, when the original work is out of print, unavailable, or available only in a language that you do not understand. If possible, as a matter of good scholarly practice, find the primary source, read it, and cite it directly rather than citing a secondary source. For example, rather than citing an instructor's lecture or a textbook or encyclopedia that in turn cites original research, find, read, and cite the original research directly (unless an instructor has directed you to do otherwise).

When citing a secondary source, provide a reference list entry for the secondary source that you used. In the text, identify the primary source and then write "as cited in" the secondary source that you used. If the year of publication of the primary source is known, also include it in the text. For example, if you read a work by Lyon et al. (2014) in which Rabbitt (1982) was cited, and you were unable to read Rabbitt's work yourself, cite Rabbitt's work as the original source, followed by Lyon et al.'s work as the secondary source. Only Lyon et al.'s work appears in the reference list.

(Rabbitt, 1982, as cited in Lyon et al., 2014)

If the year of the primary source is unknown, omit it from the in-text citation.

Allport's diary (as cited in Nicholson, 2003)

Works Requiring Special Approaches to Citation

8.7 Interviews

An *interview* is a dialogue or an exchange of information between people. Interviews used as sources can be classified into three categories: published interviews, personal interviews, and research participant interviews.

- **Published interviews** appear in a variety of places—for example, in a magazine, newspaper, recorded radio broadcast, podcast episode, YouTube video, or TV show. To cite a published interview, follow the format for the reference type (e.g., magazine article, podcast episode, radio broadcast; see Chapter 10, Examples 15, 83, and 84, respectively). The person being interviewed will not necessarily appear in the author element of the reference; in this case, integrate the person's name into the narrative of the sentence if desired (see Chapter 10, Example 77).

- **Personal interviews** are those you conducted to obtain information to support a key point in your paper (e.g., an email inquiry to an author about their published work). Because readers cannot recover this type of interview, cite it as a personal communication (see Section 8.9).

- **Research participant interviews** are those you conducted as part of your study methodology. They do not require a citation because you do not cite your own work in the paper in which you first report it. However, information gathered from research participant interviews can be presented and discussed in a paper; for guidelines, see Section 8.36 of the *Publication Manual*.

8.8 Classroom or Intranet Resources

Some works are recoverable only by certain audiences, which determines how they are cited. For example, a student writing a paper for a course assignment might cite material from the classroom website or learning management system (LMS; e.g., Canvas, Blackboard), or an employee writing an internal report might cite resources from the company intranet. These sources are recoverable by the instructor and fellow students or by other employees of the company but not the general public.

When the audience you are writing for can retrieve the works you used, cite the works using the formats shown in Chapter 10, which are organized according to reference group and category. For example, to cite a recorded lecture or PowerPoint presentation available from a classroom website or LMS, follow the format shown in Chapter 10, Example 90. The source element of these references includes the name of the classroom website or LMS and the URL (which should be the home page or login page for sites with restricted access). Likewise, for a report on a company intranet, follow the report formats shown in Section 10.4. However, if the work is for professional publication or intended for a wider audience who will not have access to these sources, cite the sources as personal communications (see Section 8.9).

8.9 Personal Communications

Works that cannot be recovered by readers (i.e., works without a source element; see Section 9.4) are cited in the text as *personal communications*. Personal communications include emails, text messages, online chats or direct messages, personal interviews, telephone conversations, live speeches, unrecorded classroom lectures, memos, letters, messages from nonarchived discussion groups or online bulletin boards, and so on.

Use a personal communication citation only when a recoverable source is not available. For example, if you learned about a topic via a classroom lecture, it would be preferable to cite the research on which the instructor based the lecture. However, if the lecture contained original content not published elsewhere, cite the lecture as a personal communication. When communications are recoverable only in an archive (e.g., a presidential library), cite them as archival materials (see https://apastyle.apa.org for more). Do not use a personal communication citation for quotes or information from participants whom you interviewed as part of your own original research (see also Section 8.36 of the *Publication Manual*).

Citing Personal Communications in the Text. Because readers cannot retrieve the information in personal communications, personal communications are not included in the reference list; they are cited in the text only. Give the initial(s) and surname of the communicator, and provide as exact a date as possible, using the following formats:

> ***Narrative citation:*** E.-M. Paradis (personal communication, August 8, 2019)
> ***Parenthetical citation:*** (T. Nguyen, personal communication, May 24, 2020)

In-Text Citations

8.10 Author–Date Citation System

Use the *author–date citation system* to cite references in the text in APA Style. In this system, each work used in a paper has two parts: an in-text citation and a corresponding reference list entry (see Figure 8.2). The in-text citation appears within the body of the paper (or in a table, figure, footnote, or appendix) and briefly identifies the cited work by its author and date of publication. This in-text citation enables readers to locate the corresponding entry in the alphabetical reference list at the end of the paper. Each reference list entry provides the author, date, title, and source of the work cited in the paper and enables readers to identify and retrieve the work (see Chapter 9 for how to create and order reference list entries).

In an in-text citation, provide the surname(s) of the author(s) or the name(s) of the group author(s). Do not include suffixes such as "Jr." in the in-text citation. (For authors with only one name or

Figure 8.2 Correspondence Between a Reference List Entry and an In-Text Citation

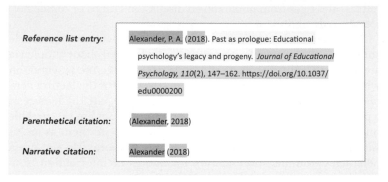

Note. The four elements of a reference list entry include the author (in purple), the date (in blue), the title (in yellow), and the source (in green). The in-text citations that correspond to this reference include the last name of the author and year of publication, which match the information in the reference list entry.

only a username, see Section 9.8.) The list of authors in an in-text citation may be shortened in certain cases (for individual authors, see Section 8.17; for group authors, see Section 8.21). To create an in-text citation for a work with an unknown or anonymous author, see Section 8.14.

The date in the in-text citation should match the date in the reference list entry. Use only the year in the in-text citation, even if the reference list entry contains a more specific date (e.g., year, month, and day). For works with no date, use "n.d." in the in-text citation (see also Section 9.17); for works that have been accepted for publication but have not yet been published, use "in press." Do not use phrases like "in progress" for draft manuscripts; instead, use the year the draft was written.

Each in-text citation must correspond to only one reference list entry. Avoid ambiguity when abbreviating the list of authors (see Sections 8.17 and 8.21), when multiple works have the same author(s) and date (see Section 8.19), and when multiple first authors share the same surname (see Section 8.20).

8.11 Parenthetical and Narrative Citations

In-text citations have two formats: parenthetical and narrative. In parenthetical citations, the author name and publication date (or equivalent information; see Section 9.12) appear in parentheses. In narrative citations, this information is incorporated into the text as part of the sentence.

Parenthetical Citation. Both the author and the date, separated by a comma, appear in parentheses for a parenthetical citation. A parenthetical citation can appear within or at the end of a sentence. When a parenthetical citation is at the end of a sentence, put the period or other end punctuation after the closing parenthesis.

Falsely balanced news coverage can distort the public's perception of expert consensus on an issue (Koehler, 2016).

- If other text appears with the parenthetical citation, use commas around the year.

(see Koehler, 2016, for more detail)

- When text and a citation appear together in parentheses, use a semicolon to separate the citation from the text; do not use parentheses within parentheses.

(e.g., falsely balanced news coverage; Koehler, 2016)

Narrative Citation. The author appears in running text and the date appears in parentheses immediately after the author name for a narrative citation.

Koehler (2016) noted the dangers of falsely balanced news coverage.

- In rare cases, the author and date might both appear in the narrative. In this case, do not use parentheses.

In 2016, Koehler noted the dangers of falsely balanced news coverage.

8.12 Citing Multiple Works

When citing multiple works parenthetically, place the citations in alphabetical order, separating them with semicolons. Listing both parenthetical in-text citations and reference list entries in alphabetical order helps readers locate and retrieve works because they are listed in the same order in both places.

(Adams et al., 2019; Shumway & Shulman, 2015; Westinghouse, 2017)

- Arrange two or more works by the same authors by year of publication. Place citations with no date first, followed by works with dates in chronological order; in-press citations appear last. Give the authors' surnames once; for each subsequent work, give only the date.

(Department of Veterans Affairs, n.d., 2017a, 2017b, 2019)

Zhou (n.d., 2000, 2016, in press)

- In the case of multiple works in which some author names have been abbreviated to "et al." (see Section 8.17), place the citations in chronological order (regardless of the order in which they appear in the reference list).

(Carraway et al., 2013, 2014, 2019)

- To highlight the work(s) most directly relevant to your point in a given sentence, place those citations first within parentheses in alphabetical order and then insert a semicolon and a phrase, such as "see also," before the first of the remaining citations, which should also be in alphabetical order. This strategy allows authors to emphasize, for example, the most recent or most important research on a topic, which would not be reflected by alphabetical order alone.

(Sampson & Hughes, 2020; see also Augustine, 2017; Melara et al., 2018; Pérez, 2014)

- Readers may find a long string of citations difficult to parse, especially if they are using assistive technology such as a screen reader; therefore, include only those citations needed to support your immediate point (for more on appropriate level of citation, see Section 8.1).

- If multiple sources are cited within the narrative of a sentence, they can appear in any order.

Suliman (2018), Gutiérrez (2012, 2017), and Medina and Reyes (2019) examined . . .

8.13 Citing Specific Parts of a Source

To cite a specific part of a source, provide an author–date citation for the work plus information about the specific part. There are many possible parts to cite, including

- pages, paragraphs, sections, tables, figures, supplemental materials, or footnotes from an article, book, report, webpage, or other work

(Centers for Disease Control and Prevention, 2019, p. 10)

(Armstrong, 2015, pp. 3–17)

(Shadid, 2020, paras. 2–3)

(Kovačič & Horvat, 2019, Table 1)

- chapters, forewords, or other sections of authored books

  (Shimamura, 2017, Chapter 3)

- time stamps of videos or audiobooks

  (Beck Institute for Cognitive Behavior Therapy, 2012, 1:30:40)

- slide numbers in PowerPoint presentations

  (Thompson, 2020, Slide 7)

For religious and classical works with canonically numbered parts common across editions (e.g., books, chapters, verses, lines, cantos), cite the part instead of a page number (see Section 9.41 for how to write the reference list entries).

(*King James Bible*, 1769/2017, 1 Cor. 13:1)

(Aristotle, ca. 350 B.C.E./1994, Part IV)

(Shakespeare, 1623/1995, 1.3.36–37)

In the reference list, provide an entry for the entire work (not only the part that you used).

It is possible to cite a specific part of a source whether you are paraphrasing (see Sections 8.23–8.24) or directly quoting (see Sections 8.25–8.27). For further guidance on quoting works without page numbers (e.g., webpages, websites, audiovisual works) and religious and classical works with canonically numbered sections, see Section 8.28.

8.14 Unknown or Anonymous Author

When the author of a work is not named, the author may be unknown (i.e., no author is listed on the work, as with a religious work) or identified specifically as "Anonymous." For works with an unknown author (see Section 9.12), include the title and publication year in the in-text citation (note that the title moves to the author position in the reference list entry as well). If the title of the work is italicized in the reference, also italicize the title in the in-text citation. If the title of the work is not italicized in the reference, use double quotation marks around the title in the in-text citation. Capitalize these titles in the text using title case (see Section 5.7), even though sentence case is used in the reference list entry. If the title is long, shorten it for the in-text citation.

> **Book with no author:** (*Interpersonal Skills*, 2019)
> **Magazine article with no author:** ("Understanding Sensory Memory," 2018)

When the author of a work is overtly designated as "Anonymous" (see Section 9.12), "Anonymous" takes the place of the author name in the in-text citation.

> (Anonymous, 2017)

8.15 Translated, Reprinted, Republished, and Reissued Dates

References to translated, reprinted, republished, or reissued works (see Sections 9.39–9.40) contain two dates in the in-text citation: the year of publication of the original work and the year of publication of the translation, reprint, republication, or reissue. Separate the years with a slash, with the earlier year first (see Chapter 10, Example 29).

> Freud (1900/1953)
> (Piaget, 1966/2000)

8.16 Omitting the Year in Repeated Narrative Citations

In general, include the author and date in every in-text citation. If you need to repeat a citation (see Section 8.1), repeat the entire citation; do not, for example, include only a page number (the abbreviation "ibid." is not used in APA Style). The year can be omitted from a citation only when multiple narrative citations to a work appear within a single paragraph (see Figure 8.3 for an example).

Once you have provided a narrative citation to a work in a paragraph, do not repeat the year in subsequent narrative citations in that same paragraph. Follow this guideline with each paragraph (i.e., include the year in the first narrative citation in a new paragraph). Include the year in every parenthetical citation.

However, if you cite multiple works by the same author or authors, regardless of the publication years, include the date in every in-text citation to prevent ambiguity. For example, if you cite Mohammed and Mahfouz (2017) and Mohammed and Mahfouz (2019), include the year with every citation, even when one of the references is cited multiple times in a single paragraph.

CITATIONS

Figure 8.3 Example of Repeated Narrative Citations With the Year Omitted

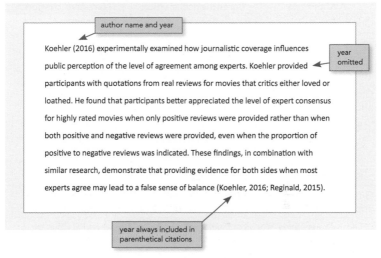

8.17 Number of Authors to Include in In-Text Citations

The format of the author element of the in-text citation changes depending on the number of authors and is abbreviated in some cases. See Table 8.1 for examples of the basic in-text citation styles.

- For a work with one or two authors, include the author name(s) in every citation.
- For a work with three or more authors, include the name of only the first author plus "et al." in every citation, including the first citation, unless doing so would create ambiguity (see Section 8.18).

In parenthetical citations, use an ampersand (&) between names for a work with two authors or before the last author when all names must be included to avoid ambiguity (see Section 8.18). In narrative citations, spell out the word "and."

(Jöreskog & Sörbom, 2007)

Eifert and Yildiz (2018)

In tables and figures, use an ampersand between names in both parenthetical and narrative citations.

The same guidelines apply when any of the authors are groups. For example, if a work is authored by three groups, the in-text citation would include the name of the first group plus "et al."

(American Educational Research Association et al., 2014)

Table 8.1 Basic In-Text Citation Styles

Author type	Parenthetical citation	Narrative citation
One author	(Luna, 2020)	Luna (2020)
Two authors	(Salas & D'Agostino, 2020)	Salas and D'Agostino (2020)
Three or more authors	(Martin et al., 2020)	Martin et al. (2020)
Group author with abbreviation		
First citation [a]	(National Institute of Mental Health [NIMH], 2020)	National Institute of Mental Health (NIMH, 2020)
Subsequent citations	(NIMH, 2020)	NIMH (2020)
Group author without abbreviation	(Stanford University, 2020)	Stanford University (2020)

[a] Define the abbreviation for a group author only once in the text, choosing either the parenthetical or the narrative format. Thereafter, use the abbreviation for all mentions of the group in the text (see Section 8.21).

8.18 Avoiding Ambiguity in In-Text Citations

Sometimes multiple works with three or more authors and the same publication year shorten to the same in-text citation form when the guidelines described in Section 8.17 are applied, which creates ambiguity. To avoid ambiguity, when the in-text citations of multiple works with three or more authors shorten to the same form, write out as many names as needed to distinguish the references, and abbreviate the rest of the names to "et al." in every citation. For example, two works have the following authors:

Kapoor, Bloom, Montez, Warner, and Hill (2017)

Kapoor, Bloom, Zucker, Tang, Köroğlu, L'Enfant, Kim, and Daly (2017)

Both these citations shorten to Kapoor et al. (2017). To avoid ambiguity when citing them both in your paper, cite them as follows:

Kapoor, Bloom, Montez, et al. (2017)

Kapoor, Bloom, Zucker, et al. (2017)

Because "et al." is plural (meaning "and others"), it cannot stand for only one name. When only the final author is different, spell out all names in every citation.

Hasan, Liang, Kahn, and Jones-Miller (2015)

Hasan, Liang, Kahn, and Weintraub (2015)

8.19 Works With the Same Author and Same Date

When multiple references have an identical author (or authors) and publication year, include a lowercase letter after the year (see Section 9.46). The year–letter combination is used in both the in-text citation and the reference list entry. Use only the year with a letter in the in-text citation, even if the reference list entry contains a more specific date.

(Judge & Kammeyer-Mueller, 2012a)

Judge and Kammeyer-Mueller (2012b)

(Sifuentes, n.d.-a, n.d.-b)

8.20 Authors With the Same Surname

If the first authors of multiple references share the same surname but have different initials, include the first authors' initials in all in-text citations, even if the year of publication differs. Initials help avoid confusion within the text and help readers locate the correct entry in the reference list (see Section 9.47).

(J. M. Taylor & Neimeyer, 2015; T. Taylor, 2014)

If the first authors of multiple references share the same surname and the same initials, cite the works in the standard author–date format.

Sometimes people publish under multiple names because of a name change (e.g., transgender authors, authors with a change in marital status). It is seldom relevant to note that two names refer to the same person. When a given name has changed, include initials with in-text citations only when the initials are different. If it is necessary to clarify that two names refer to the same person (e.g., to avoid confusion when reviewing an author's body of work), consult the person and respect their preferences in whether and how to address the name change. If it is necessary to clarify that two names refer to different people to avoid confusion, include the first name of the first author in the in-text citation: "Sarah Williams (2019) stated X, whereas Shonda Williams (2020) stated Y."

If multiple authors within a single reference share the same surname, the initials are not needed in the in-text citation; cite the work in the standard author–date format.

(Chen & Chen, 2019)

8.21 Abbreviating Group Authors

If a reference has a group author, the group name can sometimes be abbreviated—for example, "American Psychological Association" can be abbreviated to "APA." You do not have to abbreviate the name of a group author, but you can if the abbreviation is well-known, will help avoid cumbersome repetition, or will appear at least three times in the paper.

- As with other abbreviations (see Section 5.13), provide the full name of the group on first mention in the text, followed by the abbreviation.

- If the group name first appears in a narrative citation, include the abbreviation before the year in parentheses, separated with a comma.

  The American Psychological Association (APA, 2017) described . . .

- If the group name first appears in a parenthetical citation, include the abbreviation in square brackets, followed by a comma and the year.

  (American Psychological Association [APA], 2017)

- In the reference list entry, do not abbreviate the group author name. Instead, spell out the full name of the group as presented in the source.

  American Psychological Association. (2017, January). *Understanding and over-coming opioid abuse.* https://www.apa.org/helpcenter/opioid-abuse.aspx

- If several references have the same group author, introduce the abbreviation only once in the text.

- In the rare case that two different groups abbreviate to the same form (e.g., both the American Psychological Association and the American Psychiatric Association abbreviate to "APA") and you cite both groups in your paper, spell out each name every time to avoid confusion.

- If a work has three or more group authors, the in-text citation is also shortened as described in Section 8.17.

8.22 General Mentions of Websites, Periodicals, and Common Software and Apps

For a general mention of a website with no indication of particular information or a specific page from that site, no reference list entry or in-text citation is needed. Provide the name of the website in the text and include the URL in parentheses. For example, if you used a website to create a survey, mention the website in the text.

> We created our survey using Qualtrics (https://www.qualtrics.com).

A variation of this technique is also used for general mentions of periodicals. For example, if you want to include the name of a journal you searched during a literature review, provide the journal title in italic title case.

> I searched the *Journal of Abnormal Psychology* for studies to include in the literature review.

Common software and mobile apps are treated in a similar manner; in most cases, it is sufficient to mention the name of the program or app and the version used (if known) in the text, without providing an in-text citation or reference list entry (see Section 10.8).

Paraphrases and Quotations

8.23 Principles of Paraphrasing

A *paraphrase* restates another's idea (or your own previously published idea) in your own words. Paraphrasing is an effective writing strategy because it allows authors to summarize and synthesize information from one or more sources, focus on significant information, and compare and contrast relevant details. Published authors paraphrase their sources most of the time rather than directly quoting them; student authors should emulate this practice by paraphrasing more than directly quoting. Use a professional tone when describing a concept, idea, or finding in your own words (see Section 2.7).

Cite the work you paraphrase in the text using either the narrative or parenthetical format (see Section 8.11).

> Avid readers of science fiction and fantasy books are more likely than readers of other genres to believe in futuristic scenarios—for example, that it will someday be possible to travel to other galaxies or power a car on solar energy (Black et al., 2018).

Although it is not required to provide a page or paragraph number in the citation for a paraphrase, you may include one in addition to the author and year when it would help interested readers locate the relevant passage within a long or complex work (e.g., a book).

> Webster-Stratton (2016) described a case example of a 4-year-old girl who showed an insecure attachment to her mother; in working with the family dyad, the therapist focused on increasing the mother's empathy for her child (pp. 152–153).

The guidelines in this section pertain to when authors read a primary source and paraphrase it themselves. If you read a paraphrase of a primary source in a published work and want to cite that source, it is best to read and cite the primary source directly if possible; if not, use a secondary source citation (see Section 8.6).

8.24 Long Paraphrases

A paraphrase may continue for several sentences. In such cases, cite the work being paraphrased on first mention. Once the work has been cited, it is not necessary to repeat the citation as long as the context of the writing makes it clear that the same work continues to be paraphrased (see Figure 8.4 for an example). The citation may be either parenthetical or narrative; if you select the narrative approach and repeat the author names in the narrative of subsequent sentences, the year of the work can often be omitted (see Section 8.16).

If the paraphrase continues into a new paragraph, reintroduce the citation. If the paraphrase incorporates multiple sources or switches among sources, repeat the citation so the source is clear (see Figure 8.5 for an example). Read your sentences carefully to ensure you have cited sources appropriately.

Figure 8.4 Example of a Long Paraphrase With a Single In-Text Citation

Velez et al. (2018) found that for women of color, sexism and racism in the workplace were associated with poor work and mental health outcomes, including job-related burnout, turnover intentions, and psychological distress. However, self-esteem, person–organization fit, and perceived organizational support mediated these effects. Additionally, stronger womanist attitudes—which acknowledge the unique challenges faced by women of color in a sexist and racist society—weakened the association of workplace discrimination with psychological distress. These findings underscore the importance of considering multiple forms of workplace discrimination in clinical practice and research with women of color, along with efforts to challenge and reduce such discrimination.

Figure 8.5 Example of Repeated Citations Necessary to Clarify Sources

Play therapists can experience many symptoms of impaired wellness, including

emotional exhaustion or reduced ability to empathize with others (Elwood et

al., 2011; Figley, 2002), disruption in personal relationships (Elwood et al., 2011;

Robinson-Keilig, 2014), decreased satisfaction with work (Elwood et al., 2011),

avoidance of particular situations (Figley, 2002; O'Halloran & Linton, 2000), and

feelings or thoughts of helplessness (Elwood et al., 2011; Figley, 2002; O'Halloran

& Linton, 2000).

Note. In this passage, some works are cited multiple times to support multiple points. It is necessary to repeat these citations because different combinations of works support different ideas—the sources change and thus must be made clear to readers. If all ideas had the same sources, it would not be necessary to repeat the citations.

8.25 Principles of Direct Quotation

A *direct quotation* reproduces words verbatim from another work or from your own previously published work. It is best to paraphrase sources (see Sections 8.23–8.24) rather than directly quoting them because paraphrasing allows you to fit material to the context of your paper and writing style. Use direct quotations rather than paraphrasing when reproducing an exact definition (see example in Section 4.15), when an author has said something memorably or succinctly, or when you want to respond to exact wording (e.g., something someone said). Instructors and institutions may establish limits on the use of direct quotations. Consult with your instructor if you are concerned that you may have too much quoted material in your paper.

When quoting directly, always provide the author, year, and page number of the quotation in the in-text citation in either parenthetical or narrative format (see Section 8.11). To indicate a single page, use the abbreviation "p." (e.g., p. 25, p. S41, p. e221); for multiple pages, use the abbreviation "pp." and separate the page range with an en dash (e.g., pp. 34–36). If pages are discontinuous, use a comma between the page numbers (e.g., pp. 67, 72). If the work does not have page numbers, provide another way for readers to locate the quotation (see Section 8.28).

The format of a direct quotation depends on its length (fewer than 40 words vs. 40 words or more; see Sections 8.26–8.27). Regardless of quotation length, do not insert an ellipsis at the beginning and/ or end of a quotation unless the original source includes an ellipsis. If you need to make changes to a direct quotation, see Sections 8.30 and 8.31. For other uses of quotation marks, such as when presenting verbatim instructions to participants, see Section 4.7. To reproduce material that is already a direct quotation in the work you are citing, see Section 8.33.

8.26 Short Quotations (Fewer Than 40 Words)

If a quotation consists of fewer than 40 words, treat it as a short quotation: Incorporate it into the text and enclose it within double quotation marks. For a direct quotation, always include a full citation (parenthetical or narrative) in the same sentence as the quotation. Place a parenthetical citation either immediately after the quotation or at the end of the sentence. For a narrative citation, include the author and year in the sentence and then place the page number or other location information in parentheses after the quotation; if the quotation precedes the narrative citation, put the page number or location information after the year and a comma.

If the citation appears at the end of a sentence, put the end punctuation after the closing parenthesis for the citation. If the quotation includes citations, see Section 8.32; if the quotation includes material already in quotation marks, see Section 8.33. Place periods and commas within closing single or double quotation marks. Place other punctuation marks inside quotation marks only when they are part of the quoted material.

Short quotations can be presented in a variety of ways, as shown in Table 8.2.

8.27 Block Quotations (40 Words or More)

If a quotation contains 40 words or more, treat it as a block quotation. Do not use quotation marks to enclose a block quotation. Start a block quotation on a new line and indent the whole block 0.5 in. from the left margin. If there are additional paragraphs within the quotation, indent the first line of each subsequent paragraph an additional 0.5 in. Double-space the entire block quotation; do not add extra space before or after it. Either (a) cite the source in parentheses after the quotation's final punctuation or (b) cite the author and year in the narrative before the quotation and place only the

Table 8.2 Examples of Direct Quotations Cited in the Text

Correct	Incorrect	Rationale
Effective teams can be difficult to describe because "high performance along one domain does not translate to high performance along another" (Ervin et al., 2018, p. 470).	Effective teams can be difficult to describe because "high performance along one domain does not translate to high performance along another." (Ervin et al., 2018, p. 470)	The period marking the end of a sentence should follow the citation, not precede it.
"Even smart, educated, emotionally stable adults believe superstitions that they recognize are not rational," as exemplified by the existence of people who knock on wood for good luck (Risen, 2016, p. 202).	"Even smart, educated, emotionally stable adults believe superstitions that they recognize are not rational (Risen, 2016, p. 202)," as exemplified by the existence of people who knock on wood for good luck.	The citation should be outside the quotation marks, not within them.
Biebel et al. (2018) noted that "incorporating the voice of students with psychiatric disabilities into supported education services can increase access, involvement, and retention" (p. 299).	Biebel et al. (2018) noted that "incorporating the voice of students with psychiatric disabilities into supported education services can increase access, involvement, and retention." (p. 299)	The period marking the end of the sentence should follow the page number, not precede it.
"Some people are hilarious, others are painfully unfunny, and most are somewhere in between," wrote Nusbaum et al. (2017, p. 231) in their exploration of humor.	"Some people are hilarious, others are painfully unfunny, and most are somewhere in between," (p. 231) wrote Nusbaum et al. (2017) in their exploration of humor.	The page number should be within the same parentheses as the year when the quotation precedes the narrative citation.
The item read, "What were the best aspects of the program for you?" (Shayden et al., 2018, p. 304).	The item read, "What were the best aspects of the program for you"? (Shayden et al., 2018, p. 304).	The question mark that ends the quotation should appear within the quotation marks.
In 2018, Soto argued that "more similar stimuli, such as those coming from the same modality, produce more configural processing" (p. 598).	In 2018, Soto argued that "more similar stimuli, such as those coming from the same modality, produce more configural processing" (Soto, 2018, p. 598).	It is not necessary to repeat the author and year within parentheses when they already appear in the narrative.

page number in parentheses after the quotation's final punctuation. Do not add a period after the closing parenthesis in either case.

Block quotation with parenthetical citation:

Researchers have studied how people talk to themselves:

> Inner speech is a paradoxical phenomenon. It is an experience that is central to many people's everyday lives, and yet it presents considerable challenges to any effort to study it scientifically. Nevertheless, a wide range of methodologies and approaches have combined to shed light on the subjective experience of inner speech and its cognitive and neural underpinnings. (Alderson-Day & Fernyhough, 2015, p. 957)

Block quotation with narrative citation:

Flores et al. (2018) described how they addressed potential researcher bias when working with an intersectional community of transgender people of color:

> Everyone on the research team belonged to a stigmatized group but also held privileged identities. Throughout the research process, we attended to the ways in which our privileged and oppressed identities may have influenced the research process, findings, and presentation of results. (p. 311)

Block quotation consisting of two paragraphs:

Regarding implications for chronic biases in expectation formation,

> in order to accurately estimate whether people are likely to form positive or negative expectations on any given occasion, it is necessary to go beyond simply considering chronic individual differences and identify the factors that make people more likely to form expectations in line with one bias or the other.
>
> The present research sheds light on this issue by identifying a crucial distinction in the operation of these two trait biases in expectation formation. Specifically, people's valence weighting biases and self-beliefs about the future appear to shape expectations via qualitatively distinct processes. (Niese et al., 2019, p. 210)

If the block quotation includes citations, see Section 8.32; if the block quotation includes material already in quotation marks, see Section 8.33.

8.28 Direct Quotation of Material Without Page Numbers

Textual Works. To directly quote from written material that does not contain page numbers (e.g., webpages and websites, some ebooks), provide readers with another way of locating the quoted passage. Any of the following approaches is acceptable; use the approach that will best help readers find the quotation.

- Provide a heading or section name.

For people with osteoarthritis, "painful joints should be moved through a full range of motion every day to maintain flexibility and to slow deterioration of cartilage" (Gecht-Silver & Duncombe, 2015, Osteoarthritis section).

- Provide an abbreviated heading or section name in quotation marks to indicate the abbreviation if the full heading or section name is too long or unwieldy to cite in full. In the next example, the original heading was "What Can You Do to Prevent Kidney Failure?" and the items are quoted separately because they originally appeared as part of a bulleted list.

To prevent kidney failure, patients should "get active," "quit smoking," and "take medications as directed" (Centers for Disease Control and Prevention, 2017, "What Can You Do" section).

- Provide a paragraph number (count the paragraphs manually if they are not numbered).

People planning for retirement need more than just money—they also "need to stockpile their emotional reserves" to ensure adequate support from family and friends (Chamberlin, 2014, para. 1).

- Provide a heading or section name in combination with a paragraph number.

Music and language are intertwined in the brain such that "people who are better at rhythmic memory skills tend to excel at language skills as well" (DeAngelis, 2018, Musical Forays section, para. 4).

Do not include Kindle location numbers with in-text citations. Instead, provide the page number (which is available in many Kindle books, especially those based on print editions) or use the methods described in this section (e.g., provide a chapter and paragraph number, name of a heading or section) to create a page number alternative.

Note that the name of the section or other part of the work will not necessarily appear in the reference list entry for the work. For example, if you cite a particular section of a webpage or website in the text, the reference list entry should be for the page you used, not for only that section of the page.

Audiovisual Works. To directly quote from an audiovisual work (e.g., audiobook, YouTube video, TED Talk, TV show), provide a time stamp for the beginning of the quotation in place of a page number.

People make "sweeping inferences and judgments from body language" (Cuddy, 2012, 2:12).

Works With Canonically Numbered Sections. To directly quote from material with canonically numbered sections (e.g., religious or classical works; see also Section 9.41 and Chapter 10, Examples 35–37), use the name of the book, chapter, verse, line, and/or canto instead of a page number.

> The person vowed to "set me as a seal upon thine heart" (*King James Bible*, 1769/2017, Song of Solomon 8:6).

For plays, cite the act, scene, and line(s). In the following example, "1.3.36–37" refers to Act 1, Scene 3, Lines 36 and 37.

> In *Much Ado About Nothing*, Don John said, "In the meantime / let me be that I am and seek not to alter me" (Shakespeare, 1623/1995, 1.3.36–37).

See Section 8.13 for further guidance on citing specific parts of a source (e.g., chapters, paragraphs, sections, tables, and figures of articles, books, and reports; time stamps in videos or audiobooks; slide numbers of PowerPoint presentations; canonically numbered parts of religious and classical works).

8.29 Accuracy of Quotations

Direct quotations must be accurate. Except as noted here and in Sections 8.30 and 8.31, the quotation must match the wording, spelling, and interior punctuation of the original source, even if the source is incorrect. If any incorrect spelling, punctuation, or grammar in the source might confuse readers, insert the word "[*sic*]," italicized and in brackets, immediately after the error in the quotation. (See Section 8.31 regarding the use of square brackets to clarify meaning in quotations.) A quotation that includes an error may be distracting, so consider paraphrasing instead. When quoting, always check your paper against the source to ensure that there are no discrepancies.

> Nowak (2019) wrote that "people have an obligation to care for there [*sic*] pets" (p. 52).

8.30 Changes to a Quotation Requiring No Explanation

Some changes can be made to direct quotations without alerting readers:

- The first letter of the first word in a quotation may be changed to an uppercase or a lowercase letter to fit the context of the sentence in which the quotation appears.

- Some punctuation marks at the end of a quotation may be changed to fit the syntax of the sentence in which the quotation appears, as long as meaning is not changed (e.g., it might alter meaning to change a period to a question mark, depending on how the sentence is written).

- Single quotation marks may be changed to double quotation marks and vice versa.

- Footnote or endnote number callouts can be omitted (see also Section 8.32).

Any other changes (e.g., italicizing words for emphasis or omitting words; see Section 8.31) must be explicitly indicated. For more on quoting from a bulleted list without reproducing the bullets, see the second example in Section 8.28.

8.31 Changes to a Quotation Requiring Explanation

Some changes to direct quotations require explanation, as shown in the example in Figure 8.6.

Omitting Material. Use an ellipsis to indicate that you have omitted words within a quotation (e.g., to shorten a sentence or tie two sentences together). Either type three periods with spaces around each (. . .) or use the ellipsis character created by your word-processing program when you type three periods in a row (...), with a space before and after. Do not use an ellipsis at the beginning or end of any

Figure 8.6 Example of Changes Made to a Direct Quotation

"adults" added in brackets to clarify meaning

quote shortened with ellipsis

De Backer and Fisher (2012) noted that "those [adults] who read gossip magazines, watch gossip-related television shows, or read gossip articles from internet sites . . . may feel guilty about wasting their time on a leisure pursuit" (p. 421). They emphasized that "it is important to remember that *gossip helped our ancestors survive* [emphasis added], and thus by accessing gossip, one is faced with an opportunity to vicariously learn solution [sic] to adaptive problems" (De Backer & Fisher, 2012, p. 421).

error in original noted

"emphasis added" noted to indicate new italics

quotation unless the original source includes an ellipsis; start or end the quotation at the point where the source's text you are quoting begins or ends. Use four periods—that is, a period plus an ellipsis (. ...)—to show a sentence break within omitted material, such as when a quotation includes the end of one sentence and the beginning of another sentence.

Inserting Material. Use square brackets, not parentheses, to enclose material such as an addition or explanation you have inserted in a quotation.

Adding Emphasis. If you want to emphasize a word or words in a quotation, use italics. Immediately after the italicized words, insert "emphasis added" within square brackets: [emphasis added].

8.32 Quotations That Contain Citations to Other Works

When quoting material that contains embedded citations, include the citations within the quotation. Do not include these works in the reference list unless you cite them as primary sources elsewhere in your paper. In the following example, Panero et al. (2016) would appear in the reference list, but the Stanislavski citations would not:

> Students of acting "are encouraged to become immersed in a character's life (Stanislavski, 1936/1948, 1950), an activity that calls for absorption" (Panero et al., 2016, p. 234).

Footnote or endnote number callouts in the quoted material can be omitted with no explanation (see Section 8.30).

If citations appear at the end of material you want to quote, it is common practice to end the quotation before the citations and to cite only the work you read (see Figure 8.7 for an example). It is appropriate to omit the citations at the end of a quotation when the material you quote represents a new approach to or conceptualization of the ideas presented in the cited works—for example, when authors have summarized a body of work and you want to quote and cite that summary. If you want to quote the same material that was quoted in the work you are citing, see Section 8.33.

8.33 Quotations That Contain Material Already in Quotation Marks

If your source includes a direct quotation from another work, and you would like to use the same direct quotation in your paper, it is best to read and cite the original source directly. If the original source is unavailable, cite the quotation using the secondary source (see Section 8.6).

When quoting material that already includes quotation marks for some other purpose (e.g., to enclose a phrase such as a coined expression or linguistic example; see Section 4.7), you may need to change double quotation marks to single or vice versa in your paper depending on the number of words you are quoting.

Short Quotations. For quotations of fewer than 40 words, use single quotation marks within double quotation marks to set off material that was enclosed in double quotation marks in the original source.

> *Correct:* Bliese et al. (2017) noted that "mobile devices enabled employees in many jobs to work 'anywhere, anytime' and stay electronically tethered to work outside formal working hours" (p. 391).

> *Incorrect:* Bliese et al. (2017) noted that "mobile devices enabled employees in many jobs to work "anywhere, anytime" and stay electronically tethered to work outside formal working hours" (p. 391).

Figure 8.7 Example of Citations Omitted at the End of a Quotation

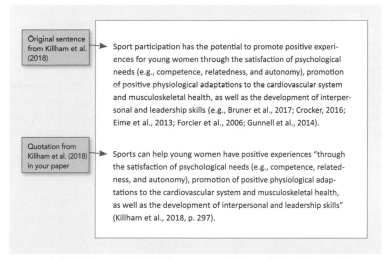

Original sentence from Killham et al. (2018) → Sport participation has the potential to promote positive experiences for young women through the satisfaction of psychological needs (e.g., competence, relatedness, and autonomy), promotion of positive physiological adaptations to the cardiovascular system and musculoskeletal health, as well as the development of interpersonal and leadership skills (e.g., Bruner et al., 2017; Crocker, 2016; Eime et al., 2013; Forcier et al., 2006; Gunnell et al., 2014).

Quotation from Killham et al. (2018) in your paper → Sports can help young women have positive experiences "through the satisfaction of psychological needs (e.g., competence, relatedness, and autonomy), promotion of positive physiological adaptations to the cardiovascular system and musculoskeletal health, as well as the development of interpersonal and leadership skills" (Killham et al., 2018, p. 297).

Note. In the original passage, Killham et al. (2018) summarized the results of many studies and cited their sources at the end of the sentence. To quote Killham et al.'s summary in your paper, cite Killham et al., and omit the citations at the end of the original sentence. Interested readers can consult Killham et al. for further information.

Block Quotations. Use double quotation marks around quoted material that appears within a block quotation. (If the original quotation marks were single quotation marks, as in British-style publications, change them to double quotation marks in your paper.)

Correct:

It is also worth considering the need for subjective certainty:

>If a conjecture is just mere guess, one would not expect the same bias to occur, because it might likely come along with the metacognition of "I know I am/was just guessing," which would counteract retrospectively increased perceptions of foreseeability. (von der Beck & Cress, 2018, p. 97)

Incorrect:

It is also worth considering the need for subjective certainty:

>If a conjecture is just mere guess, one would not expect the same bias to occur, because it might likely come along with the metacognition of 'I know I am/was just guessing,' which would counteract retrospectively increased perceptions of foreseeability. (von der Beck & Cress, 2018, p. 97)

8.34 Epigraphs

An epigraph is a quotation that is used to introduce an article, book, chapter, dissertation, or other work. Authors may use an epigraph to set the stage for what follows or to serve as a summary or counterpoint. The epigraph should appear before the first line of text and should be indented 0.5 in. from the left margin, like a block quotation, without quotation marks.

The source of an epigraph is not usually listed in the reference list unless the work is cited elsewhere in the text of the paper or is important within the context of the topic. If the source of the epigraph is not included in the reference list, then on the line below the quotation, provide the credit line—consisting of an em dash and then the author's full name, a comma, and the title of the work in which the quotation appeared—and align it to the right.

>Research is formalized curiosity. It is poking and prying with a purpose.
>
>—Zora Neale Hurston, *Dust Tracks on a Road*

However, do provide a reference list entry for an epigraph from an academic source (e.g., scholarly book or journal) or a quotation used with permission. The parenthetical citation, including the author, date, and page number, appears after the end punctuation of the quotation with no line break. The example quotation comes from a republished work (see Chapter 10, Example 29).

>If life is to be sustained, hope must remain, even where confidence is wounded, trust impaired. (Erikson, 1966/2000, p. 192)

Copyright and Permission

8.35 General Guidelines for Reprinting or Adapting Materials

Most of the time, authors need to provide only an author–date in-text citation and a reference list entry to properly credit the words or ideas of other authors. However, according to U.S. copyright law, reprinting or adapting certain kinds of works (e.g., figures published in journal articles, images from websites, lengthy quotations) requires a more comprehensive acknowledgment of the copyright status of the reprinted or adapted work in the form of a *copyright attribution*, a brief statement providing details of the original work and naming the copyright holder (see Section 8.39 for formatting guidance).

Reprinting means reproducing material exactly as it appeared originally, without modifications, in the way in which it was intended to be understood. *Adapting* refers to modifying material so that it is suitable for a new purpose (e.g., using part of a table or figure in a new table or figure in your paper). A copyright attribution is used instead of an author–date in-text citation to credit reprinted or adapted works; each of these works also should appear in the reference list. For a subset of cases (see Section 8.38), authors also need to seek and obtain explicit written permission from the copyright holder to reprint or adapt the material—a process that can take substantial time and comes with no guarantee that the copyright holder will consent to the use. These policies are a matter of law, not specifically of APA Style, and writers, including students whose work will not be formally published, should follow them.

8.36 Materials That Require a Copyright Attribution

The following are examples of materials that authors often want to reprint or adapt that may require a copyright attribution; they may also require permission (see Section 8.38). Other materials may also require a copyright attribution and permission before they can be reprinted or adapted, such as data sets, songs, poetry, and art.

- **figures, tables, and other images:** Most types of visual displays require a copyright attribution to reprint or adapt, including tables and figures published in journal articles, books, reports, webpages and websites, and other works, as well as images from the internet such as illustrations, infographics, photographs, screenshots, and most clip art. Depending on the work's place of publication and copyright status, permission may or may not be required. Copyright ownership and permission status can be particularly difficult to establish for images downloaded from the internet, but it is still necessary in most cases to check the status.

- **test and scale items, questionnaires, vignettes, and so forth:** Items reprinted or adapted from copyrighted and commercially available tests or scales (e.g., Minnesota Multiphasic Personality Inventory–2, Wechsler Adult Intelligence Scale, Stanford–Binet Intelligence Scales) require a copyright attribution and permission. Obtaining these permissions can be difficult and time consuming; a preferable alternative to reproducing the exact items in your paper may be to instead reword or paraphrase those items. Permission is required, and may be denied, to reproduce even one item from such instruments.

- **long quotations:** Although most quotations taken from a published work need only an author–date citation, long quotations, the definition of which varies by copyright holder, may require permission. When needed, request permission to reproduce the quotation and provide a copyright attribution crediting the source. It is the author's responsibility to determine the policy of each copyright holder; large publishers usually provide their permission policies on their websites.

Two special cases of material with copyright requirements are commercial stock photography and clip art. If you find photos, clip art, and other images via an online search engine, the guidelines in this section apply to those search results, too.

- **commercial stock photography:** Unless a stock image has a Creative Commons license (see Section 8.37) or is in the public domain, it is not permissible to reproduce it without purchasing a license from the vendor. Commonly used vendors of stock images are Getty Images, Shutterstock, and iStock. A license usually allows the license holder to reproduce the image without a copyright attribution; however, without your own license, you cannot reproduce the image.

- **clip art:** Most clip art does not require permission to reproduce, but it may require a copyright attribution. For clip art included with a computer program (e.g., Microsoft Word), purchase of the program provides a license for that clip art, and you can use it in an academic paper without a copyright attribution or author–date citation. If the clip art comes from a free clip art website, check the copyright status of the image to determine whether a copyright attribution or citation is needed (see Section 8.37 and Example 87 in Chapter 10).

8.37 Copyright Status

The copyright status of a work determines how you are allowed to use it in your own paper. Copyright is usually indicated on the first page of an article, on the copyright page of a book or report, below an image published online, or in the footer of a website.

The following are some common copyright statuses:

- **standard copyright:** Copyright is often indicated simply by the word "copyright" or the copyright symbol.

  Copyright 2020 by the American Psychological Association.

  © 2018 Bianca T. Burquest, all rights reserved.

  Determining who holds a copyright can sometimes be challenging, particularly for older works, because publishers may merge and copyrights may change hands. Materials described in Section 8.36 require a copyright attribution, and permission may be required as well.

- **Creative Commons copyright:** Creative Commons licenses are indicated by "Creative Commons" or "CC." Most Creative Commons licenses allow you to reprint and/or adapt a work (including images) without permission from the copyright holder as long as you give credit to the original author in the form of a copyright attribution, note the license type, and indicate whether you have adapted the original. The specific terms of Creative Commons licenses vary, so check the license associated with the work you want to reproduce to determine what you are allowed to do and what specific copyright attributions, if any, are required.

- **public domain:** Works that are not bound by copyright are considered to be in the public domain. This means that you can reprint them and/or adapt them however you want, so long as you credit the original author in the form of a copyright attribution. Assume that a work is under copyright unless you see the words "public domain" on it or the work was produced by the U.S. government (in which case it is automatically in the public domain). Although copyright does expire with time—meaning that works that were once copyrighted may now be in the public domain—the laws governing this process are complex and vary by country; consult a librarian if you have questions regarding expired copyrights.

- **no copyright indicated:** If no copyright is indicated, treat the material as copyrighted. U.S. copyright law states that a work is copyrighted as soon as it is fixed in tangible form (e.g., when you can see it on a computer screen or on paper), even if the work does not have the word "copyright" or the copyright symbol on it, and even if it is not widely distributed or professionally published. For example, students automatically own the copyright to their classroom assignments.

8.38 Permission and Fair Use

Permission is never required to reproduce works with a Creative Commons license or works in the public domain; however, a copyright attribution is still required in most cases. For copyrighted works (or works with unknown copyright), the nature of the original publication (i.e., a scholarly work vs. a commercial publication) and the concept of fair use govern whether permission is needed.

Scholarly Works. The journal publisher typically owns the copyright for material published in its journals. Many scientific, technical, and medical publishers (including APA) do not require permission or charge fees to reproduce content under the following circumstances:

- The purpose of the use is scholarly comment, noncommercial research, or educational.
- Full credit is given to the author and the publisher as copyright holders through a complete and accurate copyright attribution.
- A maximum total of three figures or tables are being reprinted or adapted from a journal article or book chapter.
- Single text extracts being reprinted are fewer than 400 words, or a series of text extracts being reprinted totals fewer than 800 words. For quotations under these thresholds, use an author–date citation (permission and copyright attributions are not required).

All publishers have their own permission policies, which may differ from guidelines provided here and may cover cases not described in this section (e.g., reproducing whole articles or chapters). Check with the publisher of the material to determine whether permission is necessary.

Fair Use. You may be able to reprint or adapt a copyrighted work as described in Section 8.36 without permission if your use is considered "fair." *Fair use* is a loosely defined and complex legal concept (for a summary, see U.S. Copyright Office, 2019) but, in general, means that under certain circumstances it is permissible to reprint or adapt a copyrighted table, figure, image, test item, questionnaire, or long quotation without obtaining permission as long as you credit the work with a copyright attribution. If in doubt, check with the copyright holder to determine what they consider fair use, especially for items from measures, questionnaires, scales, tests, or instruments. However, the use is probably fair if it meets the following criteria:

- It is for use in an academic work and not for profit (e.g., paper for a class, article in a scholarly journal).

- It represents facts or data (e.g., a chart or diagram) rather than creative self-expression (e.g., artwork, although some famous works of art are in the public domain and thus do not require permission).

- It is small in relation to the entire work (e.g., a chart within a report) and is not the whole work or the heart of the work (e.g., a whole cartoon).

- Reproducing the work will not hurt the market or potential market for the original.

Permission for Photographs of Identifiable People. If you photographed a person who is identifiable in the photograph, you must submit a signed release from that person along with the paper. This is not a matter of copyright but rather of permission from the individual to have their likeness reproduced. It is not necessary to mention the release in the paper or to write a copyright attribution for such a photograph. No release is necessary if the photograph is of one of the authors of the paper.

Securing Permission. When permission is required, you must request permission to reproduce the material in all formats (e.g., both print and electronic) from the copyright holder. Many publishers provide a way for authors to request permission on their websites (e.g., to request permission to reprint or adapt material published by APA, see https://on.apa.org/2Aswon8). The permission request should specify the details about the material (e.g., title of the work, year of publication, page number) and the nature of the reuse (e.g., in a course paper). Some publishers also require that you obtain permission from the author of the original work. Publishers normally grant permission contingent on the inclusion of a copyright attribution and payment of a fee per table, figure, or page.

Allow ample time (several weeks) to secure permission. Once permission is granted, you need to

- obtain that permission in writing;
- provide copies of permission letters when submitting the assignment; and
- include a copyright attribution in the paper, following the wording and format described in Section 8.39 or the specific wording provided by the copyright holder.

8.39 Copyright Attribution Formats

An APA Style copyright attribution contains information from the reference list entry of the work, but that information is presented in a different order than in the reference list entry and with additional information about the material's copyright and permission status. To write a copyright attribution,

- state whether the material was reprinted or adapted (use "From" for reprintings and "Adapted from" for adaptations);
- provide the title, author, year of publication, and source of the material;
- indicate the material's copyright status, which will be the copyright year and the name of the copyright holder, a statement that the work is licensed in the Creative Commons, or a statement that the work is in the public domain; and
- provide the permission statement as requested by the copyright holder if permission was sought and obtained.

Place the copyright attribution as follows:

- For a reprinted or adapted table, figure, or other image, place the copyright attribution at the end of the general note for the table or figure (see Sections 7.14 and 7.28).
- For reproduced test items, questionnaires, or long quotations, place the copyright attribution in a footnote to the reproduced text (see Section 1.13).

See Table 8.3 for copyright attribution templates and Table 8.4 for examples. See Chapter 7 for examples in context, including

- a reprinted figure that does not require permission (Figure 7.3 in Section 7.32) and
- a reprinted figure in the public domain (Figure 7.8 in Section 7.32).

When you use a copyright attribution, also provide a reference list entry for the work. However, the copyright attribution is used instead of an in-text citation; it is not necessary to include both.

Table 8.3 Copyright Attribution Templates

Source [a]	Reprinted/ adapted status	Source information	Copyright status	Permission statement [b]
Journal, magazine, newspaper, or blog	From or Adapted from	"Title of Article," by A. A. Author and B. B. Author, year, *Title of Periodical, Volume* (Issue), p. xx (DOI or URL).	Copyright year by Name of Copyright Holder. or In the public domain. or CC BY-NC. [c]	Reprinted with permission. or Adapted with permission.
Authored book or report		*Title of Book or Report* (p. xx), by A. A. Author and B. B. Author, year, Publisher (DOI or URL).		
Edited book chapter		"Title of Chapter," by A. A. Author and B. B. Author, in E. E. Editor and F. F. Editor (Eds.), *Title of Book* (any edition or volume number, p. xx), year, Publisher (DOI or URL).		
Webpage or website		*Title of Webpage*, by A. A. Author and B. B. Author, year, Site Name (DOI or URL). or *Title of Webpage*, by Group Author Same as Site Name, year (DOI or URL). [d]		

[a] For works not listed here, provide the title, author, year, and source information for the work as appropriate. [b] Include a permission statement only if permission has been sought and obtained. [c] For Creative Commons licenses (e.g., CC BY-NC, CC BY 4.0), use the specified abbreviation for the type of license associated with the material you are reprinting or adapting; "CC BY-NC" is just one example. [d] For webpages, omit the site name when the site name and author are the same, which is often the case with group authors.

Table 8.4 Example Copyright Attributions for Reprinted or Adapted Tables and Figures

Work from which the table or figure was reproduced	Example copyright attribution
Journal article, if copyrighted and if no permission needed	From "Romantic Relationship Development: The Interplay Between Age and Relationship Length," by A. Lantagne and W. Furman, 2017, *Developmental Psychology, 53*(9), p. 1744 (https://doi.org/10.1037/dev0000363). Copyright 2017 by the American Psychological Association.
Journal article, if Creative Commons license	Adapted from "Comprehensive Overview of Computer-Based Health Information Tailoring: A Systematic Scoping Review," by A. K. Ghalibaf, E. Nazari, M. Gholian-Aval, and M. Tara, 2019, *BMJ Open, 9*, p. 6 (https://doi.org/cz6h). CC BY-NC.
Whole book, if copyrighted and if no permission needed	Adapted from *Managing Therapy-Interfering Behavior: Strategies From Dialectical Behavior Therapy* (p. 172), by A. L. Chapman and M. Z. Rosenthal, 2016, American Psychological Association (https://doi.org/10.1037/14752-000). Copyright 2016 by the American Psychological Association.
Edited book chapter, if copyrighted and if permission needed	From "Pharmacokinetics," by V. Yellepeddi, in K. Whalen (Ed.), *Pharmacology* (6th ed., p. 2), 2015, Wolters Kluwer. Copyright 2015 by Wolters Kluwer. Reprinted with permission.
Webpage or website, if in the public domain	From *What Parents Can Expect in Behavior Therapy*, by Centers for Disease Control and Prevention, 2017 (https://www.cdc.gov/ncbddd/adhd/infographics/what-parents-expect.html). In the public domain.
Data from the U.S. Census Bureau, in the public domain	Data are from "Annual Estimates of the Resident Population for the United States, Regions, States, and Puerto Rico: April 1, 2010 to July 1, 2018 (NST-EST2018-01)," by the U.S. Census Bureau, 2018 (http://bit.ly/2v0bucA). In the public domain.

Note. This table shows examples of copyright attributions you would include when reprinting or adapting a table or figure from another work in an academic paper. Place the copyright attribution for a reprinted or adapted table or figure at the end of the table or figure general note (see, e.g., Figure 7.3). See Sections 8.35 to 8.38 to determine when a copyright attribution (and possibly also permission) is necessary. You may need to use different wording from that shown here depending on the requirements of the copyright holder.

9

REFERENCE LIST

The reference list at the end of a paper provides the information necessary to identify and retrieve each work cited in the text. The works included in your reference list should be only those that you used in the research for and writing of your paper. APA Style papers require reference lists unless an instructor or institution specifically requests bibliographies. A reference list cites works that specifically support the ideas, claims, and concepts in a paper; in contrast, a bibliography cites works for background or further reading and may include descriptive notes (e.g., an annotated bibliography; see Section 1.3).

This chapter provides guidelines for creating reference list entries. We include specific sections focusing on each reference element (author, date, title, source) and explain how to order entries in an APA Style reference list. For more information on crediting works in the text and formatting in-text citations, see Chapter 8; for examples of specific reference types, see Chapter 10 (these examples are cross-referenced within this chapter).

Reference Categories

9.1 Determining the Reference Category

References in the *Concise Guide* are organized by group, category, and type. *Reference groups* are textual works; data sets, software, and tests; audiovisual media; and online media. Each group contains numbered *reference categories*. For example, the textual works group contains the categories of periodicals, books and reference works, edited book chapters and reference work entries, and dissertations and theses. The online media group contains the categories of social media and webpages and websites. Within each category are different *reference types*. For example, the periodical reference category includes journal articles, magazine articles, newspaper articles, and blog posts. The social media reference category includes tweets, Facebook posts, and Instagram photos.

To create a reference list entry, first determine the reference group and category and then choose the appropriate reference type within the category and follow that example. If the work you want to cite does not match any example, choose the group, category, and type that are most similar and adapt the format using the elements shown in the relevant template. How a work was accessed or obtained (e.g., online, in print, via interlibrary loan) and how it is formatted (e.g., print, PDF, DVD, online streaming video) have little, if any, impact on the reference list entry. See Chapter 10 for reference templates and examples.

9.2 Using the Webpages and Websites Reference Category

The term "website" can cause confusion because people use it to refer to both a reference category (see Section 10.14) and a method of retrieval (i.e., online). Many types of works can be retrieved online, including articles, books, reports, and data sets, but only some works fall into the webpages and websites reference category. Use that category only when the work does not better fit within another category. First ask yourself, "What type of work is on this website?" Then choose the reference category in Chapter 10 that is most similar to the work you want to cite and follow the most relevant example. For example, to cite a report from a government website, use the reports category (Section 10.4) and follow the format for a government report (see Chapter 10, Examples 50–52). Likewise, to cite a webpage from a government website, use the webpages and websites category (Section 10.14) and follow the format for a work on a website (see Chapter 10, Examples 98–102). Note that the author of a webpage or website may be difficult to determine or may be identified through context (see Section 9.7), and webpages and websites often have unknown dates of publication (see Section 9.17).

9.3 Online and Print References

APA Style references for online and print works are largely the same. All references generally include the author, date, title, and source; differences between online and print versions are evident within the source element. The *source element* includes information about where the work came from (e.g., a periodical's title, a book's or report's publisher, a website's name). References for works with DOIs also include the DOI in the source element, and references for most online works without DOIs include the work's URL (see Section 9.34 for more on when to include DOIs and URLs). However, database information and/or database URLs are not usually included in references (see Section 9.30 for an explanation and a few exceptions). Thus, the same template can be used to create a reference for both the print and online versions of a work. Use only one template (not multiple templates) to create your reference entry.

Principles of Reference List Entries

9.4 Four Elements of a Reference

A reference generally has four elements: author, date, title, and source. Each element answers a question:

- **author:** Who is responsible for this work?
- **date:** When was this work published?
- **title:** What is this work called?
- **source:** Where can I retrieve this work?

Considering these four elements and answering these four questions will help you create a reference for any type of work, even if you do not see a specific example that matches it. See the sections on the author (Sections 9.7–9.12), date (Sections 9.13–9.17), title (Sections 9.18–9.22), and source (Sections 9.23–9.37) for more information on each element. Figure 9.1 shows an example of an article title page highlighting the locations of the reference elements and showing their placement in a reference list entry.

Sometimes reference elements are unknown or missing and the reference list entry must be adapted. See Table 9.1 for a summary of how reference elements are assembled and adjusted when information is missing.

Figure 9.1 Example of Where to Find Reference Information for a Journal Article

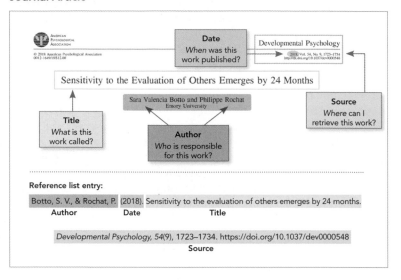

9.5 Punctuation Within Reference List Entries

Use punctuation marks within reference list entries to group information.

- Ensure that a period appears after each reference element—that is, after the author, date, title, and source. However, do not put a period after a DOI or URL because it may interfere with link functionality.

- Use punctuation marks (usually commas or parentheses) between parts of the same reference element. For example, in a reference for a journal article, use a comma between each author's last name and initials and between different authors' names, between the journal name and the volume number, and between the journal issue number and the page numbers. Do not use a comma between the journal volume and issue numbers; place the issue number in parentheses instead (see Section 9.25 and Chapter 10, Example 1).

- Italicize punctuation marks that appear within an italic reference element (e.g., a comma or colon within a book title). Do not italicize punctuation between reference elements (e.g., the period after an italic book title).

Table 9.1 How to Create a Reference When Information Is Missing

Missing element	Solution	Template	
		Reference list entry	In-text citation
Nothing— all elements are present	Provide the author, date, title, and source of the work.	Author. (Date). Title. Source.	(Author, year) Author (year)
Author	Provide the title, date, and source.	Title. (Date). Source.	(Title, year) Title (year)
Date	Provide the author, write "n.d." for "no date," and then provide the title and source.	Author. (n.d.). Title. Source.	(Author, n.d.) Author (n.d.)
Title	Provide the author and date, describe the work in square brackets, and then provide the source.	Author. (Date). [Description of work]. Source.	(Author, year) Author (year)
Author and date	Provide the title, write "n.d." for "no date," and then provide the source.	Title. (n.d.). Source.	(Title, n.d.) Title (n.d.)
Author and title	Describe the work in square brackets, and then provide the date and source.	[Description of work]. (Date). Source.	([Description of work], year) [Description of work] (year)
Date and title	Provide the author, write "n.d." for "no date," describe the work in square brackets, and then provide the source.	Author. (n.d.). [Description of work]. Source.	(Author, n.d.) Author (n.d.)
Author, date, and title	Describe the work in square brackets, write "n.d." for "no date," and then provide the source.	[Description of work]. (n.d.). Source.	([Description of work], n.d.) [Description of work] (n.d.)
Source	Cite as a personal communication (see Section 8.9) or find another work to cite (see Section 9.37).	No reference list entry	(C. C. Communicator, personal communication, month day, year) C. C. Communicator (personal communication, month day, year)

Note. This table illustrates how reference category templates change when reference elements such as the author (Section 9.12), date (Section 9.17), title (Section 9.22), and/or source (Section 9.37) are missing. Italic formatting within the title or source varies by category and is not shown here. To create a reference list entry, follow the template for the work's reference category (see Section 9.1) and adjust the information as shown here.

9.6 Accuracy and Consistency in References

Because one purpose of listing references is to enable readers to retrieve and use the cited works, reference data must be accurate and complete. The best way to ensure that information is accurate and complete is to check each reference carefully against the original publication. Authors are responsible for all information in their reference lists. Accurately prepared references help establish your credibility as a careful researcher and writer.

Consistency in reference formatting allows readers to focus on the content of your reference list, discerning both the types of works you consulted and the important reference elements (who, when, what, and where) with ease. When you present each reference in a consistent fashion, following APA Style reference guidelines, readers do not need to spend time determining how you organized the information. And when searching the literature yourself, you also save time and effort when reading reference lists in the works of others. Some works contain suggested citations; these citations often contain the information necessary to write an APA Style reference but need editing for style. When in doubt, place reference elements in the order of author, date, title, and source.

Reference Elements (Author, Date, Title, Source)

9.7 Author Element

In a reference, the *author* refers broadly to the person(s) or group responsible for a work. This element includes not only author(s) of articles, books, reports, and other works but also others who played primary roles in the creation of a work, such as the editor(s) of a book, the director of a film, the principal investigator of a grant, or a podcast host.

An author may be

- an individual,
- multiple people,
- a group (institution, government agency, organization; see Section 9.11), or
- a combination of people and groups.

Sometimes the author of a work is not listed in a traditional byline but can be determined from context. For instance, the author of an annual report is usually the organization that produced it, unless otherwise specified in the report. Thus, in the reference list entry for that annual report, the organization would be listed as the author. Likewise, in the reference for a page from an organizational or government agency website, the organization or government agency itself is considered the author, unless otherwise specified. The author of a webpage or website may also be located on an "about us" or acknowledgments page. When you cannot determine who the author is, treat the work as having no author (see Section 9.12).

9.8 Format of the Author Element

Follow these guidelines to format the author element.

- Invert all individual authors' names, providing the surname first, followed by a comma and the initials: Author, A. A.

- Use a comma to separate an author's initials from additional author names, even when there are only two authors; use an ampersand (&) before the final author's name: Author, A. A., & Author, B. B.

- Do not use a comma to separate two group authors: American Psychological Association & National Institutes of Health.

- Use a serial comma before the ampersand (&) with three or more authors.

- Provide surnames and initials for up to and including 20 authors. When there are two to 20 authors, use an ampersand before the final author's name: Author, A. A., Author, B. B., & Author, C. C.

- When there are 21 or more authors, include the first 19 authors' names, insert an ellipsis (but no ampersand), and then add the final author's name (see Chapter 10, Example 4).

- Use one space between initials.

- When given names are hyphenated, retain the hyphen and include a period after each initial but no space (e.g., Xu, A.-J., for Ai-Jun Xu). When the second element of a hyphenated name is lowercase, treat it as a single name (e.g., Raboso, L., for Lee-ann Raboso).

- Use commas to separate initials and suffixes such as Jr. and III: Author, A. A., Jr., & Author, B. B.

- If nonprimary authors are credited using the word "with" (e.g., on a book cover), include them in the reference list entry in parentheses: Meyers, K. (with Long, W. T.). The in-text citation, however, refers to the primary author only: (Meyers, 2019).

- If an author has only one name (e.g., some celebrities, some authors from Indonesia, ancient Greek and Roman authors, some group or corporate authors); an inseparable multipart name (e.g., Malcolm X, Lady Gaga); an essential title, in rare cases (Queen Elizabeth II); or a username (or screen name) only, provide the full name or username without abbreviation in both the reference list and the in-text citation. That is, cite Plato, Sukarno, or Lady Gaga; do not abbreviate these names to P.; S.; or Gaga, L. In the reference list entry, add a period after the author's name: Plato. (2017).

- Do not include titles, positions, ranks, or academic achievements with names in reference list entries (e.g., Reverend, President, General, PhD, LCSW). A few reference types include an author's role in parentheses, when needed (e.g., film director; see Chapter 10, Example 73).

- If both an author's username and real name are known, such as for some individual and group social media authors, provide the real name of the individual (in inverted format) or group, followed by the username in square brackets (see examples in Section 10.13). This approach allows the reference to be grouped with any other works by that author in the reference list and will aid readers in identifying and retrieving the cited work.

- When the @ symbol is part of a username, include that symbol with the username in brackets (see Chapter 10, Examples 91–96).

9.9 Spelling and Capitalization of Author Names

Follow these guidelines for proper spelling and capitalization of author names.

- Write the author's surname exactly as it appears in the published work, including hyphenated surnames (e.g., Santos-García) and two-part surnames (e.g., Velasco Rodríguez; see also Chapter 10, Example 25).

- If uncertain about the proper format for a name, consult other works that cite that author, bibliographic database records, or the author's website or curriculum vitae (CV) to determine the appropriate format. This will help avoid mistaking, for example, a two-part surname for a middle name and surname or vice versa. Follow the most common presentation if any ambiguity remains.

- Retain the author's preferred capitalization (e.g., hooks, b., for bell hooks) in both the reference list and the in-text citation.

AUTHOR

9.10 Identification of Specialized Roles

People in roles other than author who contributed substantially to the creation of a work are recognized for a variety of reference types. See the examples in Chapter 10 for instances when a specialized role is credited in the reference. In these references, the role is placed in parentheses after the inverted surname and initials. Put a period at the end of the author element.

- Use the abbreviation "(Ed.)" for one editor and the abbreviation "(Eds.)" for multiple editors. In the case of multiple editors, include the role once.

  Schulz, O. P. (Ed.).

  Wong, C. T., & Music, K. (Eds.).

- When a reference includes more than one specialized role type (e.g., both writers and a director), and different individuals played different roles, identify each role separately. If an individual played multiple roles, combine the roles using an ampersand (&).

  Park, O. (Writer), Gunnarsson, N. (Writer), & Botha, V. N. (Director).

  Lutz, T. (Writer & Director).

In some cases, a specialized role is identified later in the reference (e.g., an editor of a book for an edited book chapter, see Chapter 10, examples in Section 10.3; a TV series producer, see Chapter 10, Example 76).

9.11 Group Authors

Group authors may include government agencies, associations, nonprofit organizations, businesses, hospitals, task forces, and study groups (see Chapter 10, Examples 50, 53–55, 79, and 99). A group may author a publication on its own or in combination with individuals or other groups (see Chapter 10, Example 5).

- Spell out the full name of a group author in the reference list entry, followed by a period: National Institute of Mental Health.

- An abbreviation for the group author can be used in the text (see Section 8.21); however, do not include an abbreviation for a group author in a reference list entry.

- When numerous layers of government agencies are listed as the author of a work, use the most specific agency as the author in the reference (e.g., use "National Institute of Nursing Research" rather than "U.S. Department of Health and Human Services, National

Institutes of Health, National Institute of Nursing Research"). The names of parent agencies not present in the group author name appear in the source element as the publisher. This presentation aids in identifying the agency responsible for the work and in creating concise in-text citations. However, if using only the most specific responsible agency as the author would cause confusion (e.g., if you are citing both U.S. and Canadian versions of an agency and they have the same name), then include the parent agencies in the author element to differentiate them. When there are multiple layers of agencies, the parent body precedes the subdivision (e.g., The White House, Office of the Press Secretary). Agencies listed in the author element are not repeated in the source element of the reference.

- Sometimes it can be difficult to know whether to credit a group author or the individuals who wrote on behalf of that group; for example, the individuals who wrote a government agency report may be credited in an acknowledgments section. To confirm, consult the cover or title page of the work. If the cover or title page lists only the name of the group (and no names of individuals), treat the reference as having a group author (see Chapter 10, Examples 50 and 53–55). If the cover or title page lists the names of individuals, treat the reference as having individual authors, and include the name of the group as part of the source element (see Chapter 10, Examples 51–52). When a document includes a suggested reference, the author names included in that reference indicate who should be credited (note that the format of the suggested reference may need to be adjusted for APA Style).

9.12 No Author

A work is treated as having no author when its author is unknown or cannot reasonably be determined. In this case, move the title of the work to the author position (followed by a period), before the date of publication (see Chapter 10, Example 49).

Generalized anxiety disorder. (2019).

If, and only if, the work is signed "Anonymous," use "Anonymous" as the author.

Anonymous. (2017).

See Section 8.14 for how to format the in-text citation for a work with no author. See Section 9.48 for how to order works with no authors in the reference list.

9.13 Date Element

In a reference, the *date* refers to the date of publication. The date may take one of the following forms:

- year only;
- year, month, and day (i.e., an exact date);
- year and month;
- year and season; or
- range of dates (e.g., range of years, range of exact dates).

For books, use the copyright date shown on the work's copyright page as the publication date in the reference, even if the copyright date is different from the release date (e.g., 2020 would be the date in the reference for a book released in December 2019 with a 2020 copyright date). For a journal article reference, use the year of the volume, even if it is different from the copyright year.

When citing webpages and websites (see Section 10.14), ensure that the copyright date applies to the content you are citing. Do not use a copyright date from a webpage or website footer because this date may not indicate when the content on the site was published. If a note indicates the "last updated" date of the page, use that date if it applies to the content you are citing (see Section 9.15). If no separate date of publication is indicated for the work on the webpage, treat the work as having no date (see Section 9.17).

9.14 Format of the Date Element

Follow the date format and examples shown in each reference category (see Chapter 10). Use more specific dates for works that are published more frequently (e.g., year, month, and day for newspaper articles and blog posts). Most references include only the year of publication.

- Enclose the date of publication in parentheses, followed by a period: (2020).

- For works from a reference category that includes the month, day, and/or season along with the year, put the year first, followed by a comma, and then the month and date or season:

  (2020, August 26).

  (2020, Spring/Summer).

- For unpublished, informally published, or in-progress works, provide the year the work was produced (see Section 10.7). Do not use "in progress" or "submitted for publication" in the date element of a reference.

- If a work has been accepted for publication but is not yet published, use the term "in press" instead of a year (see Chapter 10, Example 8). Do not provide a date in the reference until the work has been published.

- If a work is an advance online publication, use the year of the advance online publication in the reference (see Chapter 10, Example 7).

- If a work includes both an advance online publication date and a final publication date, use the final publication date in the reference.

- When the date of original publication is approximate, use the abbreviation "ca." (which stands for "circa"; see Chapter 10, Example 36).

9.15 Updated or Reviewed Online Works

Some online works note when a work was last updated. If this date is available and is clearly attributable to the specific content you are citing rather than the overall website, use the updated date in the reference (see Chapter 10, Example 14, for a source retrieved from the UpToDate database).

Do not include a date of last review in a reference because content that has been reviewed has not necessarily been changed. If a date of last review is noted on a work, ignore it for the purposes of the reference.

9.16 Retrieval Dates

Although most online sources can be updated, some are inherently designed to change (e.g., dictionary entry, Twitter profile, Facebook page; see Chapter 10, Examples 33, 47, 92, and 94) or reflect information that changes over time (e.g., UpToDate article and work on a website that updates frequently; see Chapter 10, Examples 14 and 102). Provide a retrieval date in the source element when citing an unarchived (i.e., not stable) work that is likely or meant to change. Including this date indicates to readers that the version of the work they retrieve may be different from the version you used.

For works that may change over time but have archived versions (e.g., Cochrane reviews or *Wikipedia* articles), a retrieval date is not needed because the archived version of the page is stable and can be retrieved (e.g., via a permalink; see Chapter 10, Examples 13 and 49). Most references do not include retrieval dates; the types that might are noted in the applicable reference examples in Chapter 10. The retrieval date, when needed, appears before the URL.

Retrieved October 11, 2020, from https://xxxxx

9.17 No Date

Sometimes the publication date of a work is unknown or cannot be determined. For works with no date, write "n.d." (which stands for "no date") in parentheses. Put a period after the "n" and after the "d" with no space between the letters.

Gagnon, R. (n.d.).

Use "n.d." in the corresponding in-text citation as well.

(Gagnon, n.d.)   *or*   Gagnon (n.d.)

9.18 Title Element

In a reference, the *title* refers to the title of the work being cited. Titles fall into two broad categories: works that stand alone (e.g., books, reports, gray literature, dissertations and theses, informally published works, data sets, videos, films, TV series, podcasts, social media, and works on websites) and works that are part of a greater whole (e.g., periodical articles, edited book chapters, and TV and podcast episodes). When a work stands alone, the title of that work appears in the title element of the reference. When a work is part of a greater whole, the title of the article or chapter appears in the title element of the reference and the title of the greater whole (the journal or edited book) appears in the source element (see Sections 9.25 and 9.28, respectively).

9.19 Format of the Title Element

Follow these guidelines to format the title element.

- For works that are part of a greater whole (e.g., journal articles, edited book chapters), do not italicize the title or use quotation marks, and capitalize it using sentence case (see Section 5.7).

  The virtue gap in humor: Exploring benevolent and corrective humor.

- For works that stand alone (e.g., books, reports, webpages and websites), italicize the title, and use sentence case (see Section 5.7).

  Adoption-specific therapy: A guide to helping adopted children and their families thrive.

- For book and report references, enclose in parentheses after the title any additional information given in the publication for its identification and retrieval (e.g., edition, report number, volume number). Do not add a period between the title and the parenthetical information, and do not italicize the parenthetical information. If both edition and volume information are included, separate them with a comma, placing the edition number first.

  Nursing: A concept-based approach to learning (2nd ed., Vol. 1).

- If a numbered volume has its own title, the volume number and title are included as part of the main title, rather than in parentheses (see Chapter 10, Examples 30 and 45).

- Finish the title element with a period. However, if the title ends with a question mark or exclamation point, that punctuation mark replaces the period.

- See Section 5.7 for how to format titles that appear in the text.

9.20 Series and Multivolume Works

For a book that is part of a multivolume work, such as a handbook comprising three volumes, include the series title in the reference list entry. For examples of titled and untitled volumes, see Chapter 10, Example 30.

When a book is part of a series of conceptually related but separate works (e.g., popular book series such as Harry Potter or the Chronicles of Narnia), include only the book title, not the series title, in the reference. Depending on the publisher and the series, the series name may be either prominent or hard to find; therefore, we recommend omitting it to avoid confusion (see Chapter 10, Example 31).

9.21 Bracketed Descriptions

To help identify works outside the peer-reviewed academic literature (i.e., works other than articles, books, reports, etc.), provide a description of the work in square brackets after the title before the period. The description aids readers in identifying and retrieving the work. Examples of works that include bracketed descriptions are some audiobooks, gray literature (e.g., press releases), audiovisual works (e.g., films, YouTube videos, photographs), software and mobile apps, data sets, manuscripts in preparation, and dissertations and theses. Bracketed descriptions are also used in social media references to indicate attached links or images. Capitalize the first letter of the description, but do not italicize the description.

Comprehensive meta-analysis (Version 3.3.070) [Computer software].

The examples in Chapter 10 include bracketed descriptions where they are needed. When in doubt, include a description. Back-to-back brackets (e.g., when a translated title is followed by a description) are acceptable in references. Consistency of wording is helpful (see Section 9.6), but you may alter the wording shown in the examples to best convey the information readers need. Use succinct descriptions, as shown in the examples in Chapter 10.

9.22 No Title

For works without a title, include a description of the work in square brackets instead.

- When possible, specify the medium in the description of the untitled work (e.g., a map) rather than including two bracketed descriptions.

  [Map showing the population density of the United States as of the year 2010].

- For untitled comments on periodical articles, include up to the first 20 words of the comment or post in addition to a description (see Chapter 10, Example 18).

- For untitled social media posts, include up to the first 20 words of the comment or post (in italics) in addition to a bracketed description (see Chapter 10, Examples 91, 93, 95, and 96).

9.23 Source Element

In a reference, the *source* indicates where readers can retrieve the cited work. As with titles (see Section 9.18), sources fall into two broad categories: works that are part of a greater whole and works that stand alone.

- The source for a work that is part of a greater whole (e.g., journal article, edited book chapter) is that greater whole (i.e., the journal [see Section 9.25] or edited book [see Section 9.28]), plus any applicable DOI or URL (see Sections 9.34–9.36).

- The source for a work that stands alone (e.g., book, report, dissertation, thesis, film, TV series, podcast, data set, informally published work, social media, webpage) is the publisher of the work (see Section 9.29), database or archive (see Section 9.30), social media site (see Section 9.32), or website (see Section 9.33), plus any applicable DOI or URL (see Sections 9.34–9.36).

- Works associated with a specific location (e.g., artwork in a museum) include location information in the source (see Section 9.31) and, depending on the work, may also include a DOI or URL (see Sections 9.34–9.36).

General guidelines on the source element are provided in the following sections; see Chapter 10 for templates and examples of source components to include for each reference category.

9.24 Format of the Source Element

The source element of a reference has one or two parts, depending on the reference category. For example, the source for a print book without a DOI has one part: the book publisher. However, the source for a journal article with a DOI has two parts: the periodical information (the journal title, volume number, issue number, and page range or article number) and the DOI.

Information in the source may be omitted from the reference to avoid repetition. Namely, when the author and publisher or site name of a book, report, webpage, or website are the same, the publisher or site name is omitted from the source element. See Sections 9.25 to 9.33 for guidance on formatting the source for particular reference categories.

9.25 Periodical Sources

When a periodical (i.e., journal, magazine, newspaper, newsletter, or blog) is the source, provide the periodical title, volume number, issue number, and page range or article number (see Chapter 10, Examples 1–6, 9–12, 15, and 16).

Psychology of Popular Media Culture, 5(2), 101–118.

- Capitalize the periodical title using title case (see Section 5.7), italicize it, and place a comma (not italicized) after it.
- Reproduce periodical titles as shown on the work. If the official title includes an abbreviation, reproduce that abbreviated title in the reference (e.g., *PLOS ONE, JAMA Pediatrics*). However, do not abbreviate periodical titles yourself (e.g., do not abbreviate *The New England Journal of Medicine* to *N Engl J Med*). Likewise, do not

reproduce abbreviated titles from other reference lists or databases (e.g., if you find an article from *JAMA Pediatrics* in PubMed Central, use *JAMA Pediatrics* in the reference, not PubMed Central's abbreviation of *JAMA Pediatr*).

- Italicize the volume number.

- Include the issue number for all periodicals that have issue numbers. Place the issue number, enclosed in parentheses, immediately after the volume number (with no space in between), followed by a comma. Do not italicize the issue number, the parentheses, or the comma after the issue number.

- Insert the page range (or article number; see Section 9.27) after the issue number, without italics. Separate page numbers in a range with an en dash, followed by a period. Separate discontinuous page numbers with commas.

  39–47, 50.

- Finish the periodical information portion of the source element with a period, followed by a DOI or URL as applicable (see Sections 9.34–9.36).

9.26 Online Periodicals With Missing Information

Many online periodicals (e.g., newspapers, blogs) publish articles without volume, issue, and/or page numbers or article numbers. Omit these elements from the reference if they are not present in the cited work. For example, for an online newspaper article or blog post, only the periodical title may be present (see Chapter 10, Examples 16, 17, and 63).

  The New York Times.

9.27 Article Numbers

For articles with article numbers (which may be called "eLocators" or another term), write the word "Article" (capitalized) and then provide the article number instead of the page range (see Chapter 10, Example 6).

  PLOS ONE, 11(7), Article e0158474.

If an article with an article number also has numbered pages (such as in a PDF), those page numbers may be used for in-text citations (see Sections 8.23 and 8.25) but do not appear in the reference list entry.

SOURCE

9.28 Edited Book Chapter and Reference Work Entry Sources

For edited book chapters and entries in reference works (e.g., dictionary definitions), the source is the edited book or reference work (see Chapter 10, Examples 38–48).

- For works with editors, in the source element of the reference, write the word "In" followed by the initials and surnames (not inverted) of the editors. If there is one editor, include "(Ed.)" after the editor's name. If there are two or more editors, include "(Eds.)" after the final editor's name. Then add a comma, the title of the book or reference work in italic sentence case (see Section 5.7), the page (abbreviated "p.") number or page range (abbreviated "pp.") of the chapter or entry in parentheses (without italics), followed by a period. Then provide the name of the publisher (see Section 9.29).

  In E. E. Editor (Ed.), *Title of book* (pp. xx–xx). Publisher.

- If the edited book or reference work has edition or volume information in addition to page numbers, include them in the same parentheses in the following order: edition, volume number, page numbers (separated by commas).

  Title of book (2nd ed., Vol. 3, pp. xx–xx).

- If a numbered book volume has its own title, include the volume number and title after the main title of the book. A colon follows the main title, "Volume" is abbreviated "Vol.," and a period follows the volume number, after which the volume title appears.

  Main title of book: Vol. 2. Volume title (2nd ed., pp. xx–xx).

- For a reference work (e.g., *Merriam-Webster's Dictionary, APA Dictionary of Psychology,* mobile app) with a group author, do not repeat the group author name in the source element when the publisher is the same as the author. Simply write "In" and the name of the reference work in italics (see Chapter 10, Examples 47 and 69).

- TV episodes, podcast episodes, and songs from albums follow the same format as edited book chapters and entries from reference works (see Chapter 10, Examples 76, 81, and 83).

- Finish the source element with a period, followed by a DOI or URL as applicable (see Sections 9.34–9.36).

9.29 Publisher Sources

The name of the publisher is provided in the source element for various reference categories, including entire books, edited book chapters, reports, computer software and mobile apps, and data sets. Do not include the publisher location in the reference. Online search makes a work easily discoverable without it, and it may be unclear what location to provide for publishers with offices worldwide or online-only publishers that do not readily disclose their location.

- Write the publisher name as shown on the work, followed by a period. Do not abbreviate the publisher name unless it is shown in abbreviated form on the work.

- The format of publisher names may vary over time and across works (e.g., SAGE Publishing vs. Sage Publications); use the spelling and capitalization of the publisher name as shown on the work you used. It is not necessary to standardize the presentation of a publisher's name if it appears in multiple entries in a reference list.

- If the work is published by an imprint or division, use the imprint or division as the publisher (e.g., Magination Press, which is an imprint of the American Psychological Association, would be used as the publisher).

- Do not include designations of business structure (e.g., Inc., Ltd., LLC) in the publisher name.

- If two or more publishers are listed on the copyright page, include all of them in the order shown on the work, separated by semicolons (see Chapter 10, Example 24).

  Guilford Press; Basic Books.

- When the author is the same as the publisher (such as with an annual report written and published by the same company, a reference book published by a professional organization, or a work from an organizational website), omit the publisher from the reference to avoid repetition (see Chapter 10, Examples 32, 50, 54, and 55).

- Finish the publisher information component of the source element with a period, followed by a DOI or URL as applicable (see Sections 9.34–9.36).

9.30 Database and Archive Sources

Database and archive information is seldom needed in reference list entries. The purpose of a reference list entry is to provide readers with the details they will need to perform a search themselves if necessary, not to replicate the path the author of the work personally used. Most periodical and book content is available through a variety of databases or platforms, and different readers will have different methods or points of access. Additionally, URLs from databases or library-provided services usually require a login and/or are session specific, meaning they will not be accessible to most readers and are not suitable to include in a reference list.

- Provide database or other online archive information in a reference only when it is necessary for readers to retrieve the cited work from that exact database or archive.
  - Provide the name of the database or archive when it publishes original, proprietary works available only in that database or archive (e.g., Cochrane Database of Systematic Reviews or UpToDate; see Chapter 10, Examples 13–14). References for these works are similar to journal article references; the name of the database or archive is written in italic title case in the source element, the same as a periodical title.
  - Provide the name of the database or archive for works of limited circulation, such as
    ▷ dissertations and theses published in ProQuest Dissertations and Theses Global,
    ▷ works in a university archive,
    ▷ manuscripts posted in a preprint archive like PsyArXiv (see Chapter 10, Example 65),
    ▷ works posted in an institutional or government repository, and
    ▷ monographs published in ERIC or primary sources published in JSTOR (see Chapter 10, Example 66).

  These references are similar to report references; the name of the database or archive is provided in the source element (in title case without italics), the same as a publisher name.

- Do not include database information for works obtained from most academic research databases or platforms because these works are widely available. Examples of research databases and platforms include APA PsycNET, PsycINFO, Academic Search Complete, Ebook Central, EBSCO*host*, Google Scholar, JSTOR (excluding its primary sources collection because these are works of limited distribution), MEDLINE, Nexis Uni, Ovid, ProQuest (excluding its dissertations and theses databases because dissertations and theses are works of limited circulation), PubMed Central (excluding authors' final peer-reviewed manuscripts because these are works of limited circulation), ScienceDirect, Scopus, and Web of Science. When citing a work from one of these databases or platforms, do not include the database or platform name in the reference list entry unless the work falls under one of the exceptions.

- If you are in doubt as to whether to include database information in a reference, refer to the template for the reference type in question (see Chapter 10).

- Finish the database or archive component of the source element with a period, followed by a DOI or URL as applicable (see Sections 9.34–9.36).

9.31 Works With Specific Locations

For works associated with a specific location, such as artwork in a museum (see Chapter 10, Example 86; for more, see Section 10.5 of the *Publication Manual*), include the location in the source element of the reference to help with retrieval. Provide the city; state, province, or territory as applicable; and country. Use the two-letter postal code abbreviations for U.S. states and the analogous abbreviations (if any) for states, provinces, or territories in other countries.

New York, NY, United States	Istanbul, Turkey
Vancouver, BC, Canada	Lima, Peru
Sydney, NSW, Australia	London, England

9.32 Social Media Sources

Use social media as a source only when the content was originally published there (e.g., an original Instagram post). If you found a link to content via social media (e.g., a pin on Pinterest), cite the content you used directly and do not mention that you originally discovered it through a link on social media, except as necessary in describing your research methodology.

- When social media is the source (e.g., Instagram photo, tweet, Facebook post), provide the social media site name (in title case without italics; see Section 5.7) in the source element: Twitter.

- Include a period after the social media site name, followed by the URL (see Sections 9.34–9.36).

9.33 Website Sources

When a website is the source for a webpage (see Section 9.2), follow these guidelines to format the website source.

• Provide the website name (in title case without italics; see Section 5.7) in the source element: BBC News.

• Include a period after the website name, followed by the URL (see Sections 9.34–9.36).

• When the author of the work is the same as the website name, omit the site name from the source element to avoid repetition (see Chapter 10, Example 99). In this case, the source element will consist of only the URL of the work.

9.34 When to Include DOIs and URLs

The DOI or URL is the final component of the reference list entry. Because so much scholarship is available and/or retrieved online, most reference list entries end with either a DOI or a URL. A DOI, or *digital object identifier,* is a unique alphanumeric string that identifies content and provides a persistent link to its location on the internet. It is typically located on the first page of an article near the copyright notice, and it starts with "https://doi.org/" or "http://dx.doi.org" or "DOI:" and is followed by a string of letters and numbers. DOIs begin with the number 10 and contain a prefix and a suffix separated by a slash. The prefix is a unique number of four or more digits assigned to the organization by the International DOI Foundation (https://www.doi.org/); the suffix is assigned by the publisher and was designed to be flexible with publisher identification standards. The publisher assigns a DOI to a work when it is published, and many publishers have retroactively assigned DOIs to works published before the implementation of the DOI system in 2000. Registration agencies, such as Crossref, use DOIs to provide reference-linking services to the scientific publishing sector. DOIs can also be found in database records and the reference lists of published works. A URL, or *uniform resource locator,* specifies the location of digital information on the internet and can be found in the address bar of your internet browser.

URLs in references should link directly to the cited work when possible. For example, when citing a comment from an online newspaper article, the URL in the reference should link to the comment rather than to the article or the newspaper's home page (direct links to comments may be available if you click the time stamp and copy the URL that appears in your browser).

Follow these guidelines for including DOIs and URLs in references:

- Include a DOI for all works that have a DOI, regardless of whether you used the online version or the print version.
- If a print work does not have a DOI, do not include any DOI or URL in the reference.
- If an online work has both a DOI and a URL, include only the DOI.
- If an online work has a URL but no DOI, include the URL in the reference as follows:
    - For works without DOIs from websites (not including databases), provide a URL in the reference (as long as the URL will work for readers).
    - For works without DOIs from most academic research databases, do not include a URL or database information in the reference because these works are widely available (see Section 9.30). The reference should be the same as the reference for a print version of the work.
    - For works from databases that publish works of limited circulation (such as the ERIC database) or original, proprietary material available only in that database (such as the UpToDate database), include the name of the database or archive and the URL of the work (see Section 9.30). If the URL requires a login or is session specific, meaning it will not resolve for readers, provide the URL of the database or archive home page or login page instead of the URL for the work.
    - If the URL is no longer working or no longer provides readers access to the content you intend to cite, follow the guidance for works with no source (see Section 9.37).
- Other alphanumeric identifiers such as the International Standard Book Number (ISBN) and the International Standard Serial Number (ISSN) are not included in APA Style references.

9.35 Format of DOIs and URLs

Follow these guidelines to format DOIs and URLs.

- Present both DOIs and URLs as hyperlinks (i.e., beginning with "http://" or "https://"). Because a hyperlink leads readers directly to the content, it is not necessary to include the words "Retrieved from" or "Accessed from" before a DOI or URL.

- It is acceptable to use either the default display settings for hyperlinks in your word-processing program (e.g., usually blue font, underlined) or plain text that is not underlined.

- Links should be live if the work is to be published or read online.

- Follow the current recommendation of the International DOI Foundation to format DOIs in the reference list, which as of this publication is as follows:

https://doi.org/xxxxx

Here, "https://doi.org/" is a way of presenting a DOI as a link, and "xxxxx" refers to the DOI number. The preferred format of the DOI has changed over time; although older works use previous formats (e.g., "http://dx.doi.org/" or "doi:" or "DOI:" before the DOI number), in your reference list, standardize DOIs into the current preferred format for all entries. For example, use https://doi.org/10.1037/a0040251 in your reference even though that article, published in 2016, displayed the DOI in an older format.

> **Why use the new DOI format?** The current DOI format presents the DOI as a direct link to the work rather than as an unlinked number or a link through a proxy server. It simplifies and standardizes retrieval.

- Copy and paste the DOI or URL from your web browser directly into your reference list to avoid transcription errors. Do not change the capitalization or punctuation of the DOI or URL. Do not add line breaks manually to the hyperlink; it is acceptable if your word-processing program automatically adds a break or moves the hyperlink to its own line.

- Do not add a period after the DOI or URL because it may interfere with link functionality.

9.36 DOI or URL Shorteners

When a DOI or URL is long or complex, you may use shortDOIs or shortened URLs if desired. Use the shortDOI service provided by the International DOI Foundation (http://shortdoi.org/) to create shortDOIs. A work can have only one DOI and only one shortDOI; the shortDOI service will either produce a new shortDOI for a work that has never had one or retrieve an existing shortDOI.

Some websites provide their own branded shortened URLs, and independent URL shortening services are also available. Any shortened URL is acceptable in a reference as long as the link takes you to the correct location. If you choose to use a shortened URL, it is best to use well-known services (e.g., bitly, perma.cc) or the shortened URL that is provided by the site of the long URL (e.g., Amazon provides amzn.com links for its URLs). See Chapter 10, Examples 4 and 18, for a shortDOI and a shortened URL, respectively.

9.37 No Source

A reference without a recoverable source should not be included in the reference list because readers cannot retrieve the work. In most cases, nonrecoverable sources such as personal emails, classroom lectures, and intranet sources should be cited only in the text as personal communications (see Section 8.9).

Online works that are no longer accessible are considered nonrecoverable sources. Before submitting a paper, test the URLs in your reference list to ensure that they work and update them as necessary. Do not include broken URLs in your paper. If the content you cited is no longer available online, search for an archived version of the page on the Internet Archive (https://archive.org/) and use the archived URL. If no archived version of the URL is available, delete the reference list entry and substitute another reference if possible.

Reference Variations

Some works may be in another language or translated, reprinted, reissued, or republished. For these reference variations, additional information about the work and/or its publication history is included in the reference list entry.

9.38 Works in Another Language

Multilingual authors may cite works published in a language other than the language in which they are writing. For example, an author who understands both English and Spanish may write a paper in English and cite both English and Spanish works. From the reader's perspective, the language in which the paper is written (in this example, English) is considered the main language and any other language in the paper (in this example, Spanish) is considered "another language."

To cite a work that is in another language, provide the author, date, title, and source of the work in the original language as well as a translation of the title in square brackets after the title and before the period (see Chapter 10, Examples 9, 27, and 74). In the case of a work that is part of a greater whole (e.g., an edited book chapter), translate only the title of the work being cited (e.g., the chapter title; see Chapter 10, Example 41); it is not necessary to translate the title of the greater whole (e.g., the book title). For example, if you are writing in English and cite a Spanish work, provide the author, date, title, and source in the original Spanish in the reference list, and also provide the title of the work translated into English in square brackets.

If the other language uses a different alphabet from the one you are writing in, transliterate the alphabet into the Roman alphabet. If transliteration is not possible or advisable, it is acceptable to reproduce the original alphabet in the paper. In that case, alphabetize the reference list entry the same way as in published articles or place the entry at the end of the list.

9.39 Translated Works

Cite translated works in the language in which the translation was published. For example, if a Spanish article was translated into English and you read the English translation, your reference list entry should be in English. Credit the translator in the reference for a translated work (see Chapter 10, Examples 10, 28, 29, 35, 36, and 42). For translated works, also provide the year the work was originally published (in its original language) at the end of the reference in parentheses in the following format:

(Original work published 1955)

See Section 8.15 for how to format in-text citations for translated works.

9.40 Reprinted, Republished, or Reissued Works

A *reprinted work* is one that has been published in two places and is available in both (e.g., a journal article that was reprinted as an edited book chapter). A *republished work* is one that went out of print (i.e., was no longer available) and then was published again; this is common for older works as well as for music (for which the term "reissued" is used rather than "republished").

The reference list entry for a reprinted work contains information about the work that you used, followed by details about the original publication in parentheses (see Chapter 10, Examples 11 and 43). The reference list entry for a republished or reissued work (see Chapter 10, Examples 28, 29, and 46) contains information about the new publication that you used, followed by the year the work was originally published in parentheses at the end of the reference in the following format:

(Original work published 1922)

See Section 8.15 for how to format in-text citations for reprinted, republished, or reissued works.

9.41 Religious and Classical Works

Religious works (e.g., Bible, Qur'an, Torah, Bhagavad Gita), classical works (e.g., ancient Greek and Roman works), and classical literature (e.g., by Shakespeare) are all cited like books (see Section 10.2).

- Religious works (see Chapter 10, Example 35) are usually treated as having no author (see Section 9.12). However, an annotated version of a religious work would be treated as having an editor.

- The original publication year of a religious work may be unknown or in dispute and is not included in the reference in those cases. However, versions of religious works such as the Bible may be republished; these republished dates are included in the reference (see Section 9.40 and Chapter 10, Example 35).

- For translated religious and classical works, include the translator's name in the reference (see Section 9.39 and Chapter 10, Example 28).

- Classical works (e.g., ancient Greek and Roman works; see Chapter 10, Example 36) and works of classical literature (e.g., by Shakespeare; see Chapter 10, Example 37) are treated as republished works (see Section 9.40).

- When the date of original publication for a classical work is ancient, use the abbreviation "B.C.E." (which stands for "before the common era"), and if that date is approximate, use the abbreviation "ca." (which stands for "circa"; see Chapter 10, Example 36). Dates in the common era do not need to be noted as "C.E." ("common era") or "A.D." ("anno Domini").

- If a religious or classical work has canonically numbered parts common across editions (e.g., books, chapters, verses, lines, cantos), use these numbers instead of page numbers when referring to a specific part of the work (see Section 8.13) or directly quoting the work (see Section 8.28).

See Section 8.28 for how to format the in-text citation for these works.

Reference List Format and Order

9.42 Format of the Reference List

The following guidelines will help you properly format your reference list in APA Style:

- Begin the reference list on a new page after the text.
- Place the section label "References" in bold at the top of the page, centered.
- Order the reference list entries alphabetically by author, as described in Sections 9.43 to 9.47.
- Double-space the entire reference list (both within and between entries).
- Apply a hanging indent of 0.5 in. to each reference list entry, meaning that the first line of the reference is flush left and subsequent lines are indented 0.5 in. from the left margin. Use the paragraph-formatting function of your word-processing program to apply the hanging indent.

9.43 Order of Works in the Reference List

Works are listed in alphabetical order in the reference list by the first word of the reference list entry, according to the following principles:

- Arrange entries in alphabetical order by the surname of the first author followed by the initials of the author's given name(s). In APA Style for alphabetizing names, "nothing precedes something": Loft, V. H. precedes Loftus, E. F., even though "u" precedes "v" in the alphabet.
- When alphabetizing names, disregard any spaces or punctuation marks (e.g., apostrophes, hyphens) in two-word surnames. Also disregard anything in parentheses (e.g., roles like "Eds.") or square brackets (e.g., usernames).
- Alphabetize entries by authors who have the same given name and surname with suffixes indicating birth order chronologically, oldest first.

See Figure 9.2 for examples of how to order works in the reference list. For further examples, review the reference lists of published articles or the sample papers on the APA Style website (https://apastyle.apa.org).

Figure 9.2 Examples of the Order of Works in a Reference List

Benjamin, A. S., *precedes* ben Yaakov, D.

Denzin, N. K., *precedes* de Onís, C., *precedes* Devlin, J. T.

Girard, J.-B., *precedes* Girard-Perregaux, A. S.

Ibn Abdulaziz, T., *precedes* Ibn Nidal, A. K. M.

López, M. E., *precedes* López de Molina, G.

MacCallum, T., II, *precedes* MacCallum, T., III

MacNeil, E., *precedes* McAdoo, Z. C. E., *precedes* M'Carthy, L. L.

Olson, S. R., *precedes* O'Neil, U., *precedes* Oppenheimer, R.

Partridge, F., *precedes* Plato

San Martin, Q. E., *precedes* Santa Maria, M., *precedes* Santayana, F. E.

Santiago, J., Sr., *precedes* Santiago, J., Jr.

Villafuerte, S. A., *precedes* Villa-Lobos, J.

9.44 Order of Surname and Given Name

Naming practices for the order of given name and surname vary by culture; in some cultures, the given name appears before the surname, whereas in others, the surname appears first. If you are uncertain of which name order you are reading, check the author's preferred form (e.g., by visiting their website or their institution's website or by reading their bio or CV), or consult the author's previous publications to see how their name was presented there. For example, an author may publish as "Zhang Yi-Chen" in China but as "Yi-Chen Zhang" in the United States; in either case, according to APA Style, this author would be listed as "Zhang, Y.-C.," in the reference list. See Section 9.9 for more.

9.45 Order of Multiple Works by the Same First Author

When ordering multiple works by the same first author in the reference list, include the author's name in every entry.

- One-author entries should be arranged by year of publication, the earliest first. References with no date precede references with dates, and in-press references are listed last.

Patel, S. N. (n.d.).

Patel, S. N. (2016).

Patel, S. N. (2020a).

Patel, S. N. (2020b, April).

Patel, S. N. (in press).

- One-author entries should precede multiple-author entries beginning with the same first author, even if the multiple-author work was published earlier.

Davison, T. E. (2019).

Davison, T. E., & McCabe, M. P. (2015).

- Multiple-author entries in which all authors appear in the same order should be arranged by the year of publication (the same as one-author entries).

Costa, P. T., Jr., & McCrae, R. R. (2013).

Costa, P. T., Jr., & McCrae, R. R. (2014).

- Multiple-author entries with the same first author and different subsequent authors should be arranged alphabetically by the surname of the second author or, if the second author is the same, the surname of the third author, and so forth.

Jacobson, T. E., Duncan, B., & Young, S. E. (2019).

Jacobson, T. E., & Raymond, K. M. (2017).

Pfeiffer, S. J., Chu, W.-W., & Park, S. H. (2018).

Pfeiffer, S. J., Chu, W.-W., & Wall, T. L. (2018).

9.46 Order of Works With the Same Author and Same Date

Ambiguity can arise when multiple works cited in a paper have the same author and date (i.e., the same author[s] in the same order and the same year of publication) because the same in-text citation would then correspond to multiple reference list entries. To differentiate references with the same author and year, put a lowercase letter after the year in both the in-text citation and the reference list entry.

- The letter format for references with years is "2020a," "2020b."
- The letter format for references with no date is "n.d.-a," "n.d.-b."
- The letter format for in-press references is in "in press-a," "in press-b."

Assigning the letters is a two-step process. First, compare the dates. References with only a year precede those with more specific dates, and specific dates are placed in chronological order.

Azikiwe, H., & Bello, A. (2020a).

Azikiwe, H., & Bello, A. (2020b, March 26).

Azikiwe, H., & Bello, A. (2020c, April 2).

Second, if the references have identical dates, alphabetize the references by title (disregarding the words "A," "An," and "The" at the beginning of a reference title). The following are examples of references in the proper order.

Judge, T. A., & Kammeyer-Mueller, J. D. (2012a). General and specific measures in organizational behavior research: Considerations, examples, and recommendations for researchers. *Journal of Organizational Behavior, 33*(2), 161–174. https://doi.org/10.1002/job.764

Judge, T. A., & Kammeyer-Mueller, J. D. (2012b). On the value of aiming high: The causes and consequences of ambition. *Journal of Applied Psychology, 97*(4), 758–775. https://doi.org/10.1037/a0028084

However, if references with the same author and date are identified as articles in a series (e.g., Part 1 and Part 2), order the references in the series order, regardless of the titles' alphabetical order.

For citing works with the same author and date in text, see Section 8.19.

9.47 Order of Works by First Authors With the Same Surname

Arrange works by first authors with the same surname and different initials alphabetically by first initial(s).

Taylor, J. M., & Neimeyer, G. J. (2015).

Taylor, T. (2014).

The in-text citations for these references also include the initials of the first author (see Section 8.20). These guidelines apply to only the first author in each reference.

If multiple first authors share the same surname and the same initials, order the works as described in Sections 9.45 and 9.46. This guideline applies regardless of whether the authors are different people or the same person with a name change. For guidance on the corresponding in-text citations, see Section 8.20.

9.48 Order of Works With No Author or an Anonymous Author

Before treating a work as though it has no author, consider whether a group or organization is the author (see Section 9.11). If, and only if, the work is signed "Anonymous," begin the entry with the word "Anonymous," and alphabetize the entry as if Anonymous were a true name.

If there is no author and the work is not signed "Anonymous," the reference begins with the work's title (see Section 9.12); alphabetize the entry by the first significant word of the title (i.e., ignoring the words "A," "An," and "The" at the beginning of the title).

Alphabetize numerals as though they were spelled out (e.g., alphabetize 22 as though it were "twenty-two"). Thus, "Top 100 business schools" precedes "Top 10 nursing specialties" because when spelled out, "one hundred" appears alphabetically before "ten." Likewise, "Theological studies" precedes "200 years" because "theological" precedes "two hundred."

For citing works with no author in text, see Section 8.14.

9.49 Abbreviations in References

Some parts of books, reports, and other publications are abbreviated in the reference list to save space, including the following examples. Many, but not all, reference abbreviations are capitalized.

Abbreviation	Book or publication part
ed.	edition
Rev. ed.	revised edition
2nd ed.	second edition
Ed. (Eds.)	editor (editors)
Trans.	translator(s)
Narr. (Narrs.)	narrator (narrators)
n.d.	no date
p. (pp.)	page (pages)
para. (paras.)	paragraph (paragraphs)
Vol. (Vols.)	volume (volumes)
No.	number
Pt.	part
Tech. Rep.	technical report
Suppl.	supplement

10 ॐ

REFERENCE EXAMPLES

Appropriately crediting the contributions of past scholars on which your research and writing are based is a hallmark of scholarly discourse. These contributions must be cited accurately and consistently so that future scholars can identify and retrieve the works cited in the text.

This chapter provides examples of references in APA Style and their corresponding in-text citations. The examples are organized first by group, then by category, and then by type, as follows:

- The **textual works group** (Sections 10.1–10.7) contains the categories of periodicals, books and reference works, edited book chapters and reference work entries, reports and gray literature, dissertations and theses, reviews of other works, and informally published works. Within those categories are examples by type (e.g., journal article, edited book chapter, government report, dissertation).

- The **software and tests group** (Sections 10.8–10.9) contains the categories of computer software and mobile apps and tests, scales, and inventories. Within those categories are examples by type (e.g., entry in a mobile reference work, test scoring manual).

- The **audiovisual media group** (Sections 10.10–10.12) contains the categories of audiovisual works, audio works, and visual works. Within those categories are examples by type (e.g., YouTube video, speech audio recording, podcast episode, PowerPoint slides).

- The **online media group** (Sections 10.13–10.14) contains the categories of social media and webpages and websites. Within those categories are examples by type (e.g., Instagram photo, tweet, webpage on a news website).

As described in Chapter 9, the key elements of a reference are the author (who), date (when), title (what), and source (where; see also Figure 9.1). For each reference category, a corresponding template illustrates the order and format in which these elements should appear, and examples of the most common reference types follow. If you do not see an example that matches the work you want to cite, use the template for the work's reference category as a starting point for writing the reference list entry. Then select the appropriate option from each column of the template to write the reference. Mix and match elements within a template; it is not necessary to use multiple templates. When in doubt, provide more information rather than less. For every reference, the in-text citation contains the first two parts of the reference—usually the "who" (author) and the "when" (date; see Section 8.11), although this can change if reference information is missing (see Table 9.1).

Legal References. Most legal references (e.g., court cases and laws) are formatted in a legal reference style, which is different in several ways from the author–date–title–source pattern of other APA Style references. Legal references are described with examples in Sections 10.15 to 10.18.

Additional References. Additional reference examples, including conference sessions and presentations, issue briefs, data sets, apparatuses and equipment, unpublished works, and archival documents, are available in Chapter 10 of the *Publication Manual*, on the APA Style website (https://apastyle.apa.org), and on the APA Style blog (https://apastyle.apa.org/blog).

The following index of reference examples is organized by variations in each reference element. The numbers after each index entry refer to the numbered reference examples in this chapter.

Author Variations

Type of author
    artist (recording), 80, 81
    artist (visual), 86, 87, 88
    composer, 80, 81
    director, 73, 74, 76

Date Variations

Title Variations

Source Variations

Textual Works

10.1 Periodicals

Periodicals are generally published on a continuous basis and include journals, magazines, newspapers, newsletters, and even blogs and other online platforms that publish articles. Sometimes the distinctions between periodical types are ambiguous—for example, a blog that is hosted on a newspaper website. Regardless of where the work appears, its reference list entry follows the same pattern. The date element is presented in different formats for journal, magazine, and newspaper articles and blog posts (see Examples 1, 15, 16, and 17, respectively). When periodical information (e.g., volume number, issue number, page range) is missing, omit it from the reference. For online news websites, see Section 10.14 and Example 98. Use the template shown next to construct references for periodical articles.

Author	Date	Title	Source	
			Periodical information	DOI or URL
Author, A. A., & Author, B. B.	(2020). (2020, January).	Title of article.	*Title of Periodical, 34*(2), 5–14.	https://doi.org/xxxx
Name of Group.	(2020, May 16)		*Title of Periodical, 2*(1–2), Article 12.	https://xxxxx
Author, C. C. [username].				
Username.			*Title of Periodical.*	

1. Journal article with a DOI

McCauley, S. M., & Christiansen, M. H. (2019). Language learning as language use: A cross-linguistic model of child language development. *Psychological Review, 126*(1), 1–51. https://doi.org/10.1037/rev0000126

> ***Parenthetical citation:*** (McCauley & Christiansen, 2019)
> ***Narrative citation:*** McCauley and Christiansen (2019)

2. Journal article without a DOI, with a nondatabase URL

Ahmann, E., Tuttle, L. J., Saviet, M., & Wright, S. D. (2018). A descriptive review of ADHD coaching research: Implications for college students. *Journal of Postsecondary Education and Disability, 31*(1), 17–39. https://www.ahead.org/professional-resources/publications/jped/archived-jped/jped-volume-31

Parenthetical citation: (Ahmann et al., 2018)
Narrative citation: Ahmann et al. (2018)

3. Journal, magazine, or newspaper article without a DOI, from most academic research databases or print version

Anderson, M. (2018). Getting consistent with consequences. *Educational Leadership, 76*(1), 26–33.

Goldman, C. (2018, November 28). The complicated calibration of love, especially in adoption. *Chicago Tribune.*

Parenthetical citations: (Anderson, 2018; Goldman, 2018)
Narrative citations: Anderson (2018) and Goldman (2018)

- Do not include the database name or URL. See Section 9.30 for more on excluding or including database information in references.

4. Journal article with a DOI, 21 or more authors

Kalnay, E., Kanamitsu, M., Kistler, R., Collins, W., Deaven, D., Gandin, L., Iredell, M., Saha, S., White, G., Woollen, J., Zhu, Y., Chelliah, M., Ebisuzaki, W., Higgins, W., Janowiak, J., Mo, K. C., Ropelewski, C., Wang, J., Leetmaa, A., … Joseph, D. (1996). The NCEP/NCAR 40-year reanalysis project. *Bulletin of the American Meteorological Society, 77*(3), 437–471. http://doi.org/fg6rf9

Parenthetical citation: (Kalnay et al., 1996)
Narrative citation: Kalnay et al. (1996)

- Because the original DOI was long and complex, a shortDOI is used (see Section 9.36). Either the long or short form of the DOI is acceptable.

5. Journal article with a DOI, combination of individual and group authors

De Vries, R., Nieuwenhuijze, M., Buitendijk, S. E., & the members of Midwifery Science Work Group. (2013). What does it take to have a strong and independent profession of midwifery? Lessons from the Netherlands. *Midwifery, 29*(10), 1122–1128. https://doi.org/10.1016/j.midw.2013.07.007

Parenthetical citation: (De Vries et al., 2013)
Narrative citation: De Vries et al. (2013)

- Write the name of the group author as shown on the source (see Section 9.11). This byline included the wording "the members of."

6. Journal article with an article number or eLocator

Burin, D., Kilteni, K., Rabuffetti, M., Slater, M., & Pia, L. (2019). Body ownership increases the interference between observed and executed movements. *PLOS ONE, 14*(1), Article e0209899. https://doi.org/10.1371/journal.pone. 0209899

Parenthetical citation: (Burin et al., 2019)
Narrative citation: Burin et al. (2019)

- Capitalize the word "Article" before the article number or eLocator.

7. Journal article, advance online publication

Huestegge, S. M., Raettig, T., & Huestegge, L. (2019). Are face-incongruent voices harder to process? Effects of face–voice gender incongruency on basic cognitive information processing. *Experimental Psychology.* Advance online publication. https://doi.org/10.1027/1618-3169/a000440

Parenthetical citation: (Huestegge et al., 2019)
Narrative citation: Huestegge et al. (2019)

- See Section 8.5 for more information on which version of an article to cite.

8. Journal article, in press

Pachur, T., & Scheibehenne, B. (in press). Unpacking buyer–seller differences in valuation from experience: A cognitive modeling approach. *Psychonomic Bulletin & Review.*

Parenthetical citation: (Pachur & Scheibehenne, in press)
Narrative citation: Pachur and Scheibehenne (in press)

9. Journal article, published in another language

Chaves-Morillo, V., Gómez Calero, C., Fernández-Muñoz, J. J., Toledano-Muñoz, A., Fernández-Huete, J., Martínez-Monge, N., Palacios-Ceña, D., & Peñacoba-Puente, C. (2018). La anosmia neurosensorial: Relación entre subtipo, tiempo de reconocimiento y edad [Sensorineural anosmia: Relationship between subtype, recognition time, and age]. *Clínica y Salud, 28*(3), 155–161. https://doi.org/10.1016/j.clysa.2017.04.002

Parenthetical citation: (Chaves-Morillo et al., 2018)
Narrative citation: Chaves-Morillo et al. (2018)

- When an article is in a different language from your paper, include a translation of the article title in square brackets (see Section 9.38).

10. Journal article, republished in translation

Piaget, J. (1972). Intellectual evolution from adolescence to adulthood (J. Bliss & H. Furth, Trans.). *Human Development, 15*(1), 1–12. https://doi.org/10.1159/000271225 (Original work published 1970)

> *Parenthetical citation:* (Piaget, 1970/1972)
> *Narrative citation:* Piaget (1970/1972)

- For more on translated works, see Section 9.39.

11. Journal article, reprinted from another source

Shore, M. F. (2014). Marking time in the land of plenty: Reflections on mental health in the United States. *American Journal of Orthopsychiatry, 84*(6), 611–618. https://doi.org/10.1037/h0100165 (Reprinted from "Marking time in the land of plenty: Reflections on mental health in the United States," 1981, *American Journal of Orthopsychiatry, 51*[3], 391–402, https://doi.org/10.1111/j.1939-0025.1981.tb01388.x)

> *Parenthetical citation:* (Shore, 1981/2014)
> *Narrative citation:* Shore (1981/2014)

- Provide information for the reprinted version that you used; then provide in parentheses the original article title (even if the title did not change), year, and source information (see Section 9.40).
- Place the original issue number in square brackets rather than in parentheses to avoid nested parentheses.

12. Special section or special issue in a journal

Lilienfeld, S. O. (Ed.). (2018). Heterodox issues in psychology [Special section]. *Archives of Scientific Psychology, 6*(1), 51–104.

McDaniel, S. H., Salas, E., & Kazak, A. E. (Eds.). (2018). The science of teamwork [Special issue]. *American Psychologist, 73*(4).

> *Parenthetical citations:* (Lilienfeld, 2018; McDaniel et al., 2018)
> *Narrative citations:* Lilienfeld (2018) and McDaniel et al. (2018)

- List the editor(s) of the special section or issue in the author position and the title of the special section or issue in the title position.
- Provide the page range for a special section. Do not provide a page range for a special issue.
- Some publishers include an "S" in issue numbers for special issues. In the reference, write the issue number exactly as shown in the publication.

PERIODICALS

- For an article within a special section or special issue, follow the format for a journal article (see Examples 1–3), in which case the title of the special section or issue does not appear in the reference.

13. Article from the Cochrane Database of Systematic Reviews

Mehrholz, J., Pohl, M., Platz, T., Kugler, J., & Elsner, B. (2018). Electromechanical and robot-assisted arm training for improving activities of daily living, arm function, and arm muscle strength after stroke. *Cochrane Database of Systematic Reviews*. https://doi.org/10.1002/14651858.CD006876.pub5

> *Parenthetical citation:* (Mehrholz et al., 2018)
> *Narrative citation:* Mehrholz et al. (2018)

- Articles in the Cochrane Database of Systematic Reviews are available only in that database (see Section 9.30). In the reference list, format Cochrane articles like periodical articles. Do not italicize the database name if it appears in text.

14. Article from the UpToDate database

Morey, M. C. (2019). Physical activity and exercise in older adults. *UpToDate*. Retrieved August 22, 2019, from https://www.uptodate.com/contents/physical-activity-and-exercise-in-older-adults

> *Parenthetical citation:* (Morey, 2019)
> *Narrative citation:* Morey (2019)

- Articles in the UpToDate database are available only in that database (see Section 9.30) and have information that changes over time. In the reference list, format UpToDate articles like periodical articles. Do not italicize the database name if it appears in text.
- Use the year of last update in the date element (see Section 9.15).
- Include a retrieval date because the content is designed to change over time and versions of the page are not archived (see Section 9.16).

15. Magazine article

Bergeson, S. (2019, January 4). Really cool neutral plasmas. *Science, 363*(6422), 33–34. https://doi.org/10.1126/science.aau7988

Bustillos, M. (2013, March 19). On video games and storytelling: An interview with Tom Bissell. *The New Yorker.* https://www.newyorker.com/books/page-turner/on-video-games-and-storytelling-an-interview-with-tom-bissell

Weir, K. (2017, January). Forgiveness can improve mental and physical health. *Monitor on Psychology, 48*(1), 30.

> *Parenthetical citations:* (Bergeson, 2019; Bustillos, 2013; Weir, 2017)
> *Narrative citations:* Bergeson (2019), Bustillos (2013), and Weir (2017)

16. Newspaper article

Guarino, B. (2017, December 4). How will humanity react to alien life? Psychologists have some predictions. *The Washington Post.* https://www.washingtonpost.com/news/speaking-of-science/wp/2017/12/04/how-will-humanity-react-to-alien-life-psychologists-have-some-predictions

Hess, A. (2019, January 3). Cats who take direction. *The New York Times,* C1.

> *Parenthetical citations:* (Guarino, 2017; Hess, 2019)
> *Narrative citations:* Guarino (2017) and Hess (2019)

- To cite articles from online news websites (vs. online newspapers as shown here), see Example 98.

17. Blog post

Klymkowsky, M. (2018, September 15). Can we talk scientifically about free will? *Sci-Ed.* https://blogs.plos.org/scied/2018/09/15/can-we-talk-scientifically-about-free-will/

> *Parenthetical citation:* (Klymkowsky, 2018)
> *Narrative citation:* Klymkowsky (2018)

18. Comment on an online periodical article or post

KS in NJ. (2019, January 15). From this article, it sounds like men are figuring something out that women have known forever. I know of many [Comment on the article "How workout buddies can help stave off loneliness"]. *The Washington Post.* https://wapo.st/2HDToGJ

> *Parenthetical citation:* (KS in NJ, 2019)
> *Narrative citation:* KS in NJ (2019)

- Credit the person who left the comment as the author using the format that appears with the comment (i.e., a real name or a username).

- Provide the comment title or up to the first 20 words of the comment; then write "Comment on the article" and the title of the article on which the comment appeared (in quotation marks and sentence case, enclosed within square brackets).
- Link to the comment itself when possible (see Sections 9.33–9.34).
- Because the comment URL was long and complex, it has been shortened (see Section 9.36). Either the long or the short form of the URL is acceptable.

19. Editorial

Cuellar, N. G. (2016). Study abroad programs [Editorial]. *Journal of Transcultural Nursing, 27*(3), 209. https://doi.org/10.1177/1043659616638722

Parenthetical citation: (Cuellar, 2016)
Narrative citation: Cuellar (2016)

- Use the reference format for the publication in which the editorial was published. This example shows an editorial from a journal; editorials also appear in magazines, newspapers, and other publications.
- Include the notation "Editorial" in square brackets after the title (except when the word "Editorial" is included in the title).
- If the editorial is unsigned, follow the guidelines in Sections 8.14 and 9.12 for the in-text citation and reference list entry, respectively.

10.2 Books and Reference Works

The books category includes authored books, edited books, anthologies, religious works, and classical works. The reference works category includes dictionaries, encyclopedias (including *Wikipedia*), and diagnostic manuals. For ebooks, the format, platform, or device (e.g., Kindle) is not included in the reference. For audiobooks, include the narrator and audiobook notation only in specific cases (see Examples 22 and 29). For a chapter in an authored book, create a reference for the whole book (see Examples 20–23) and provide the chapter number with the in-text citation only (see Section 8.13). Use the template shown next to construct references for books and reference works.

Author or editor	Date	Title	Source	
			Publisher information	DOI or URL
Author, A. A., & Author, B. B.	(2020).	*Title of book.*	Publisher Name.	https://doi.org/xxxx
Name of Group.		*Title of book* (2nd ed., Vol. 4).	First Publisher Name; Second Publisher Name.	https://xxxxx
Editor, E. E. (Ed.).		*Title of book* [Audiobook].		
Editor, E. E., & Editor, F. F. (Eds.).		*Title of book* (E. E. Editor, Ed.).		
		Title of book (T. Translator, Trans.; N. Narrator, Narr.).		

20. Authored book with a DOI

Brown, L. S. (2018). *Feminist therapy* (2nd ed.). American Psychological Association. https://doi.org/10.1037/0000092-000

> ***Parenthetical citation:*** (Brown, 2018)
> ***Narrative citation:*** Brown (2018)

21. Authored book without a DOI, from most academic research databases or print version

Burgess, R. (2019). *Rethinking global health: Frameworks of power.* Routledge.

> ***Parenthetical citation:*** (Burgess, 2019)
> ***Narrative citation:*** Burgess (2019)

- See Section 9.30 for more on including database information in references.

22. Authored ebook (e.g., Kindle book) or audiobook without a DOI, with a nondatabase URL

Cain, S. (2012). *Quiet: The power of introverts in a world that can't stop talking* (K. Mazur, Narr.) [Audiobook]. Random House Audio. http://bit.ly/2G0Bpbl

Christian, B., & Griffiths, T. (2016). *Algorithms to live by: The computer science of human decisions.* Henry Holt and Co. http://a.co/7qGBZAk

> ***Parenthetical citations:*** (Cain, 2012; Christian & Griffiths, 2016)
> ***Narrative citations:*** Cain (2012) and Christian and Griffiths (2016)

- It is not necessary to note when you used an audiobook versus a print book or an ebook when the content is the same, even if the format is different. However, do note that the work is an audiobook in the title element when the content is different (e.g., abridged), if you want to note something special about the audiobook (e.g., the impact of the narration on the listener), or if you quote from the audiobook (see Section 8.28).
- If the audiobook was released in a different year from the text version of the book, treat the work as republished (see Example 29).

23. Authored book with editor credited on the book cover

Meadows, D. H. (2008). *Thinking in systems: A primer* (D. Wright, Ed.). Chelsea Green Publishing.

> **Parenthetical citation:** (Meadows, 2008)
> **Narrative citation:** Meadows (2008)

- When an editor is credited on the cover of an authored book, provide the editor's name in parentheses after the book title with "Ed." or "Eds." in parentheses (see Section 9.10).

24. Edited book with a DOI, with multiple publishers

Schmid, H.-J. (Ed.). (2017). *Entrenchment and the psychology of language learning: How we reorganize and adapt linguistic knowledge.* American Psychological Association; De Gruyter Mouton. https://doi.org/10.1037/15969-000

> **Parenthetical citation:** (Schmid, 2017)
> **Narrative citation:** Schmid (2017)

- Separate multiple publisher names using semicolons.

25. Edited book without a DOI, from most academic research databases or print version

Hacker Hughes, J. (Ed.). (2017). *Military veteran psychological health and social care: Contemporary approaches.* Routledge.

> **Parenthetical citation:** (Hacker Hughes, 2017)
> **Narrative citation:** Hacker Hughes (2017)

- See Section 9.30 for more on including database information in references.

BOOKS

26. Edited ebook (e.g., Kindle book) or audiobook without a DOI, with a nondatabase URL

Pridham, K. F., Limbo, R., & Schroeder, M. (Eds.). (2018). *Guided partici-pation in pediatric nursing practice: Relationship-based teaching and learning with parents, children, and adolescents.* Springer Publishing Company. http://a.co/0IAiVgt

Parenthetical citation: (Pridham et al., 2018)
Narrative citation: Pridham et al. (2018)

- An ebook example is shown. See Example 22 for information about when a notation is needed after an audiobook title.

27. Book in another language

Amano, N., & Kondo, H. (2000). *Nihongo no goi tokusei* [Lexical character-istics of Japanese language] (Vol. 7). Sansei-do.

Piaget, J., & Inhelder, B. (1966). *La psychologie de l'enfant* [The psychology of the child]. Quadrige.

Parenthetical citations: (Amano & Kondo, 2000; Piaget & Inhelder, 1966)
Narrative citations: Amano and Kondo (2000) and Piaget and Inhelder (1966)

- When a book is in a different language from your paper, in-clude a translation of the book title in square brackets (see Section 9.38).

28. Book republished in translation

Piaget, J., & Inhelder, B. (1969). *The psychology of the child* (H. Weaver, Trans.; 2nd ed.). Basic Books. (Original work published 1966)

Parenthetical citation: (Piaget & Inhelder, 1966/1969)
Narrative citation: Piaget and Inhelder (1966/1969)

- For more on translated works, see Section 9.39.

29. Republished book, ebook, or audiobook

Freud, S. (2010). *The interpretation of dreams: The complete and definitive text* (J. Strachey, Ed. & Trans.). Basic Books. (Original work published 1900)

Rowling, J. K. (2015). *Harry Potter and the sorcerer's stone* (J. Dale, Narr.) [Audiobook]. Pottermore Publishing. http://bit.ly/2TcHchx (Original work published 1997)

Parenthetical citations: (Freud, 1900/2010; Rowling, 1997/2015)
Narrative citations: Freud (1900/2010) and Rowling (1997/2015)

- If the new version has been edited and/or translated from the original, provide the name(s) of the editor(s) and/or translator(s) after the title in parentheses.
- If an audiobook was released in a different year from the text version of the book, treat the audiobook as republished (see also Example 22 and Section 9.40).

30. One volume of a multivolume work

Fiske, S. T., Gilbert, D. T., & Lindzey, G. (2010). *Handbook of social psychology* (5th ed., Vol. 1). John Wiley & Sons. https://doi.org/10.1002/9780470561119

Travis, C. B., & White, J. W. (Eds.). (2018). *APA handbook of the psychology of women: Vol. 1. History, theory, and battlegrounds.* American Psychological Association. https://doi.org/10.1037/0000059-000

> *Parenthetical citations:* (Fiske et al., 2010; Travis & White, 2018)
> *Narrative citations:* Fiske et al. (2010) and Travis and White (2018)

- If the volume has both series editors (or editors-in-chief) and volume editors, only the volume editors appear in the author element.
- If the volume does not have its own title, include the volume number in parentheses without italics (as in the Fiske et al. example).
- If the volume has its own title, include the volume number and title after the main title in italics (as in the Travis & White example).

31. Book in a series

Madigan, S. (2019). *Narrative therapy* (2nd ed.). American Psychological Association. https://doi.org/10.1037/0000131-000

> *Parenthetical citation:* (Madigan, 2019)
> *Narrative citation:* Madigan (2019)

- For a series of conceptually related titles, the series title is not included in the reference (this book is part of the Theories of Psychotherapy Series; see Section 9.20).

32. Diagnostic manual (*DSM, ICD*)

American Psychiatric Association. (2013). *Diagnostic and statistical manual of mental disorders* (5th ed.). https://doi.org/10.1176/appi.books.9780890425596

World Health Organization. (2019). *International statistical classification of diseases and related health problems* (11th ed.). https://icd.who.int/

Parenthetical citation with abbreviation included:
Diagnostic and Statistical Manual of Mental Disorders (5th ed.; *DSM-5*; American Psychiatric Association, 2013)

International Statistical Classification of Diseases and Related Health Problems (11th ed.; *ICD-11*; World Health Organization, 2019)

Narrative citation with abbreviation included:
American Psychiatric Association's (2013) *Diagnostic and Statistical Manual of Mental Disorders* (5th ed.; *DSM-5*)

World Health Organization's (2019) *International Statistical Classification of Diseases and Related Health Problems* (11th ed.; *ICD-11*)

Subsequent parenthetical citations: (American Psychiatric Association, 2013; World Health Organization, 2019)

Subsequent narrative citations: American Psychiatric Association (2013) and World Health Organization (2019)

- When the author and publisher are the same, omit the publisher from the source element.
- It is common, but not required, to identify the title (and edition) of a diagnostic manual in the text. Group authors and manual titles can be abbreviated in the text (with a few exceptions) but not the reference list (see Sections 5.13 and 8.21).
- Generally, include a citation for a manual the first time it is mentioned in the text. If the first mention appears in a heading, do not cite the manual in the heading; rather, cite it within the first paragraph of that section or soon thereafter.
- Do not repeat the citation for a subsequent general mention of a manual. Repeat a citation only when it directly supports a statement (e.g., quoting, paraphrasing).
- Additional examples and guidance for citing other editions of and entries in the *DSM* and *ICD* are available on the APA Style website (https://apastyle.apa.org).

33. Dictionary, thesaurus, or encyclopedia

American Psychological Association. (n.d.). *APA dictionary of psychology.* Retrieved June 14, 2019, from https://dictionary.apa.org/

Merriam-Webster. (n.d.). *Merriam-Webster.com dictionary.* Retrieved May 5, 2019, from https://www.merriam-webster.com/

Zalta, E. N. (Ed.). (2019). *The Stanford encyclopedia of philosophy* (Summer 2019 ed.). Stanford University. https://plato.stanford.edu/archives/sum2019/

Parenthetical citations: (American Psychological Association, n.d.; Merriam-Webster, n.d.; Zalta, 2019)

Narrative citations: American Psychological Association (n.d.), Merriam-Webster (n.d.), and Zalta (2019)

- When a stable or archived version of the work is cited (as shown for the Zalta example), a retrieval date is not needed.
- When an online reference work is continuously updated (see Section 9.15) and the versions are not archived (as with the *APA Dictionary of Psychology* and the *Merriam-Webster.com Dictionary* examples), use "n.d." as the year of publication and include a retrieval date (see Section 9.16).

34. Anthology

Gold, M. (Ed.). (1999). *The complete social scientist: A Kurt Lewin reader.* American Psychological Association. https://doi.org/10.1037/10319-000

Parenthetical citation: (Gold, 1999)
Narrative citation: Gold (1999)

- Provide the editor(s) of the anthology in the author position of the reference.
- The date refers to the year the anthology was published (for a work included in an anthology, see Example 46).

35. Religious work

King James Bible. (2017). King James Bible Online. https://www.kingjamesbibleonline.org/ (Original work published 1769)

The Qur'an (M. A. S. Abdel Haleem, Trans.). (2004). Oxford University Press.

The Torah: The five books of Moses (3rd ed.). (2015). The Jewish Publication Society. (Original work published 1962)

Parenthetical citations: (*King James Bible*, 1769/2017; *The Qur'an*, 2004; *The Torah*, 1962/2015)
Narrative citations: *King James Bible* (1769/2017), *The Qur'an* (2004), and *The Torah* (1962/2015)

- For more on citing religious works, see Section 9.41; to cite a specific book or verse, see Section 8.13; to quote a passage, see Section 8.28.
- Additional examples of religious texts are available on the APA Style website (https://apastyle.apa.org).

36. Ancient Greek or Roman work

Aristotle. (1994). *Poetics* (S. H. Butcher, Trans.). The Internet Classics Archive. http://classics.mit.edu/Aristotle/poetics.html (Original work published ca. 350 B.C.E.)

Parenthetical citation: (Aristotle, ca. 350 B.C.E./1994)
Narrative citation: Aristotle (ca. 350 B.C.E./1994)

BOOKS

- For ancient Greek or Roman works, include the copyright date of the version used in the date element and the date of the original (ancient) publication in parentheses at the end of the entry. When the date of original publication is approximate, use the abbreviation "ca." (which stands for "circa").
- For more on citing classical works, see Section 9.41; to cite a canonically numbered part of a classical work, see Section 8.13; to quote a passage, see Section 8.28.

37. Shakespeare

Shakespeare, W. (1995). *Much ado about nothing* (B. A. Mowat & P. Werstine, Eds.). Washington Square Press. (Original work published 1623)

Parenthetical citation: (Shakespeare, 1623/1995)
Narrative citation: Shakespeare (1623/1995)

- For more on citing Shakespeare and other classical works of literature, see Section 9.41; to cite a specific act, scene, or line, see Section 8.13; to quote a passage, see Section 8.28.

10.3 Edited Book Chapters and Entries in Reference Works

The edited book chapter category includes chapters of edited books and works in anthologies. The entries in reference works category includes dictionary, thesaurus, and encyclopedia entries. For ebook chapters or entries, the format, platform, or device (e.g., Kindle) is not included in the reference. For audiobook chapters or entries, include the narrator and audiobook notation only in specific cases (see Example 22). For a chapter in an authored book, create a reference for the whole book (see Examples 20–23) and provide the chapter number with the in-text citation only (see Section 8.13). Use the template shown next to construct references for edited book chapters and entries in reference works.

Chapter author	Date	Chapter title	Source	
			Edited book information	DOI or URL
Author, A. A., & Author, B. B. Name of Group.	(2020).	Title of chapter.	In E. E. Editor (Ed.), *Title of book* (pp. 3–13). Publisher Name. In E. E. Editor & F. F. Editor (Eds.), *Title of book* (3rd ed., Vol. 2, pp. 212–255). Publisher Name.	https://doi.org/xxxx https://xxxxx

38. Chapter in an edited book with a DOI

Balsam, K. F., Martell, C. R., Jones, K. P., & Safren, S. A. (2019). Affirmative cognitive behavior therapy with sexual and gender minority people. In G. Y. Iwamasa & P. A. Hays (Eds.), *Culturally responsive cognitive behavior therapy: Practice and supervision* (2nd ed., pp. 287–314). American Psychological Association. https://doi.org/10.1037/0000119-012

Parenthetical citation: (Balsam et al., 2019)
Narrative citation: Balsam et al. (2019)

39. Chapter in an edited book without a DOI, from most academic research databases or print version

Weinstock, R., Leong, G. B., & Silva, J. A. (2003). Defining forensic psychiatry: Roles and responsibilities. In R. Rosner (Ed.), *Principles and practice of forensic psychiatry* (2nd ed., pp. 7–13). CRC Press.

Parenthetical citation: (Weinstock et al., 2003)
Narrative citation: Weinstock et al. (2003)

- See Section 9.30 for more on including database information in references.

40. Chapter in an edited ebook (e.g., Kindle book) or audiobook without a DOI, with nondatabase URL

Tafoya, N., & Del Vecchio, A. (2005). Back to the future: An examination of the Native American Holocaust experience. In M. McGoldrick, J. Giordano, & N. Garcia-Preto (Eds.), *Ethnicity and family therapy* (3rd ed., pp. 55–63). Guilford Press. http://a.co/36xRhBT

Parenthetical citation: (Tafoya & Del Vecchio, 2005)
Narrative citation: Tafoya and Del Vecchio (2005)

- See Examples 22 and 29 for more information on audiobooks.

41. Chapter in an edited book in another language

Carcavilla González, N. (2015). Terapia sensorial auditiva: Activación cerebral por medio de la música [Auditory sensory therapy: Brain activation through music]. In J. J. García Meilán (Ed.), *Guía práctica de terapias estimulativas en el Alzhéimer* (pp. 67–86). Editorial Síntesis. https://www.sintesis.com/guias-profesionales-203/guia-practica-de-terapias-estimulativas-en-el-alzheimer-libro-1943.html

Parenthetical citation: (Carcavilla González, 2015)
Narrative citation: Carcavilla González (2015)

CHAPTERS

- When a chapter is in a different language from your paper, include a translation of the chapter title in square brackets (see Section 9.38 for more).

42. Chapter in an edited book, republished in translation

Heidegger, M. (2008). On the essence of truth (J. Sallis, Trans.). In D. F. Krell (Ed.), *Basic writings* (pp. 111–138). Harper Perennial Modern Thought. (Original work published 1961)

Parenthetical citation: (Heidegger, 1961/2008)
Narrative citation: Heidegger (1961/2008)

- For more on translated works, see Section 9.39.

43. Chapter in an edited book, reprinted from a journal article

Sacchett, C., & Humphreys, G. W. (2004). Calling a squirrel a squirrel but a canoe a wigwam: A category-specific deficit for artefactual objects and body parts. In D. A. Balota & E. J. Marsh (Eds.), *Cognitive psychology: Key readings in cognition* (pp. 100–108). Psychology Press. (Reprinted from "Calling a squirrel a squirrel but a canoe a wigwam: A category-specific deficit for artefactual objects and body parts," 1992, *Cognitive Neuropsychology, 9*[1], 73–86, http://doi.org/d4vb59)

Parenthetical citation: (Sacchett & Humphreys, 1992/2004)
Narrative citation: Sacchett and Humphreys (1992/2004)

- Provide the information for the reprinted version you used, then provide in parentheses the original article title (even if the title did not change), year, and source information (see Section 9.40 for more).
- Place the original journal article issue number in square brackets instead of parentheses to avoid nested parentheses.

44. Chapter in an edited book, reprinted from another book

Bronfenbrenner, U. (2005). The social ecology of human development: A retrospective conclusion. In U. Bronfenbrenner (Ed.), *Making human beings human: Bioecological perspectives on human development* (pp. 27–40). SAGE Publications. (Reprinted from *Brain and intelligence: The ecology of child development*, pp. 113–123, by F. Richardson, Ed., 1973, National Educational Press)

Parenthetical citation: (Bronfenbrenner, 1973/2005)
Narrative citation: Bronfenbrenner (1973/2005)

- Provide information for the reprinted version you used, then provide in parentheses the original book title, page range, author or editor name (including "Ed." for an editor), year, and publisher (see Section 9.40 for more).

45. Chapter in a volume of a multivolume work

Goldin-Meadow, S. (2015). Gesture and cognitive development. In L. S. Liben & U. Mueller (Eds.), *Handbook of child psychology and developmental science: Vol. 2. Cognitive processes* (7th ed., pp. 339–380). John Wiley & Sons. https://doi.org/10.1002/9781118963418.childpsy209

Parenthetical citation: (Goldin-Meadow, 2015)
Narrative citation: Goldin-Meadow (2015)

- If the volume has both series editors (or editors-in-chief) and volume editors, only the volume editors appear in the reference.
- The volume in this example has its own title. See Example 30 for how to include untitled volume information in parentheses after the book title.

46. Work in an anthology

Lewin, K. (1999). Group decision and social change. In M. Gold (Ed.), *The complete social scientist: A Kurt Lewin reader* (pp. 265–284). American Psychological Association. https://doi.org/10.1037/10319-010 (Original work published 1948)

Parenthetical citation: (Lewin, 1948/1999)
Narrative citation: Lewin (1948/1999)

- Works that have been published elsewhere before appearing in an anthology are treated as being republished (see Section 9.40) rather than reprinted.

47. Entry in a dictionary, thesaurus, or encyclopedia, with group author

American Psychological Association. (n.d.). Positive transference. In *APA dictionary of psychology*. Retrieved September 30, 2019, from https://dictionary.apa.org/positive-transference

Merriam-Webster. (n.d.). Self-report. In *Merriam-Webster.com dictionary*. Retrieved September 12, 2019, from https://www.merriam-webster.com/dictionary/self-report

Parenthetical citations: (American Psychological Association, n.d.; Merriam-Webster, n.d.)
Narrative citations: American Psychological Association (n.d.) and Merriam-Webster (n.d.)

- When an online reference work is continuously updated (see Section 9.15) and the versions are not archived, use "n.d." as the year of publication and include a retrieval date (see Section 9.16).

48. Entry in a dictionary, thesaurus, or encyclopedia, with individual author

Graham, G. (2019). Behaviorism. In E. N. Zalta (Ed.), *The Stanford encyclopedia of philosophy* (Summer 2019 ed.). Stanford University. https://plato.stanford.edu/archives/sum2019/entries/behaviorism/

> **Parenthetical citation:** (Graham, 2019)
> **Narrative citation:** Graham (2019)

- This example is structured similarly to the reference for a chapter in an edited book because the entry has an individual author, the encyclopedia has an editor, and the whole work has a publisher.
- Because this version of the entry is archived, a retrieval date is not needed.

49. *Wikipedia* entry

List of oldest companies. (2019, January 13). In *Wikipedia*. https://en.wikipedia.org/w/index.php?title=List_of_oldest_companies&oldid=878158136

> **Parenthetical citation:** ("List of Oldest Companies," 2019)
> **Narrative citation:** "List of Oldest Companies" (2019)

- Cite the archived version of the page so that readers can retrieve the version you used. Access the archived version on *Wikipedia* by selecting "View history" and then the time and date of the version you used. If a wiki does not provide permanent links to archived versions of the page, include the URL for the entry and the retrieval date.

10.4 Reports and Gray Literature

There are many kinds of reports, including government reports, technical reports, and research reports. These reports, like journal articles, usually cover original research, but they may or may not be peer reviewed. They are part of a body of literature sometimes referred to as *gray literature*. The category of gray literature includes press releases, codes of ethics, grants, policy briefs, issue briefs, and so forth. It is optional—but often helpful—to describe these less common types of gray literature in square brackets after the title. Reports sometimes include a suggested reference format, which usually contains the information necessary to write an APA Style reference (author, date, title, and source), but you may need to adjust the order of the elements and other formatting to conform to APA Style. When the publisher is the same as the author, which is often the case for group authors (see Examples 50 and 54), omit the publisher from the source element. Use the template shown next to construct references for reports and gray literature.

| | | | Source | |
| | | | Publisher | |
Author	Date	Title	information	DOI or URL
Author, A. A., & Author, B. B. Name of Group.	(2020). (2020, May 2).	Title of report. Title of report (Report No. 123). Title of gray literature [Description].	Publisher Name.	https://doi.org/xxxx https://xxxxx

REPORTS

50. Report by a government agency or other organization

Australian Government Productivity Commission & New Zealand Productivity Commission. (2012). *Strengthening trans-Tasman economic relations.* https://www.pc.gov.au/inquiries/completed/australia-new-zealand/report/trans-tasman.pdf

Canada Council for the Arts. (2013). *What we heard: Summary of key findings: 2013 Canada Council's Inter-Arts Office consultation.* http://publications.gc.ca/collections/collection_2017/canadacouncil/K23-65-2013-eng.pdf

National Cancer Institute. (2018). *Facing forward: Life after cancer treatment* (NIH Publication No. 18-2424). U.S. Department of Health and Human Services, National Institutes of Health. https://www.cancer.gov/publications/patient-education/life-after-treatment.pdf

Parenthetical citations: (Australian Government Productivity Commission & New Zealand Productivity Commission, 2012; Canada Council for the Arts, 2013; National Cancer Institute, 2018)
Narrative citations: Australian Government Productivity Commission and New Zealand Productivity Commission (2012), Canada Council for the Arts (2013), and National Cancer Institute (2018)

• See Section 9.11 for how to treat the names of group authors.

- The names of parent agencies not included in the group author name appear in the source element as the publisher (see Section 9.11).
- If multiple agencies authored a report together, join the names with an ampersand, using commas to separate the names of three or more agencies.

51. Report by individual authors at a government agency or other organization

Fried, D., & Polyakova, A. (2018). *Democratic defense against disinformation.* Atlantic Council. https://www.atlanticcouncil.org/images/publications/ Democratic_Defense_Against_Disinformation_FINAL.pdf

Segaert, A., & Bauer, A. (2015). *The extent and nature of veteran homelessness in Canada.* Employment and Social Development Canada. https://www.canada.ca/en/employment-social-development/programs/ communities/homelessness/publications-bulletins/veterans-report.html

Parenthetical citations: (Fried & Polyakova, 2018; Segaert & Bauer, 2015)

Narrative citations: Fried and Polyakova (2018) and Segaert and Bauer (2015)

52. Report by individual authors at a government agency, published as part of a series

Blackwell, D. L., Lucas, J. W., & Clarke, T. C. (2014). *Summary health statistics for U.S. adults: National Health Interview Survey, 2012* (Vital and Health Statistics Series 10, Issue 260). Centers for Disease Control and Prevention. https://www.cdc.gov/nchs/data/series/sr_10/sr10_260.pdf

Parenthetical citation: (Blackwell et al., 2014)
Narrative citation: Blackwell et al. (2014)

53. Report by a task force, working group, or other group

British Cardiovascular Society Working Group. (2016). *British Cardiovascular Society Working Group report: Out-of-hours cardiovascular care: Management of cardiac emergencies and hospital in-patients.* British Cardiovascular Society. http://www.bcs.com/documents/BCSOOHWP_ Final_Report_05092016.pdf

Parenthetical citation: (British Cardiovascular Society Working Group, 2016)
Narrative citation: British Cardiovascular Society Working Group (2016)

- Capitalize the name of the task force or working group because it is a proper noun.

54. Annual report

U.S. Securities and Exchange Commission. (2017). *Agency financial report: Fiscal year 2017.* https://www.sec.gov/files/sec-2017-agency-financial-report.pdf

Parenthetical citation: (U.S. Securities and Exchange Commission, 2017)
Narrative citation: U.S. Securities and Exchange Commission (2017)

55. Code of ethics

American Counseling Association. (2014). *2014 ACA code of ethics.* https://www.counseling.org/knowledge-center

American Nurses Association. (2015). *Code of ethics for nurses with interpretive statements.* https://www.nursingworld.org/coe-view-only

American Psychological Association. (2017). *Ethical principles of psychologists and code of conduct* (2002, amended effective June 1, 2010, and January 1, 2017). https://www.apa.org/ethics/code/index.aspx

Parenthetical citations: (American Counseling Association, 2014; American Nurses Association, 2015; American Psychological Association, 2017)
Narrative citations: American Counseling Association (2014), American Nurses Association (2015), and American Psychological Association (2017)

56. Grant

Blair, C. B. (Principal Investigator). (2015–2020). *Stress, self-regulation and psychopathology in middle childhood* (Project No. 5R01HD081252-04) [Grant]. Eunice Kennedy Shriver National Institute of Child Health & Human Development. https://projectreporter.nih.gov/project_info_details.cfm?aid=9473071&icde=40092311

Parenthetical citation: (Blair, 2015–2020)
Narrative citation: Blair (2015–2020)

- List the principal investigator as the author with their role in parentheses, the project start and end year(s) as the date, the project title as the title, and the funding agency as the source.
- The National Institutes of Health (NIH) refers to grant numbers as project numbers; use the appropriate terminology for the grant in your reference and include the number in parentheses after the title.
- A grant application is not a recoverable source and should be discussed as part of the methodology but not included in the reference list.

57. Policy brief

> Harwell, M. (2018). *Don't expect too much: The limited usefulness of common SES measures and a prescription for change* [Policy brief]. National Education Policy Center. https://nepc.colorado.edu/publication/SES
>
> **Parenthetical citation:** (Harwell, 2018)
> **Narrative citation:** Harwell (2018)

58. Press release

> U.S. Food and Drug Administration. (2019, February 14). *FDA authorizes first interoperable insulin pump intended to allow patients to customize treatment through their individual diabetes management devices* [Press release]. https://www.fda.gov/NewsEvents/Newsroom/PressAnnouncements/ucm631412.htm
>
> **Parenthetical citation:** (U.S. Food and Drug Administration, 2019)
> **Narrative citation:** U.S. Food and Drug Administration (2019)

10.5 Dissertations and Theses

References for doctoral dissertations and master's and undergraduate theses are divided by whether they are unpublished or published; unpublished works generally must be retrieved directly from the college or university in print form, whereas published works are available from a database (e.g., the ProQuest Dissertations and Theses Global database), a university archive, or a personal website. Thus, for unpublished dissertations and theses, the university name appears in the source element of the reference, whereas for published dissertations and theses, the university name appears in square brackets after the title.

Use the template shown next to construct references for unpublished dissertations and theses.

Author	Date	Title	Source
Author, A. A.	(2020).	*Title of dissertation* [Unpublished doctoral dissertation].	Name of Institution Awarding the Degree.
		Title of thesis [Unpublished master's thesis].	
		Title of undergraduate thesis [Unpublished undergraduate thesis].	

Use the template shown next to construct references for published dissertations and theses.

			Source	
			Database or archive name	URL
Author	**Date**	**Title**		
Author, A. A.	(2020).	*Title of dissertation* [Doctoral dissertation, Name of Institution Awarding the Degree]. *Title of thesis* [Master's thesis, Name of Institution Awarding the Degree].	Database Name. Archive Name.	https://xxxxx

59. Unpublished dissertation or thesis

Harris, L. (2014). *Instructional leadership perceptions and practices of elementary school leaders* [Unpublished doctoral dissertation]. University of Virginia.

Parenthetical citation: (Harris, 2014)
Narrative citation: Harris (2014)

60. Dissertation or thesis from a database

Hollander, M. M. (2017). *Resistance to authority: Methodological innovations and new lessons from the Milgram experiment* (Publication No. 10289373) [Doctoral dissertation, University of Wisconsin–Madison]. ProQuest Dissertations and Theses Global.

Parenthetical citation: (Hollander, 2017)
Narrative citation: Hollander (2017)

61. Dissertation or thesis published online (not in a database)

Hutcheson, V. H. (2012). *Dealing with dual differences: Social coping strategies of gifted and lesbian, gay, bisexual, transgender, and queer adolescents* [Master's thesis, The College of William & Mary]. William & Mary Digital Archive. https://digitalarchive.wm.edu/bitstream/handle/10288/16594/HutchesonVirginia2012.pdf

Parenthetical citation: (Hutcheson, 2012)
Narrative citation: Hutcheson (2012)

10.6 Reviews

Reviews of books, films, TV shows, albums, and other entertainment are published in a variety of outlets, including journals, magazines, newspapers, websites, and blogs. The reference format for a review should be the same as the format for the type of content appearing within that source, with the addition of information about the item being reviewed in square brackets after the review title. Within the square brackets, write "Review of the" and then the type of work being reviewed (e.g., film, book, TV series episode, video game); its title (in sentence case, described in Section 5.7; see also Section 9.19 for whether to format the title in italics or quotation marks); and its author or editor, director, writer, and so forth, with a designation of role for all except regular authors of books. Use the template shown next to construct references for reviews.

		Title		Source	
Author	**Date**	**Review title**	**Details of reviewed work**	**Periodical information**	**DOI or URL**
Reviewer, A. A.	(2020). (2020, May 3).	Title of review	[Review of the book *Book title*, by A. A. Author]. [Review of the book *Book title*, by E. E. Editor, Ed.]. [Review of the film *Film title*, by D. D. Director, Dir.]. [Review of the TV series episode "Episode title," by W. W. Writer, Writer, & D. D. Director, Dir.].	*Periodical Title, 34*(2), 14–15. *Blog Title.*	https://doi.org/xxxxx https://xxxxxx

62. Film review published in a journal

Mirabito, L. A., & Heck, N. C. (2016). Bringing LGBTQ youth theater into the spotlight [Review of the film *The year we thought about love*, by E. Brodsky, Dir.]. *Psychology of Sexual Orientation and Gender Diversity, 3*(4), 499–500. https://doi.org/10.1037/sgd0000205

Parenthetical citation: (Mirabito & Heck, 2016)
Narrative citation: Mirabito and Heck (2016)

63. Book review published in a newspaper

Santos, F. (2019, January 11). Reframing refugee children's stories [Review of the book *We are displaced: My journey and stories from refugee girls around the world*, by M. Yousafzai]. *The New York Times.* https://nyti. ms/2Hlgjk3

Parenthetical citation: (Santos, 2019)
Narrative citation: Santos (2019)

64. TV series episode review published on a website

Perkins, D. (2018, February 1). The good place *ends its remarkable second season with irrational hope, unexpected gifts, and a smile* [Review of the TV series episode "Somewhere else," by M. Schur, Writer & Dir.]. A.V. Club. https://www.avclub.com/the-good-place-ends-its-remarkable-second-season-with-i-1822649316

Parenthetical citation: (Perkins, 2018)
Narrative citation: Perkins (2018)

- The title is italicized because this work is a webpage on a website (see Example 100). In the reference, the title of the show appears in reverse italics (see Section 4.16) and sentence case.

10.7 Informally Published Works

Informally published works include those available from a preprint archive or repository such as PsyArXiv, an electronic archive such as ERIC, an institutional archive, a government archive, a personal website, and so forth. For informally published works, the date should be the year the work was completed or the year the draft was written. Include a DOI or URL when available.

Use the template shown next to construct references for informally published works.

| | | | Source | |
| | | | Database or archive | |
Author	Date	Title	information	DOI or URL
Author, A. A., & Author, B. B.	(2020).	*Title of the work.* *Title of the work* (Publication No. 123).	Name of Database. Name of Archive.	https://doi. org/xxxxx https:// xxxxxx

65. Informally published work, from a preprint archive or an institutional repository

Leuker, C., Samartzidis, L., Hertwig, R., & Pleskac, T. J. (2018). *When money talks: Judging risk and coercion in high-paying clinical trials.* PsyArXiv. https://doi.org/10.17605/OSF.IO/9P7CB

Stults-Kolehmainen, M. A., & Sinha, R. (2015). *The effects of stress on physical activity and exercise.* PubMed Central. https://www.ncbi.nlm.nih.gov/pmc/articles/PMC3894304

> **Parenthetical citations:** (Leuker et al., 2018; Stults-Kolehmainen & Sinha, 2015)
> **Narrative citations:** Leuker et al. (2018) and Stults-Kolehmainen and Sinha (2015)

- The informally published work may not be peer reviewed (as with Leuker et al.'s preprint article from PsyArXiv), or it may be the author's final, peer-reviewed manuscript as accepted for publication (as with Stults-Kolehmainen & Sinha's manuscript from PubMed Central). See Section 8.5 for more on use of an archival version.

66. Informally published work, from ERIC database

Ho, H.-K. (2014). *Teacher preparation for early childhood special education in Taiwan* (ED545393). ERIC. https://files.eric.ed.gov/fulltext/ED545393.pdf

> **Parenthetical citation:** (Ho, 2014)
> **Narrative citation:** Ho (2014)

- ERIC assigns document numbers to works in its database. Include this number in parentheses after the title of the work.

Software and Tests

10.8 Computer Software and Mobile Apps

Common software and mobile apps mentioned in text, but not paraphrased or quoted, do not need citations, nor do programming languages. "Common" is relative to your field and audience—examples of software or apps that do not require citations include Microsoft Office (e.g., Word, Excel, PowerPoint), social media apps (e.g., Facebook, Instagram, Twitter), survey software (e.g., Qualtrics, Survey Monkey), Adobe products (e.g., Adobe Reader, Photoshop, Adobe Acrobat), Java, and statistical programs (e.g., R, SPSS, SAS). If you used common software or mobile apps during your research, simply give the proper name of the software or app along with the version number in the text, if relevant.

Data were analyzed with IBM SPSS Statistics (Version 25).

Clients had installed the Facebook app on their mobile devices.

However, include reference list entries and in-text citations if you have paraphrased or quoted from any software or apps. Also provide reference list entries and in-text citations when mentioning software, apps, and apparatuses or equipment of limited distribution—meaning your audience is unlikely to be familiar with them. The date of a computer software or mobile app reference is the year of publication of the version used. The titles of software and apps should be italicized in the reference list entry but not italicized in the text. To cite content on a social media app, see Section 10.13. Use the template shown next to construct references for software and mobile apps of limited distribution.

| | | | Source | |
Author	Date	Title	Publisher	URL
Author, A. A., & Author, B. B. Name of Group.	(2020).	*Title of work* (Version 1.2) [Computer software]. *Title of work* (Version 4.6) [Mobile app].	Publisher. App Store. Google Play Store.	https:// xxxxxx

Use the template shown next to construct references for entries in mobile app reference works. The format for an entry in a mobile app reference work is similar to that for a chapter in an edited book. The most common case, in which the same author is responsible for the whole work and all entries, is shown here.

| | | Entry | Source | |
Author	Date	title	Mobile app information	URL
Author, A. A., & Author, B. B. Name of Group.	(2020).	Title of entry.	In *Title of work* (Version 1.2) [Mobile app]. Publisher Name or App Store.	https:// xxxxxx

67. Software

Borenstein, M., Hedges, L., Higgins, J., & Rothstein, H. (2014). *Comprehensive meta-analysis* (Version 3.3.070) [Computer software]. Biostat. https:// www.meta-analysis.com/

Parenthetical citation: (Borenstein et al., 2014)
Narrative citation: Borenstein et al. (2014)

68. Mobile app

Epocrates. (2019). *Epocrates medical references* (Version 18.12) [Mobile app]. App Store. https://itunes.apple.com/us/app/epocrates/id281935788?mt=8

Parenthetical citation: (Epocrates, 2019)
Narrative citation: Epocrates (2019)

69. Entry in a mobile app reference work

Epocrates. (2019). Interaction check: Aspirin + sertraline. In *Epocrates medical references* (Version 18.12) [Mobile app]. Google Play Store. https://play.google.com/store/apps/details?id=com.epocrates&hl=en_US

Parenthetical citation: (Epocrates, 2019)
Narrative citation: Epocrates (2019)

10.9 Tests, Scales, and Inventories

To cite a test, scale, or inventory, provide a citation for its supporting literature (e.g., its manual, which may be an authored or an edited book, or the journal article in which it was published; see Example 70). If supporting literature is not available, it is also possible to cite the test itself (see Example 71) and/or a database record for a test (see Example 72). The title of a test, a scale, or an inventory should be capitalized using title case whenever it appears in a paper. Although the test title may be italicized in a reference (e.g., in the name of a manual or when the test itself is cited), in the text, the title of a test should appear in title case in standard (nonitalic) type. A test database name (e.g., PsycTESTS, ETS TestLink) is included only for test database records (see Example 72). Use the template shown next to construct references for tests, scales, inventories, or test database records.

| | | | Source | |
Author	Date	Title	Database	DOI or URL
Author, A. A., & Author, B. B.	(2020).	*Title of the Test.* *Title of the Test Database Record* [Database record].	Test Database Name.	https://doi.org/xxxxx https://xxxxxx

70. Manual for a test, scale, or inventory

Tellegen, A., & Ben-Porath, Y. S. (2011). *Minnesota Multiphasic Personality Inventory–2 Restructured Form (MMPI-2-RF): Technical manual.* Pearson.

Parenthetical citation: (Tellegen & Ben-Porath, 2011)
Narrative citation: Tellegen and Ben-Porath (2011)

71. Test, scale, or inventory itself

Project Implicit. (n.d.). *Gender–Science IAT*. https://implicit.harvard.edu/implicit/takeatest.html

> **Parenthetical citation:** (Project Implicit, n.d.)
> **Narrative citation:** Project Implicit (n.d.)

- Cite the test, scale, or inventory only if a manual or other supporting literature is not available; if a manual is available for a test, cite the manual, not the test (see Example 70).

72. Database record for a test

Alonso-Tapia, J., Nieto, C., Merino-Tejedor, E., Huertas, J. A., & Ruiz, M. (2018). *Situated Goals Questionnaire for University Students (SGQ-U, CMS-U)* [Database record]. PsycTESTS. https://doi.org/10.1037/t66267-000

Cardoza, D., Morris, J. K., Myers, H. F., & Rodriguez, N. (2000). *Acculturative Stress Inventory (ASI)* (TC022704) [Database record]. ETS TestLink.

> **Parenthetical citations:** (Alonso-Tapia et al., 2018; Cardoza et al., 2000)
> **Narrative citations:** Alonso-Tapia et al. (2018) and Cardoza et al. (2000)

- Test database records (e.g., records from PsycTESTS, the ETS TestLink collection, or the CINAHL database) typically provide unique descriptive and administrative information about tests; cite the database record if you use this unique information. Otherwise, cite the test's supporting literature, if available.

Audiovisual Media

Audiovisual media may have both visual and audio components (e.g., films, TV shows, YouTube videos; see Section 10.10), audio components only (e.g., music, speech recordings; see Section 10.11), or visual components only (e.g., artwork, PowerPoint slides, photographs; see Section 10.12). The reference examples that follow are divided into those categories as an aid to readers of this manual; however, they follow the same formats, so the guidance is presented together here.

The formats for audiovisual references follow a pattern based on whether the work stands alone (e.g., films, whole TV series, podcasts, webinars, music albums, artwork, YouTube videos) or is part of a greater whole (e.g., TV series episodes, podcast episodes, songs from a music album).

The author of an audiovisual work is determined by media type, as shown next. Describe the audiovisual work in square brackets—for example, "[Film]," "[TV series]," "[Audio podcast episode]," "[Song]," "[Painting]," and so forth—in the title element of the reference. In the source element of the reference, provide the name of the production company for films, TV series, or podcasts; the label for music albums; the museum name and location for artwork; or the name of the streaming video site that hosts a streaming video. To cite a direct quotation from an audiovisual work (e.g., from a film), see Section 8.28; for interviews, see Section 8.7. If you want to reproduce an audiovisual work (e.g., a photograph or clip art) rather than just cite it, you may need to seek permission from the copyright owner and/or provide a copyright attribution per the terms of the image license (see Section 8.36 for more).

Use the template shown next to construct references for audiovisual media that stand alone.

Author	Date	Title	Source	
			Publisher	**URL**
Director, D. D. (Director).	(2020).	*Title of work* [Description].	Production Company.	https:// xxxxxx
Producer, P. P. (Executive Producer).	(1989–present). (2013–2019). (2019, July 21).		Label. Museum Name, Museum Location.	
Host, H. H. (Host).				
Artist, A. A.			Department Name, University Name.	
Uploader, U. U.				

Use the template shown next to construct references for audiovisual media that are part of a greater whole.

Author	Date	Title	Source	
			Publisher	**URL**
Writer, W. W. (Writer), & Director, D. D. (Director).	(2020). (2020, March 26).	Title of episode (Season No., Episode No.) [Description].	In P. P. Producer (Executive Producer), *Title of TV series*. Production Company.	https:// xxxxxx
Host, H. H. (Host).				
Producer, P. P. (Producer).		Title of song [Description].	In *Title of podcast*. Production Company.	
Composer, C. C.			On *Title of album*. Label.	
Artist, A. A.				

10.10 Audiovisual Works
73. Film or video

Forman, M. (Director). (1975). *One flew over the cuckoo's nest* [Film]. United Artists.

Fosha, D. (Guest Expert), & Levenson, H. (Host). (2017). *Accelerated experiential dynamic psychotherapy (AEDP) supervision* [Film; educational DVD]. American Psychological Association. https://www.apa.org/pubs/videos/4310958.aspx

Jackson, P. (Director). (2001). *The lord of the rings: The fellowship of the ring* [Film; four-disc special extended ed. on DVD]. WingNut Films; The Saul Zaentz Company.

> **Parenthetical citations:** (Forman, 1975; Fosha & Levenson, 2017; Jackson, 2001)
> **Narrative citations:** Forman (1975), Fosha and Levenson (2017), and Jackson (2001)

- The director should be credited as the author of a film. However, if the director is unknown (as with the Fosha & Levenson example), someone in a similar role can be credited instead to aid readers in retrieving the work; the description of role in this case matches what is on the work and is flexible.
- It is not necessary to specify how you watched a film (e.g., in a theater, on DVD, streaming online). However, the format or other descriptive information may be included—within the square brackets, following the word "Film" and a semicolon—when you need to specify the version used (e.g., when the film's DVD release includes a commentary or special feature that you used, or when the film is a limited-release educational video or DVD). Adjust this wording as needed.

74. Film or video in another language

Malle, L. (Director). (1987). *Au revoir les enfants* [Goodbye children] [Film]. Nouvelles Éditions de Films.

> **Parenthetical citation:** (Malle, 1987)
> **Narrative citation:** Malle (1987)

- When a film title is in a different language from your paper, include a translation of the title in square brackets (see Section 9.38).

75. TV series

Simon, D., Colesberry, R. F., & Kostroff Noble, N. (Executive Producers). (2002–2008). *The wire* [TV series]. Blown Deadline Productions; HBO.

Parenthetical citation: (Simon et al., 2002–2008)
Narrative citation: Simon et al. (2002–2008)

- When the series spans multiple years, separate the years with an en dash. If the series is still airing, replace the second year with the word "present": (2015–present).

76. TV series episode or webisode

Barris, K. (Writer & Director). (2017, January 11). Lemons (Season 3, Episode 12) [TV series episode]. In K. Barris, J. Groff, A. Anderson, E. B. Dobbins, L. Fishburne, & H. Sugland (Executive Producers), *Black-ish*. Wilmore Films; Artists First; Cinema Gypsy Productions; ABC Studios.

Oakley, B. (Writer), Weinstein, J. (Writer), & Lynch, J. (Director). (1995, May 21). Who shot Mr. Burns? (Part one) (Season 6, Episode 25) [TV series episode]. In D. Mirkin, J. L. Brooks, M. Groening, & S. Simon (Executive Producers), *The Simpsons*. Gracie Films; Twentieth Century Fox Film Corporation.

Parenthetical citations: (Barris, 2017; Oakley et al., 1995)
Narrative citations: Barris (2017) and Oakley et al. (1995)

- Include writer(s) and the director for the episode. Include the contributor roles in parentheses after each contributor's name. "Writer" and "Director" are shown here, but "Executive Director" or other role descriptions might also be used.
- Provide the season number and episode number after the title in parentheses.

77. TED Talk

Giertz, S. (2018, April). *Why you should make useless things* [Video]. TED Conferences. https://www.ted.com/talks/simone_giertz_why_you_should_make_useless_things

TED. (2012, March 16). *Brené Brown: Listening to shame* [Video]. YouTube. https://www.youtube.com/watch?v=psN1DORYYV0

Parenthetical citations: (Giertz, 2018; TED, 2012)
Narrative citations: Giertz (2018) and TED (2012)

- When the TED Talk comes from TED's website (as with the Giertz example), use the name of the speaker as the author. When the TED Talk is on YouTube, list the owner of the YouTube account (here, TED) as the author to aid in retrieval.
- When the speaker is not listed as the author, integrate their name into the narrative if desired: "Brown discussed shame as a human experience (TED, 2012)."
- To cite a quotation from a TED Talk, see Section 8.28.

78. Webinar, recorded

Goldberg, J. F. (2018). *Evaluating adverse drug effects* [Webinar]. American Psychiatric Association. https://education.psychiatry.org/Users/Product Details.aspx?ActivityID=6172

Parenthetical citation: (Goldberg, 2018)
Narrative citation: Goldberg (2018)

- Use this format only for recorded, retrievable webinars.
- Cite unrecorded webinars as personal communications (see Section 8.9).

79. YouTube video or other streaming video

Cutts, S. (2017, November 24). *Happiness* [Video]. Vimeo. https://vimeo.com/244405542

Fogarty, M. [Grammar Girl]. (2016, September 30). *How to diagram a sentence (absolute basics)* [Video]. YouTube. https://youtu.be/deiEY5Yq1ql

University of Oxford. (2018, December 6). *How do geckos walk on water?* [Video]. YouTube. https://www.youtube.com/watch?v=qm1xGfO7Jc8

Parenthetical citations: (Cutts, 2017; Fogarty, 2016; University of Oxford, 2018)
Narrative citations: Cutts (2017), Fogarty (2016), and University of Oxford (2018)

- The person or group who uploaded the video is credited as the author for retrievability, even if they did not create the work. Note the contributions of others who appear in the video in the text narrative if desired (see Example 77).
- See Section 9.8 for how to present usernames. To cite a quotation from a YouTube or other streaming video, see Section 8.28.

10.11 Audio Works

See the introduction to the Audiovisual Media section for templates for audio works.

80. Music album

Bach, J. S. (2010). *The Brandenburg concertos: Concertos BWV 1043 & 1060* [Album recorded by Academy of St Martin in the Fields]. Decca. (Original work published 1721)

Bowie, D. (2016). *Blackstar* [Album]. Columbia.

Parenthetical citations: (Bach, 1721/2010; Bowie, 2016)
Narrative citations: Bach (1721/2010) and Bowie (2016)

- For a recording of a classical work, provide the composer as the author, and note (in square brackets) following the title the individual or group who recorded the version you used. Provide the publication date for the version you used, and then provide the year of original composition in parentheses at the end of the reference.
- For all other recordings, provide the name of the recording artist or group as the author.
- It is not usually necessary to specify how you listened to an album (e.g., streaming on Spotify, iTunes, Amazon Music, Pandora, on CD). However, the format or other descriptive information may be included—in square brackets, following the word "Album" and a semicolon—when you need to specify the version you used (e.g., when a version of an album includes special tracks or features you accessed). Adjust this wording as needed.
- Include a URL in the reference if that location is the only means of retrieval (e.g., for artists who provide music in only one location, such as on SoundCloud or their website).

81. Single song or track

Beethoven, L. van. (2012). Symphony No. 3 in E-flat major [Song recorded by Staatskapelle Dresden]. On *Beethoven: Complete symphonies*. Brilliant Classics. (Original work published 1804)

Beyoncé. (2016). Formation [Song]. On *Lemonade*. Parkwood; Columbia.

Childish Gambino. (2018). This is America [Song]. mcDJ; RCA.

Lamar, K. (2017). Humble [Song]. On *Damn*. Aftermath Entertainment; Interscope Records; Top Dawg Entertainment.

Parenthetical citations: (Beethoven, 1804/2012; Beyoncé, 2016; Childish Gambino, 2018; Lamar, 2017)
Narrative citations: Beethoven (1804/2012), Beyoncé (2016), Childish Gambino (2018), and Lamar (2017)

- If the song has no associated album (as in the Childish Gambino example), omit that part of the reference.
- Include a URL in the reference if that location is the only means of retrieval (e.g., for artists who provide music in only one location, such as on SoundCloud or their website).

82. Podcast

Vedantam, S. (Host). (2015–present). *Hidden brain* [Audio podcast]. NPR. https://www.npr.org/series/423302056/hidden-brain

Parenthetical citation: (Vedantam, 2015–present)
Narrative citation: Vedantam (2015–present)

- List the host of the podcast as the author. Alternatively, provide the executive producers, if known. In either case, include their role in parentheses.
- Specify the podcast type (audio or video) in square brackets.
- If the URL of the podcast is unknown (e.g., if accessed via an app), omit the URL.

83. Podcast episode

Glass, I. (Host). (2011, August 12). Amusement park (No. 443) [Audio podcast episode]. In *This American life*. WBEZ Chicago. https://www.thisamericanlife.org/radio-archives/episode/443/amusement-park

Parenthetical citation: (Glass, 2011)
Narrative citation: Glass (2011)

- List the host of the podcast as the author and include their role in parentheses.
- Provide the episode number after the title in parentheses. If the podcast does not number episodes, omit the number from the reference.
- Specify the podcast type (audio or video) in square brackets.
- If the URL of the podcast is unknown (e.g., if accessed via an app), omit the URL.

84. Radio interview recording in a digital archive

de Beauvoir, S. (1960, May 4). *Simone de Beauvoir discusses the art of writing* [Interview]. Studs Terkel Radio Archive; The Chicago History Museum. https://studsterkel.wfmt.com/programs/simone-de-beauvoir-discusses-art-writing

Parenthetical citation: (de Beauvoir, 1960)
Narrative citation: de Beauvoir (1960)

- For interviews that are housed in digital or physical archives (whether in audio or audiovisual form), credit the interviewee as the author. For more on interviews, see Section 8.7.

85. Speech audio recording

King, M. L., Jr. (1963, August 28). *I have a dream* [Speech audio recording]. American Rhetoric. https://www.americanrhetoric.com/speeches/mlkihaveadream.htm

Parenthetical citation: (King, 1963)
Narrative citation: King (1963)

10.12 Visual Works

See the introduction to the Audiovisual Media section for templates for visual works.

86. Artwork in a museum or on a museum website

Delacroix, E. (1826–1827). *Faust attempts to seduce Marguerite* [Lithograph]. The Louvre, Paris, France.

Wood, G. (1930). *American gothic* [Painting]. Art Institute of Chicago, Chicago, IL, United States. https://www.artic.edu/aic/collections/artwork/6565

> *Parenthetical citations:* (Delacroix, 1826–1827; Wood, 1930)
> *Narrative citations:* Delacroix (1826–1827) and Wood (1930)

- Use this format to cite all types of museum artwork, including paintings, sculptures, photographs, prints, drawings, and installations; always include a description of the medium or format in square brackets after the title.
- For untitled art, include a description in square brackets in place of a title.

87. Clip art or stock image

GDJ. (2018). *Neural network deep learning prismatic* [Clip art]. Openclipart. https://openclipart.org/detail/309343/neural-network-deep-learning-prismatic

> *Parenthetical citation:* (GDJ, 2018)
> *Narrative citation:* GDJ (2018)

- Use this format to cite (but not reproduce) most clip art or stock images. To reproduce clip art or stock images, permission and/or a copyright attribution may be necessary in addition to the reference. No citation, permission, or copyright attribution is necessary for clip art from programs like Microsoft Word or PowerPoint (see Section 8.36).

88. Infographic

Rossman, J., & Palmer, R. (2015). *Sorting through our space junk* [Infographic]. World Science Festival. https://www.worldsciencefestival.com/2015/11/space-junk-infographic/

> *Parenthetical citation:* (Rossman & Palmer, 2015)
> *Narrative citation:* Rossman and Palmer (2015)

- Use this format to cite (but not reproduce) an infographic. To reproduce an infographic, permission and/or a copyright attribution may be necessary in addition to the reference (see Section 8.36).

89. Photograph

McCurry, S. (1985). *Afghan girl* [Photograph]. National Geographic. https://www.nationalgeographic.com/magazine/national-geographic-magazine-50-years-of-covers/#/ngm-1985-jun-714.jpg

Rinaldi, J. (2016). [Photograph series of a boy who finds his footing after abuse by those he trusted]. The Pulitzer Prizes. https://www.pulitzer.org/winners/jessica-rinaldi

Parenthetical citations: (McCurry, 1985; Rinaldi, 2016)
Narrative citations: McCurry (1985) and Rinaldi (2016)

- Use this format to cite (but not reproduce) photographs or other artwork not connected to a museum (for museum artwork, see Example 86). To reproduce a photograph, permission and/or a copyright attribution may be necessary in addition to the reference (see Section 8.36).
- The source is the name of the site from which the photograph was retrieved.
- For an untitled photograph, include a description in square brackets in place of a title.
- If you took the photograph yourself, see Section 7.30.

90. PowerPoint slides or lecture notes

Canan, E., & Vasilev, J. (2019, May 22). [Lecture notes on resource allocation]. Department of Management Control and Information Systems, University of Chile. https://uchilefau.academia.edu/ElseZCanan

Housand, B. (2016). *Game on! Integrating games and simulations in the classroom* [PowerPoint slides]. SlideShare. https://www.slideshare.net/brianhousand/game-on-iagc-2016/

Mack, R., & Spake, G. (2018). *Citing open source images and formatting references for presentations* [PowerPoint slides]. Canvas@FNU. https://fnu.onelogin.com/login

Parenthetical citations: (Canan & Vasilev, 2019; Housand, 2016; Mack & Spake, 2018)
Narrative citations: Canan and Vasilev (2019), Housand (2016), and Mack and Spake (2018)

- If the slides come from a classroom website, learning management system (e.g., Canvas, Blackboard), or company intranet and you are writing for an audience with access to

VISUAL

that resource, provide the name of the site and its URL (use the login page URL for sites requiring login; see Section 8.8).

Online Media

10.13 Social Media

Cite only original content from social media sites such as Twitter, Facebook, Reddit, Instagram, Tumblr, LinkedIn, and so forth. That is, if you used social media to discover content (e.g., you found a link to a blog post on Pinterest or Twitter) and you want to cite the content, cite it directly—it is not necessary to mention that you found it through a link on social media.

Social media posts may contain text only, text with audiovisuals (e.g., photos, videos), or audiovisuals alone. Include the text of a social media post up to the first 20 words. Note the presence of audiovisuals (in square brackets) after the text of the post (see Example 93).

Social media posts might also contain nonstandard spelling and capitalization, hashtags, links, and emojis. Do not alter the spelling and capitalization in a social media reference. Retain hashtags and links. Replicate emojis, if possible. If you are not able to create the emoji, provide the emoji's name in square brackets, for example, "[face with tears of joy emoji]" for 😂. The full list of emoji names can be found on the Unicode Consortium's website (http://unicode.org/emoji/charts/index.html). When calculating the number of words in your paper, count an emoji as one word.

Use the template shown next to construct references for social media content.

Author	Date	Title	Source Social media site name	URL
Twitter and Instagram: Author, A. A. [@username]. Name of Group [@username]. **Facebook and others:** Author, A. A. Name of Group. Name of Group [Username]. Username.	(n.d.). (2019, May 8).	*Content of the post up to the first 20 words.* *Content of the post up to the first 20 words* [Description of audiovisuals]. [Description of audiovisuals].	Site Name.	https://xxxxxx Retrieved August 27, 2020, from https://xxxxxx

91. Tweet

APA Education [@APAEducation]. (2018, June 29). *College students are form-ing mental-health clubs—and they're making a difference @washingtonpost* [Thumbnail with link attached] [Tweet]. Twitter. https://twitter.com/apaeducation/status/1012810490530140161

Badlands National Park [@BadlandsNPS]. (2018, February 26). *Biologists have identified more than 400 different plant species growing in @ BadlandsNPS #DYK #biodiversity* [Tweet]. Twitter. https://twitter.com/BadlandsNPS/status/968196500412133379

White, B. [@BettyMWhite]. (2018, June 21). *I treasure every minute we spent together #koko* [Image attached] [Tweet]. Twitter. https://twitter.com/BettyMWhite/status/1009951892846227456

Parenthetical citations: (APA Education, 2018; Badlands National Park, 2018; White, 2018)
Narrative citations: APA Education (2018), Badlands National Park (2018), and White (2018)

- If the tweet includes images (including animated gifs), vid-eos, thumbnail links to outside sources, links to other tweets (as in a retweet with comment), or a poll, indicate that in square brackets. For tweet replies, do not include the "reply-ing to" information; if that is important to note, do so within the in-text citation.
- Replicate emojis if possible (see introduction to Section 10.13).

92. Twitter profile

APA Style [@APA_Style]. (n.d.). *Tweets* [Twitter profile]. Twitter. Retrieved November 1, 2019, from https://twitter.com/APA_Style

Parenthetical citation: (APA Style, n.d.)
Narrative citation: APA Style (n.d.)

- Provide a retrieval date because the contents of the page can change over time.
- A Twitter profile has several tabs ("Tweets" is the default). To reference one of the other tabs (e.g., "Lists" or "Moments"), substitute that tab name for "Tweets."
- Include the notation "Twitter profile" in square brackets.

93. Facebook post

Gaiman, N. (2018, March 22). *100,000+ Rohingya refugees could be at serious risk during Bangladesh's monsoon season. My fellow UNHCR Goodwill Ambassador Cate Blanchett is* [Image attached] [Status up-date]. Facebook. http://bit.ly/2JQxPAD

National Institute of Mental Health. (2018, November 28). *Suicide affects all ages, genders, races, and ethnicities. Check out these 5 Action Steps for Helping Someone in Emotional Pain* [Infographic]. Facebook. http://bit.ly/321Qstq

News From Science. (2018, June 26). *These frogs walk instead of hop: https://scim.ag/2KlriwH* [Video]. Facebook. https://www.facebook.com/ScienceNOW/videos/10155508587605108/

Parenthetical citations: (Gaiman, 2018; National Institute of Mental Health, 2018; News From Science, 2018)
Narrative citations: Gaiman (2018), National Institute of Mental Health (2018), and News From Science (2018)

- This format can be used for posts to other social media services, including Tumblr, LinkedIn, and so forth.
- If a status update includes images, videos, thumbnail links to outside sources, or content from another Facebook post (such as when sharing a link), indicate that in square brackets.
- Replicate emojis if possible (see the introduction to Section 10.13 for more).

94. Facebook page

Smithsonian's National Zoo and Conservation Biology Institute. (n.d.). *Home* [Facebook page]. Facebook. Retrieved July 22, 2019, from https://www.facebook.com/nationalzoo

Parenthetical citation: (Smithsonian's National Zoo and Conservation Biology Institute, n.d.)
Narrative citation: Smithsonian's National Zoo and Conservation Biology Institute (n.d.)

- Use the page title in the reference (e.g., "Timeline," "Home," "Photos," "About").
- Include the notation "Facebook page" in square brackets.
- This format can be used or adapted for references to other platform or profile pages, including YouTube, Instagram, Tumblr, LinkedIn, and so forth.

95. Instagram photo or video

Zeitz MOCAA [@zeitzmocaa]. (2018, November 26). *Grade 6 learners from Parkfields Primary School in Hanover Park visited the museum for a tour and workshop hosted by* [Photographs]. Instagram. https://www.instagram.com/p/BqpHpjFBs3b/

Parenthetical citation: (Zeitz MOCAA, 2018)
Narrative citation: Zeitz MOCAA (2018)

96. Instagram highlight

The New York Public Library [@nypl]. (n.d.). *The raven* [Highlight]. Instagram. Retrieved April 16, 2019, from https://bitly.com/2FV8bu3

Parenthetical citation: (The New York Public Library, n.d.)
Narrative citation: The New York Public Library (n.d.)

- Use "n.d." for the date; although each story within a highlight is dated, the highlight itself is not dated and may include stories from multiple dates.
- Because highlights can change at any time, include the retrieval date.
- Because the URL was long and complex, it has been shortened (see Section 9.36). Either the long or the short form of the URL is acceptable.

97. Online forum post

National Aeronautics and Space Administration [nasa]. (2018, September 12). *I'm NASA astronaut Scott Tingle. Ask me anything about adjusting to being back on Earth after my first spaceflight!* [Online forum post]. Reddit. https://www.reddit.com/r/IAmA/comments/9fagqy/im_nasa_astronaut_scott_tingle_ask_me_anything/

Parenthetical citation: (National Aeronautics and Space Administration, 2018)
Narrative citation: National Aeronautics and Space Administration (2018)

- For more on formatting usernames, see Section 9.8.

10.14 Webpages and Websites

Use the webpages and websites category if there is no other reference category that fits and the work has no parent or overarching publication (e.g., journal, blog, conference proceedings) other than the website itself (see Section 9.2). If you cite multiple webpages from a website, create a reference for each. To mention a website in general, do not create a reference list entry or an in-text citation. Instead, include the name of the website in the text and provide the URL in parentheses (see Section 8.22 for an example).

For help in determining the author of a webpage or website reference, including how the author can be inferred from context or found on an "about us" or acknowledgments page, see Example 101 as well as Section 9.7. Provide the most specific date possible (see Section 9.15 for information on how to handle updated dates or reviewed dates)—for example, a year, month, and day; year and month; or year only. When the author name and the site name are the same, omit the site name from the source element. Include a retrieval date only when the content is designed to change over time and the page is not archived (see Section 9.16).

Use the template shown next to construct references for webpages or websites.

| | | | Source | |
| | | | Website | |
Author	Date	Title	name	URL
Author, A. A., & Author, B. B. Name of Group.	(2020). (2020, August). (2020, May 28). (n.d.).	*Title of work.*	Site Name.	https://xxxxxx Retrieved December 22, 2020, from https://xxxxx

98. Webpage on a news website

Avramova, N. (2019, January 3). *The secret to a long, happy, healthy life? Think age-positive.* CNN. https://www.cnn.com/2019/01/03/health/respect-toward-elderly-leads-to-long-life-intl/index.html

Bologna, C. (2018, June 27). *What happens to your mind and body when you feel homesick?* HuffPost. https://www.huffingtonpost.com/entry/what-happens-mind-body-homesick_us_5b201ebde4b09d7a3d77eee1

Parenthetical citations: (Avramova, 2019; Bologna, 2018)
Narrative citations: Avramova (2019) and Bologna (2018)

• Use this format for articles published in online news sources (e.g., BBC News, Bloomberg, CNN, HuffPost, MSNBC, Salon, Vox). To cite articles from online magazines or newspapers, see Examples 15 and 16.

99. Webpage on a website with a group author

Centers for Disease Control and Prevention. (2018, January 23). *People at high risk of developing flu-related complications.* https://www.cdc.gov/flu/about/disease/high_risk.htm

World Health Organization. (2018, March). *Questions and answers on immunization and vaccine safety.* https://www.who.int/features/qa/84/en/

Parenthetical citations: (Centers for Disease Control and Prevention, 2018; World Health Organization, 2018)
Narrative citations: Centers for Disease Control and Prevention (2018) and World Health Organization (2018)

- When the author and site name are the same, omit the site name from the source element.

100. Webpage on a website with an individual author

Martin Lillie, C. M. (2016, December 29). *Be kind to yourself: How self-compassion can improve your resiliency.* Mayo Clinic. https://www.mayoclinic.org/healthy-lifestyle/adult-health/in-depth/self-compassion-can-improve-your-resiliency/art-20267193

Parenthetical citation: (Martin Lillie, 2016)
Narrative citation: Martin Lillie (2016)

101. Webpage on a website with no date

Boddy, J., Neumann, T., Jennings, S., Morrow, V., Alderson, P., Rees, R., & Gibson, W. (n.d.). *Ethics principles.* The Research Ethics Guidebook: A Resource for Social Scientists. http://www.ethicsguidebook.ac.uk/EthicsPrinciples

National Nurses United. (n.d.). *What employers should do to protect nurses from Zika.* https://www.nationalnursesunited.org/pages/what-employers-should-do-to-protect-rns-from-zika

Parenthetical citations: (Boddy et al., n.d.; National Nurses United, n.d.)
Narrative citations: Boddy et al. (n.d.) and National Nurses United (n.d.)

- In the Boddy et al. example, the authors are listed on the acknowledgments page of the site (see Section 9.7 for more on determining the author).
- When the author and site name are the same, omit the site name from the source element.

102. Webpage on a website with a retrieval date

U.S. Census Bureau. (n.d.). *U.S. and world population clock.* U.S. Department of Commerce. Retrieved July 3, 2019, from https://www.census.gov/popclock/

Parenthetical citation: (U.S. Census Bureau, n.d.)
Narrative citation: U.S. Census Bureau (n.d.)

- When the author and site name are the same, omit the site name from the source element.
- Include a retrieval date because the contents of the page are designed to change over time and the page itself is not archived (see Section 9.16).

Legal References

In APA Style, most legal materials are cited in the standard legal citation style used for legal references across all disciplines, which has notable differences from other APA Style references. However, existing legal references are usually already written in legal style and require few, if any, changes for an APA Style paper. Abbreviations are often used to shorten legal references; for examples of common legal abbreviations, see Table 11.2 of the *Publication Manual*. The following table summarizes the key differences between APA Style references and legal references.

Issue	APA Style	Legal style
Order of elements in the reference list entry	Usually the author, date, title, and source, in that order	Usually the title, source, and date, in that order
In-text citation	Usually the author and year	Usually the title and year
Version of source being referenced	The exact version used	The version of record as published in an official legal publication such as the *United States Code* or the *Federal Register*, plus a URL for the version used
Use of standard abbreviations	Used for parts of a work (e.g., "2nd ed." for a second edition)	Used for common legal entities and publications (e.g., "S." for the Senate and "H.R." for the House of Representatives)

In-text citations for legal references are formed in basically the same way and serve the same purpose as standard APA Style author–date citations. Most legal reference entries begin with the title of the work; as a result, most in-text citations consist of the title and year (e.g., Americans With Disabilities Act, 1990; *Brown v. Board of Education*, 1954). If the title is long (e.g., for federal testimony), shorten it for the in-text citation (e.g., *Federal real property reform: How cutting red tape and better management could achieve billions in savings* in the reference list could be shortened to *Federal Real Property Reform* in the text); give enough information in the in-text citation to enable readers to locate the entry in the reference list.

Examples of in-text citations and reference entries for legal materials are given in the sections that follow. Only the most common United States and United Nations legal examples are provided in this chapter. See the seventh edition of the *Publication Manual* (Sections 11.5–11.8) for references to other legal works, including legislative materials, administrative and executive materials, and patents. For more information on preparing these and other kinds of legal references, consult the latest edition of *The Bluebook: A Uniform System of Citation* (*Bluebook*, 2015).

10.15 Cases or Court Decisions

A reference for a case or court decision includes the following information:

- **title or name of the case**, usually one party versus another (e.g., *Brown v. Board of Education*);

- **citation**, usually to a volume and page of one of the various sets of books where published cases can be found called *reporters* (e.g., *Federal Reporter, Second Series*), which typically contain decisions of courts in particular political divisions, which are called *jurisdictions*;

- **precise jurisdiction of the court writing the decision** (e.g., U.S. district court, New York Court of Appeals), in parentheses;

- **date of the decision**, in parentheses (in the same set of parentheses as the jurisdiction if both are present); and

- **URL** from which you retrieved the case information (optional; this is not strictly required for legal citations but may aid readers in retrieval).

To create a reference list entry for the case you want to cite, first identify the court that decided the case and then follow the relevant example. Often, the document about the case will have the relevant citation included, or it can easily be retrieved by searching the internet for the name of the court decision and the word "citation." When a case or court decision is reported over multiple pages, provide only the first page number in the reference list entry (see Example 103). Do not provide the page range for the whole case or decision. For cases or court decisions that have not been assigned a page number, include three underscores instead of the page number in the reference list entry (see Example 104).

Federal Court Decisions. The United States has both federal and state court systems. Within federal courts there are multiple levels of authority, and decisions from these courts are published in different publications.

- **U.S. Supreme Court:** Decisions from the U.S. Supreme Court, the highest federal court, are published in the *United States Reports* (other reporters may also publish Supreme Court decisions). The template for Supreme Court decisions is as follows:

  Reference list: Name v. Name, Volume U.S. Page (Year). URL

  Parenthetical citation: (*Name v. Name*, Year)

  Narrative citation: *Name v. Name* (Year)

- **U.S. Circuit Court:** Decisions from the U.S. Circuit Court are published in the *Federal Reporter*. The template for U.S. Circuit Court decisions is as follows:

  Reference list: Name v. Name, Volume F. [*or* F.2d, F.3d] Page (Court Year). URL

  Parenthetical citation: (*Name v. Name*, Year)

  Narrative citation: *Name v. Name* (Year)

- **U.S. District Court:** Decisions from the U.S. District Court are published in the *Federal Supplements*. The template for U.S. District Court decisions is as follows:

  Reference list: Name v. Name, Volume F. Supp. Page (Court Year). URL

  Parenthetical citation: (*Name v. Name*, Year)

  Narrative citation: *Name v. Name* (Year)

State Court Decisions. At the state level, courts also operate at different levels of authority, although different states have different names for the levels. For example, the state supreme court is generally the highest state court (the state of New York is one exception; the court of appeals is the highest court in that state). The template for state court decisions is as follows:

  Reference list: Name v. Name, Volume Reporter Page (Court Year). URL

  Parenthetical citation: (*Name v. Name*, Year)

  Narrative citation: *Name v. Name* (Year)

103. U.S. Supreme Court case, with a page number

Brown v. Board of Education, 347 U.S. 483 (1954). https://www.oyez.org/cases/1940-1955/347us483

Parenthetical citation: (*Brown v. Board of Education*, 1954)
Narrative citation: Brown v. Board of Education (1954)

- U.S. Supreme Court decisions are published in the *United States Reports* (abbreviated "U.S." in the reference). For example, the decision to eliminate racial segregation in public schools, *Brown v. Board of Education,* was published in Volume 347 of the *United States Reports,* on page 483, in the year 1954. Cite Supreme Court decisions as published in the *United States Reports* whenever possible; cite the *Supreme Court Reporter* for cases that have not yet been published in *United States Reports.*

104. U.S. Supreme Court case, without a page number

Obergefell v. Hodges, 576 U.S. ___ (2015). https://www.supremecourt.gov/opinions/14pdf/14-556_3204.pdf

Parenthetical citation: (*Obergefell v. Hodges*, 2015)
Narrative citation: Obergefell v. Hodges (2015)

- The court decision to legalize same-sex marriage in the United States, *Obergefell v. Hodges,* occurred in 2015 and was published in Volume 576 of the *United States Reports.* However, as of the printing of this *Concise Guide,* the paginated volumes of the *United States Reports* have been published only for decisions through the 2012 Supreme Court term. For cases that have not been assigned a page number (like *Obergefell v. Hodges*), include three underscores instead of the page number in the reference list entry.

105. U.S. circuit court case

Daubert v. Merrell Dow Pharmaceuticals, Inc., 951 F.2d 1128 (9th Cir. 1991). https://openjurist.org/951/f2d/1128/william-daubert-v-merrell-dow-pharmaceuticals

Parenthetical citation: (*Daubert v. Merrell Dow Pharmaceuticals, Inc.*, 1991)
Narrative citation: Daubert v. Merrell Dow Pharmaceuticals, Inc. (1991)

- This court decision regarding birth defects resulting from medication use during pregnancy appeared in Volume 951 of the *Federal Reporter, Second Series,* on page 1128, and was decided by the 9th Circuit Court in the year 1991.

106. U.S. district court case

Burriola v. Greater Toledo YMCA, 133 F. Supp. 2d 1034 (N.D. Ohio 2001). https://law.justia.com/cases/federal/district-courts/FSupp2/133/1034/2293141/

> **Parenthetical citation:** (*Burriola v. Greater Toledo YMCA*, 2001)
> **Narrative citation:** *Burriola v. Greater Toledo YMCA* (2001)

- This court decision stating that children with special needs should receive accommodations for services at public after-school-care providers under the Americans With Disabilities Act of 1990 appeared in Volume 133 of the *Federal Supplement, Second Series*, on page 1034. It was decided by the U.S. District Court for the Northern District of Ohio in the year 2001.

107. U.S. district court case with appeal

Durflinger v. Artiles, 563 F. Supp. 322 (D. Kan. 1981), *aff'd*, 727 F.2d 888 (10th Cir. 1984). https://openjurist.org/727/f2d/888/durflinger-v-artiles

> **Parenthetical citation:** (*Durflinger v. Artiles*, 1981/1984)
> **Narrative citation:** *Durflinger v. Artiles* (1981/1984)

- This court decision regarding whether third parties should be protected from involuntarily committed psychiatric patients in state custody was rendered by the federal district court for the District of Kansas in the year 1981. On appeal, the decision was affirmed by the federal-level 10th Circuit Court of Appeals in 1984. Information about both the original decision and the appealed decision appears in the reference list entry.
- If on appeal the decision is affirmed, the abbreviation "*aff'd*" is used between the two components, in italics and set off by commas; if the decision is overturned or reversed, the abbreviation "*rev'd*" is used, in italics and set off by commas.
- Consult the *Bluebook* for the proper forms of the various stages in a case's history.

108. State supreme court case

Tarasoff v. Regents of the University of California, 17 Cal.3d 425, 131 Cal. Rptr. 14, 551 P.2d 334 (1976). https://www.casebriefs.com/blog/law/torts/torts-keyed-to-dobbs/the-duty-to-protect-from-third-persons/tarasoff-v-regents-of-university-of-california

Parenthetical citation: (Tarasoff v. Regents of the University of California, 1976)
Narrative citation: Tarasoff v. Regents of the University of California (1976)

- This court decision held that mental health professionals have a duty to protect individuals who are being threatened with bodily harm by a patient. It was decided by the Supreme Court of the State of California in the year 1976.
- Some court decisions are reported in multiple places, known as *parallel citation*. When a work has parallel citations, include all the citations in your reference list entry. Existing legal citations usually include the parallel citations, so you should not need to do additional research to find them. In this case, the court decision was reported in three places, which are all included in the parallel citation, shown here separated with commas. These three sources are Volume 17 of the *California Reports, Third Series* (Cal.3d), page 425; Volume 131 of the *California Reporter* (Cal. Rptr.), page 14; and Volume 551 of the *Pacific Reporter, Second Series* (P.2d), page 334.

10.16 Statutes (Laws and Acts)

A *statute* is a law or act passed by a legislative body. Federal statutes are published in the *United States Code* (U.S.C.). The U.S.C. is divided into sections called *titles*—for example, Title 42 refers to public health and welfare. New laws are then added to the appropriate title as a way of keeping the law organized. State statutes are published in state-specific compilations; for example, statutes pertaining to the state of Florida are published in the *Florida Statutes*. State statutes are also typically organized into titles.

In the reference list entry for a federal or state statute, include the name of the act; the title, source (abbreviated as specified in the *Bluebook*), and section number of the statute; and, in parentheses, the publication date of the statutory compilation you used (e.g., the U.S.C. or a state-specific compilation). You may include the URL from which you retrieved the statute after the year. This is not strictly required for legal citations but may aid readers in retrieval.

In the in-text citation, give the popular or official name of the act (if any) and the year of the act. The year in the reference list entry and in-text citation should refer to the year in which the statute was published in the source being cited, which may be different from the year in the name of the act.

The template for federal or state statutes is as follows:

Reference list: Name of Act, Title Source § Section Number (Year). URL

Parenthetical citation: (Name of Act, Year)

Narrative citation: Name of Act (Year)

For a federal statute (i.e., law or act), the source is usually the *United States Code.* You may see a public law number on the act as well; include a public law number in the reference list entry when the act is codified in scattered sections (see Example 110) or to refer to an act before it is codified (otherwise leave the public law number out of the reference). The format for state statutes may differ depending on the state but generally follows the same format as for federal statutes. Consult the *Bluebook* or another legal resource for further information on your state.

109. Federal statute, Americans With Disabilities Act of 1990

Americans With Disabilities Act of 1990, 42 U.S.C. § 12101 *et seq.* (1990). https://www.ada.gov/pubs/adastatute08.htm

> **Parenthetical citation:** (Americans With Disabilities Act, 1990)
> **Narrative citation:** Americans With Disabilities Act (1990)

- This act can be located beginning at Section 12101 of Title 42 of the *United States Code* and was codified in the year 1990. The phrase "*et seq.*" is Latin for "and what follows" and is a shorthand way of showing that the act covers not only the initial section cited but also others that follow.

110. Federal statute, Civil Rights Act of 1964

Civil Rights Act of 1964, Pub. L. No. 88-352, 78 Stat. 241 (1964). https://www.govinfo.gov/content/pkg/STATUTE-78/pdf/STATUTE-78-Pg241.pdf

> **Parenthetical citation:** (Civil Rights Act, 1964)
> **Narrative citation:** Civil Rights Act (1964)

- The Civil Rights Act of 1964 is codified in the *United States Code* in three scattered sections: 2 U.S.C., 28 U.S.C., and 42 U.S.C. To cite the entire act, use the public law number as shown in the example.

111. Federal statute, Every Student Succeeds Act

Every Student Succeeds Act, 20 U.S.C. § 6301 (2015). https://www.congress.gov/114/plaws/publ95/PLAW-114publ95.pdf

Parenthetical citation: (Every Student Succeeds Act, 2015)
Narrative citation: Every Student Succeeds Act (2015)

- The Every Student Succeeds Act pertains to educational policy for students in public primary and secondary schools. It was codified in Title 20 of the *United States Code* in Section 6301 in the year 2015.

112. State statute in state code

Florida Mental Health Act, Fla. Stat. § 394 (1971 & rev. 2009). http://www.leg.state.fl.us/statutes/index.cfm?App_mode=Display_Statute&URL=0300-0399/0394/0394.html

Parenthetical citation: (Florida Mental Health Act, 1971/2009)
Narrative citation: Florida Mental Health Act (1971/2009)

- This Florida act can be found in the *Florida Statutes*, Section 394. It was first codified in the year 1971 and then revised in 2009. Both years appear in the in-text citation, separated by a slash.
- Consult the *Bluebook* for formats for other states.

10.17 Constitutions and Charters

To cite a whole federal or state constitution, a citation is not necessary. Simply refer to the constitution in text.

The U.S. Constitution has 26 amendments.

The Massachusetts Constitution was ratified in 1780.

Create reference list entries and in-text citations for citations to articles and amendments of constitutions. In the reference list and in parenthetical citations, abbreviate U.S. Constitution to "U.S. Const." and use the legal state abbreviation for a state constitution (e.g. "Md. Const." for the Maryland Constitution; see a list of state abbreviations for legal references at the Legal Information Institute at https://www.law.cornell.edu/citation/4-500). In the narrative, use either "U.S." or "United States" for the U.S. Constitution, and spell out the name of the state for a state constitution—for example, "the Wisconsin Constitution." U.S. Constitution article and amendment numbers are Roman numerals. State constitution article numbers are also Roman numerals, but state constitution amendment numbers are Arabic numerals. URLs are not necessary for the reference. Additional information about the cited source can be included in the narrative, if desired.

LEGAL

113. Article of the U.S. Constitution

Template:
U.S. Const. art. xxx, § x.

Example:
U.S. Const. art. IV, § 3.

Parenthetical citation: (U.S. Const. art. IV, § 3)
Narrative citation: Article IV, Section 3, of the U.S. Constitution

114. Article of a state constitution

Template:
State Const. art. xxx, § x.

Example:
S.C. Const. art. XI, § 3.

Parenthetical citation: (S.C. Const. art. IX, § 3)
Narrative citation: Article IX, Section 3, of the South Carolina Constitution

115. Amendment to the U.S. Constitution

Template:
U.S. Const. amend. xxx.

Example:
U.S. Const. amend. XIX.

Parenthetical citation: (U.S. Const. amend. XIX)
Narrative citation: Amendment XIX to the U.S. Constitution

- Amendments to state constitutions are cited in the same way as amendments to the U.S. Constitution.
- No date is needed in the reference unless the amendment has been repealed. (For an example of a repealed amendment to the U.S. Constitution, see Chapter 11, Example 26 of the *Publication Manual*.)

116. U.S. Bill of Rights

U.S. Const. amend. I–X.

Parenthetical citation: (U.S. Const. amend. I–X)
Narrative citation: Amendments I–X to the U.S. Constitution

- The first 10 amendments to the U.S. Constitution are collectively referred to as the Bill of Rights. The citation is the same as that for an amendment to the constitution, except that the range of amendments is included in the citation.

117. Charter of the United Nations

Template:
U.N. Charter art. xx, para. xx.

Example:
U.N. Charter art. 1, para. 3.

Parenthetical citation: (U.N. Charter art. 1, para. 3)
Narrative citation: Article 1, paragraph 3, of the United Nations Charter

- A citation to the charter of the United Nations should include the name of the agreement, the article number, and the paragraph number. To cite an entire article, omit the paragraph number.

10.18 Treaties and International Conventions

References for treaties or international conventions should include the name of the treaty, convention, or other agreement; the signing or approval date; and a URL if available. In text, provide the name of the treaty or convention and the year.

Reference list: Name of Treaty or Convention, Month Day, Year, URL
Parenthetical citation: (Name of Treaty or Convention, Year)
Narrative citation: Name of Treaty or Convention (Year)

118. United Nations convention

United Nations Convention on the Rights of the Child, November 20, 1989, https://www.ohchr.org/en/professionalinterest/pages/crc.aspx

Parenthetical citation: (United Nations Convention on the Rights of the Child, 1989)
Narrative citation: United Nations Convention on the Rights of the Child (1989)

CREDITS FOR ADAPTED TABLES AND FIGURES

Many tables and figures presented in the *Concise Guide* were adapted from published works. The copyright attributions for those works are presented here, ordered by chapter. The other tables and figures and the student sample paper were created by the APA Style team.

Figure 1.4: Adapted from "Age and Gender Differences in Self-Esteem—A Cross-Cultural Window," by W. Bleidorn, R. C. Arslan, J. J. A. Denissen, P. J. Rentfrow, J. E. Gebauer, J. Potter, and S. D. Gosling, 2016, *Journal of Personality and Social Psychology*, *111*(3), pp. 396–410 (https://doi.org/10.1037/pspp0000078). Copyright 2015 by the American Psychological Association.

Table 7.2: Adapted from "Internet-Based Cognitive–Behavior Therapy for Procrastination: A Randomized Controlled Trial," by A. Rozental, E. Forsell, A. Svensson, G. Andersson, and P. Carlbring, 2015, *Journal of Consulting and Clinical Psychology*, *83*(4), p. 815 (https://doi.org/10.1037/ccp0000023). Copyright 2015 by the American Psychological Association.

Table 7.3: Adapted from "Introduction of the *DSM-5* Levels of Personality Functioning Questionnaire," by S. K. Huprich, S. M. Nelson, K. B. Meehan, C. J. Siefert, G. Haggerty, J. Sexton, V. B. Dauphin, M. Macaluso, J. Jackson, R. Zackula, and L. Baade, 2018, *Personality Disorders: Theory, Research, and Treatment*, *9*(6), p. 557 (https://doi.org/10.1037/per0000264). Copyright 2017 by the American Psychological Association.

Table 7.4: Adapted from "Low Social Rhythm Regularity Predicts First Onset of Bipolar Spectrum Disorders Among At-Risk Individuals With Reward Hypersensitivity," by L. B. Alloy, E. M. Boland, T. H. Ng, W. G. Whitehouse, and L. Y. Abramson, 2015, *Journal of Abnormal Psychology*, *124*(4), p. 946 (https://doi.org/10.1037/abn0000107). Copyright 2015 by the American Psychological Association.

H. I. Strømsø, 2016, *Journal of Educational Psychology*, *108*(2), p. 157 (https://doi.org/10.1037/edu0000057). Copyright 2015 by the American Psychological Association.

Figure 7.2: Adapted from "Framing of Online Risk: Young Adults' and Adolescents' Representations of Risky Gambles," by C. M. White, M. Gummerum, and Y. Hanoch, 2018, *Decision*, *5*(2), p. 124 (https://doi.org/10.1037/dec0000066). Copyright 2016 by the American Psychological Association.

Figure 7.3: Adapted from "Large Continuous Perspective Change With Noncoplanar Points Enables Accurate Slant Perception," by X. M. Wang, M. Lind, and G. P. Bingham, 2018, *Journal of Experimental Psychology: Human Perception and Performance*, *44*(10), p. 1513 (https://doi.org/10.1037/xhp0000553). Copyright 2018 by the American Psychological Association.

Figure 7.4: Adapted from "Meeting the Mental Health Needs of Children and Youth Through Integrated Care: A Systems and Policy Perspective," by D. de Voursney and L. N. Huang, 2016, *Psychological Services*, *13*(1), p. 84 (https://doi.org/10.1037/ser0000045). In the public domain.

Figure 7.5: Adapted from "Racial Microaggression Experiences and Coping Strategies of Black Women in Corporate Leadership," by A. M. B. Holder, M. A. Jackson, and J. G. Ponterotto, 2015, *Qualitative Psychology*, *2*(2), p. 171 (https://doi.org/10.1037/qup0000024). Copyright 2015 by the American Psychological Association.

Figure 7.6: Adapted from "Traditions and Alcohol Use: A Mixed-Methods Analysis," by F. G. Castro and K. Coe, 2007, *Cultural Diversity and Ethnic Minority Psychology*, *13*(4), p. 271 (https://doi.org/10.1037/1099-9809.13.4.269). Copyright 2007 by the American Psychological Association.

Figure 7.7: Adapted from "The Limits of Learning: Exploration, Generalization, and the Development of Learning Traps," by A. S. Rich and T. M. Gureckis, 2018, *Journal of Experimental Psychology: General*, *147*(11), p. 1560 (https://doi.org/10.1037/xge0000466). Copyright 2018 by the American Psychological Association.

Figure 7.8: Adapted from *2017 Poverty Rate in the United States*, by U.S. Census Bureau, 2017 (https://www.census.gov/library/visualizations/2018/comm/acs-poverty-map.html). In the public domain.

Figure 7.9: Adapted from "Empathic Accuracy for Happiness in the Daily Lives of Older Couples: Fluid Cognitive Performance Predicts Pattern Accuracy Among Men," by G. Hülür, C. A. Hoppmann, A. Rauers, H. Schade, N. Ram, and D. Gerstorf, 2016, *Psychology and Aging*, *31*(5), p. 550 (https://doi.org/10.1037/pag0000109). Copyright 2016 by the American Psychological Association.

Figure 7.10: Adapted from "Out of Place, Out of Mind: Schema-Driven False Memory Effects for Object-Location Bindings," by A. R. Lew and M. L. Howe, *Journal of Experimental Psychology: Learning, Memory, and Cognition*, *43*(3), p. 405 (https://doi.org/10.1037/xlm0000317). Copyright 2016 by the American Psychological Association.

Figure 8.1: Adapted from "Clever People: Intelligence and Humor Production Ability," by A. P. Christensen, P. J. Silvia, E. C. Nusbaum, and R. E. Beaty, 2018, *Psychology of Aesthetics, Creativity, and the Arts*, *12*(2), p. 136 (https://doi.org/10.1037/aca0000109). Copyright 2018 by the American Psychological Association.

Figure 8.3: Adapted from "Can Journalistic 'False Balance' Distort Public Perception of Consensus in Expert Opinion?" by D. J. Koehler, 2016, *Journal of Experimental Psychology: Applied*, *22*(1), pp. 24–38 (https://doi.org/10.1037/xap0000073). Copyright 2016 by the American Psychological Association.

Figure 8.4: Adapted from "Discrimination, Work Outcomes, and Mental Health Among Women of Color: The Protective Role of Womanist Attitudes," by B. L. Velez, R. Cox Jr., C. J. Polihronakis, and B. Moradi, 2018, *Journal of Counseling Psychology*, *65*(2), pp. 178, 193 (http://doi.org/10.1037/cou0000274). Copyright 2018 by the American Psychological Association.

Figure 8.5: Adapted from "Play Therapists' Perceptions of Wellness and Self-Care Practices," by K. K. Meany-Walen, A. Cobie-Nuss, E. Eittreim, S. Teeling, S. Wilson, and C. Xander, 2018, *International Journal of Play Therapy*, *27*(3), p. 177 (https://doi.org/10.1037/pla0000067). Copyright 2018 by the American Psychological Association.

Figure 8.6: Adapted from "Tabloids as Windows Into Our Interpersonal Relationships: A Content Analysis of Mass Media Gossip From an Evolutionary Perspective," by C. J. S. De Backer and M. L. Fisher, 2012, *Journal of Social, Evolutionary, and Cultural Psychology*, *6*(3), p. 421 (https://doi.org/10.1037/h0099244). Copyright 2012 by the American Psychological Association.

Figure 8.7: Adapted from "Women Athletes' Self-Compassion, Self-Criticism, and Perceived Sport Performance," by M. E. Killham, A. D. Mosewich, D. E. Mack, K. E. Gunnell, and L. J. Ferguson, 2018, *Sport, Exercise, and Performance Psychology*, *7*(3), p. 297 (https://doi.org/10.1037/spy0000127). Copyright 2018 by the American Psychological Association.

Figure 9.1: Adapted from "Sensitivity to the Evaluation of Others Emerges by 24 Months," by S. V. Botto and P. Rochat, 2018, *Developmental Psychology*, *54*(9), p. 1723 (https://doi.org/10.1037/dev0000548). Copyright 2018 by the American Psychological Association.

REFERENCES

Accord Alliance. (n.d.). *Learn about DSD*. http://www.accordalliance.org/learn-about-dsd/

American Psychological Association. (n.d.). *Definitions related to sexual orientation and gender diversity in APA documents*. https://www.apa.org/pi/lgbt/resources/sexuality-definitions.pdf

American Psychological Association. (2012a). Guidelines for psychological practice with lesbian, gay, and bisexual clients. *American Psychologist, 67*(1), 10–42. https://doi.org/10.1037/a0024659

American Psychological Association. (2012b). Guidelines for the evaluation of dementia and age-related cognitive change. *American Psychologist, 67*(1), 1–9. https://doi.org/10.1037/a0024643

American Psychological Association. (2014). Guidelines for psychological practice with older adults. *American Psychologist, 69*(1), 34–65. https://doi.org/10.1037/a0035063

American Psychological Association. (2015a). Guidelines for psychological practice with transgender and gender nonconforming people. *American Psychologist, 70*(9), 832–864. https://doi.org/10.1037/a0039906

American Psychological Association. (2015b). *Key terms and concepts in understanding gender diversity and sexual orientation among students*. https://www.apa.org/pi/lgbt/programs/safe-supportive/lgbt/key-terms.pdf

American Psychological Association. (2017). *Multicultural guidelines: An ecological approach to context, identity, and intersectionality*. https://www.apa.org/about/policy/multicultural-guidelines.aspx

American Psychological Association. (2018). *APA resolution for the use of the term* patient *in American Psychological Association policies, rules, and public relations activities when referring to the health-related and scientific activities of health service psychologists and scientists in health care services and settings*. https://www.apa.org/about/policy/resolution-term-patient.pdf

American Psychological Association. (2020). *Publication manual of the American Psychological Association* (7th ed.). https://doi.org/10.1037/0000165-000

American Psychological Association of Graduate Students. (2015). *Proud and prepared: A guide for LGBT students navigating graduate training*. American Psychological Association. https://www.apa.org/apags/resources/lgbt-guide.aspx

The Asexual Visibility & Education Network. (n.d.). *General FAQ: Definitions.* https://www.asexuality.org/?q=general.html#def

Blackless, M., Charuvastra, A., Derryck, A., Fausto-Sterling, A., Lauzanne, K., & Lee, E. (2000). How sexually dimorphic are we? Review and synthesis. *American Journal of Human Biology, 12*(2), 151–166. http://doi.org/bttkh4

The bluebook: A uniform system of citation (20th ed.). (2015). Harvard Law Review Association.

Bowleg, L. (2008). When Black + woman + lesbian ≠ Black lesbian woman: The methodological challenges of quantitative and qualitative intersectionality research. *Sex Roles, 59*(5–6), 312–325. https://doi.org/10.1007/s11199-008-9400-z

Brown, L. (n.d.). *Identity-first language.* Autistic Self Advocacy Network. https://autisticadvocacy.org/home/about-asan/identity-first-language (Original work published 2011)

Brueggemann, B. J. (2013). Disability studies/disability culture. In M. L. Wehmeyer (Ed.), *The Oxford handbook of positive psychology and disability* (pp. 279–299). Oxford University Press. https://doi.org/10.1093/oxfordhb/9780195398786.013.013.0019

Cooper, H. (2016, May 12). Principles of good writing: Avoiding plagiarism. *APA Style.* https://blog.apastyle.org/apastyle/2016/05/avoiding-plagiarism.html

Crenshaw, K. W. (1989). Demarginalizing the intersections of race and sex: A Black feminist critique of antidiscrimination doctrine, feminist theory, and antiracist politics. *University of Chicago Legal Forum, 1989*(1), Article 8. https://chicagounbound.uchicago.edu/uclf/vol1989/iss1/8/

de Onis, C. M. (2017). What's in an "x"? An exchange about the politics of "Latinx." *Chiricú Journal: Latina/o Literatures, Arts, and Cultures, 1*(2), 78–91. https://doi.org/10.2979/chiricu.1.2.07

Diemer, M. A., Mistry, R. S., Wadsworth, M. E., Lopez, I., & Reimers, F. (2013). Best practices in conceptualizing and measuring social class in psychological research. *Analyses of Social Issues and Public Policy, 13*(1), 77–113. https://doi.org/10.1111/asap.12001

Dunn, D. S., & Andrews, E. E. (n.d.). *Choosing words for talking about disability.* American Psychological Association. https://www.apa.org/pi/disability/resources/choosing-words.aspx

Dunn, D. S., & Andrews, E. E. (2015). Person-first *and* identity-first language: Developing psychologists' cultural competence using disability language. *American Psychologist, 70*(3), 255–264. https://doi.org/10.1037/a0038636

Gastil, J. (1990). Generic pronouns and sexist language: The oxymoronic character of masculine generics. *Sex Roles, 23*(11–12), 629–643. https://doi.org/10.1007/BF00289252

Hegarty, P., & Buechel, C. (2006). Androcentric reporting of gender differences in APA journals: 1965–2004. *Review of General Psychology, 10*(4), 377–389. https://doi.org/10.1037/1089-2680.10.4.377

Howard, J. A., & Renfrow, D. G. (2014). Intersectionality. In J. D. McLeod, E. J. Lawler, & M. Schwalbe (Eds.), *Handbook of the social psychology of inequality* (pp. 95–121). Springer. https://doi.org/10.1007/978-94-017-9002-4

International Journal of Indigenous Health. (n.d.). *Defining Aboriginal Peoples within Canada.* https://journals.uvic.ca/journalinfo/ijih/IJIHDefiningIndigenousPeoplesWithinCanada.pdf

Intersex Society of North America. (n.d.). *How common is intersex?* http://www.isna.org/faq/frequency

Knatterud, M. E. (1991). Writing with the patient in mind: Don't add insult to injury. *American Medical Writers Association Journal*, *6*(1), 10–17.

Lindland, E., Fond, M., Haydon, A., & Kendall-Taylor, N. (2015). *Gauging aging: Mapping the gaps between expert and public understandings of aging in America*. FrameWorks Institute. https://frameworksinstitute.org/assets/files/aging_mtg.pdf

Lundebjerg, N. E., Trucil, D. E., Hammond, E. C., & Applegate, W. B. (2017). When it comes to older adults, language matters: *Journal of the American Geriatrics Society* adopts modified American Medical Association Style. *Journal of the American Geriatrics Society*, *65*(7), 1386–1388. https://doi.org/10.1111/jgs.14941

Merriam-Webster. (n.d.-a). *Words we're watching: 'Patchwriting': Paraphrasing in a cut-and-pasteworld*.https://www.merriam-webster.com/words-at-play/words-were-watching-patchwriting

Merriam-Webster. (n.d.-b). *Words we're watching: Singular 'they': Though singular 'they' is old, 'they' as a nonbinary pronoun is new—and useful*. https://www.merriam-webster.com/words-at-play/singular-nonbinary-they

Moulton, J., Robinson, G. M., & Elias, C. (1978). Sex bias in language use: "Neutral" pronouns that aren't. *American Psychologist*, *33*(11), 1032–1036. https://doi.org/10.1037/0003-066X.33.11.1032

Rappaport, J. (1977). *Community psychology: Values, research and action*. Holt, Rinehart, & Winston.

Singh, A. A. (2017). Understanding trauma and supporting resilience with LGBT people of color. In K. L. Eckstrand & J. Potter (Eds.), *Trauma, resilience, and health promotion in LGBT patients: What every healthcare provider should know* (pp. 113–119). Springer.

Solomon, A. (2012). *Far from the tree: Parents, children, and the search for identity*. Scribner.

Stout, J. G., & Dasgupta, N. (2011). When *he* doesn't mean *you*: Gender-exclusive language as ostracism. *Personality and Social Psychology Bulletin*, *37*(6), 757–769. https://doi.org/10.1177/0146167211406434

Sweetland, J., Volmert, A., & O'Neil, M. (2017). *Finding the frame: An empirical approach to reframing aging and ageism*. FrameWorks Institute. http://frameworksinstitute.org/assets/files/aging_elder_abuse/aging_research_report_final_2017.pdf

University of Kansas, Research and Training Center on Independent Living. (2013). *Guidelines: How to write and report about people with disabilities* (8th ed.). https://rtcil.drupal.ku.edu/sites/rtcil.drupal.ku.edu/files/images/galleries/Guidelines%208th%20edition.pdf

U.S. Copyright Office. (2019). *More information on fair use*. Copyright.gov. https://www.copyright.gov/fair-use/more-info.html

Web Accessibility Initiative. (2018). *Web content accessibility guidelines (WCAG) overview*. https://www.w3.org/WAI/standards-guidelines/wcag

World Health Organization. (2001). *International classification of functioning, disability and health (ICF)*. https://www.who.int/classifications/icf/en/

World Health Organization. (2011). *World report on disability*. https://www.who.int/disabilities/world_report/2011/en/

Zell, E., Krizan, Z., & Teeter, S. R. (2015). Evaluating gender similarities and differences using metasynthesis. *American Psychologist*, *70*(1), 10–20. https://doi.org/10.1037/a0038208

INDEX

Numbers in **bold** refer to section numbers.